CW01637726

PRESTWICK AIRPORT
THROUGH TIME

Peter C. Brown

AMBERLEY

International Air Transport Association (IATA) Code: PIK
International Civil Aviation Organisation (ICAO) Code: EGPK

First published 2018

Amberley Publishing
The Hill, Stroud, Gloucestershire, GL5 4EP
www.amberley-books.com

ISBN 978 1 4456 7769 9 (print)
ISBN 978 1 4456 7770 5 (ebook)

British Library Cataloguing in Publication Data.
A catalogue record for this book is available from the British Library.

Origination by Amberley Publishing.
Printed in Great Britain.

Introduction

Prestwick, Glasgow's second airport, occupies an area of 880 acres on the coastal side of South Ayrshire, where it receives unobstructed approaches over the sea. It was initially the only Scottish airport permitted to operate a transatlantic link, largely due to the very benign weather conditions and a much lower incidence of fog than any other airport in Great Britain thanks to a geological anomaly. This is probably the main reason that it managed to avoid total closure when it appeared that BAA plc seemed to be running down operations in the early 1990s, and silenced the political bodies that questioned why Glasgow needed two airports when Glasgow Corporation had already invested money in building Glasgow Airport.

Simply known as 'The Meadow', at the end of Monkton village, the site that would become Prestwick Airport was bare of structures (no building developments were made until after the First World War) but was attractive to aviators due to its long, flat fields. The first aircraft recorded to have flown from the site was a Royal Aircraft Factory BE2a from the recently formed Royal Flying Corps on 25 July 1913.

Throughout the 1920s, small-scale airlines in Scotland were using the town's beach and fields as landing strips, and it wasn't until 1934 that the airfield at Monkton would see the start of planned development, when Group Captain David Fowler McIntyre and Douglas Douglas-Hamilton, the 14th Duke of Hamilton and Marquis of Douglas and Clydesdale, who were both members of No. 602 City of Glasgow Auxiliary Air Force Squadron, and had achieved fame on 3 April 1933 by becoming the first men to fly over the world's highest mountain, Mount Everest, acquired 348 acres of the vast green fields just behind Orangefield House to set up a training ground. Previously known as Monkton House, Orangefield House was renamed in 1736 by the then owner James Macrae, who was a great admirer of William of Orange, and served for a while as the control tower from February 1941.

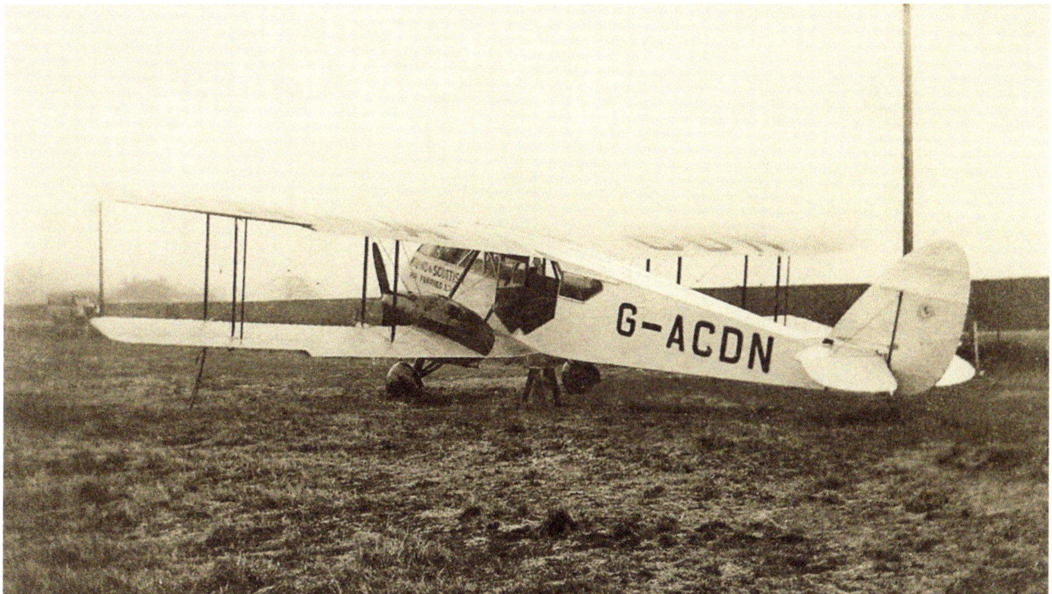

1930s

De Havilland twin-engined biplane DH.84 Dragon G-ACDN of Midland & Scottish Air Ferries Ltd at The Meadow, Monkton, in 1934. (James B. Aird)

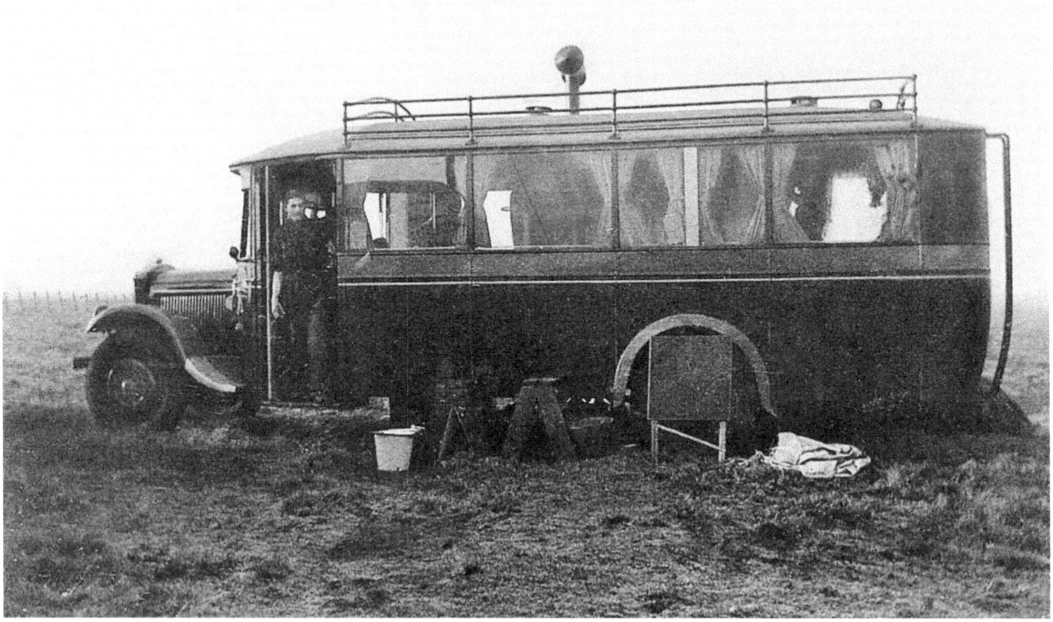

Ground engineers standing in the doorway of a Midland & Scottish Air Ferries' Reo speedwagon (the ancestor of the pick-up truck) at The Meadow, Monkton, in 1934. The chassis had been fitted to a passenger bus body and subsequently converted. (James B. Aird)

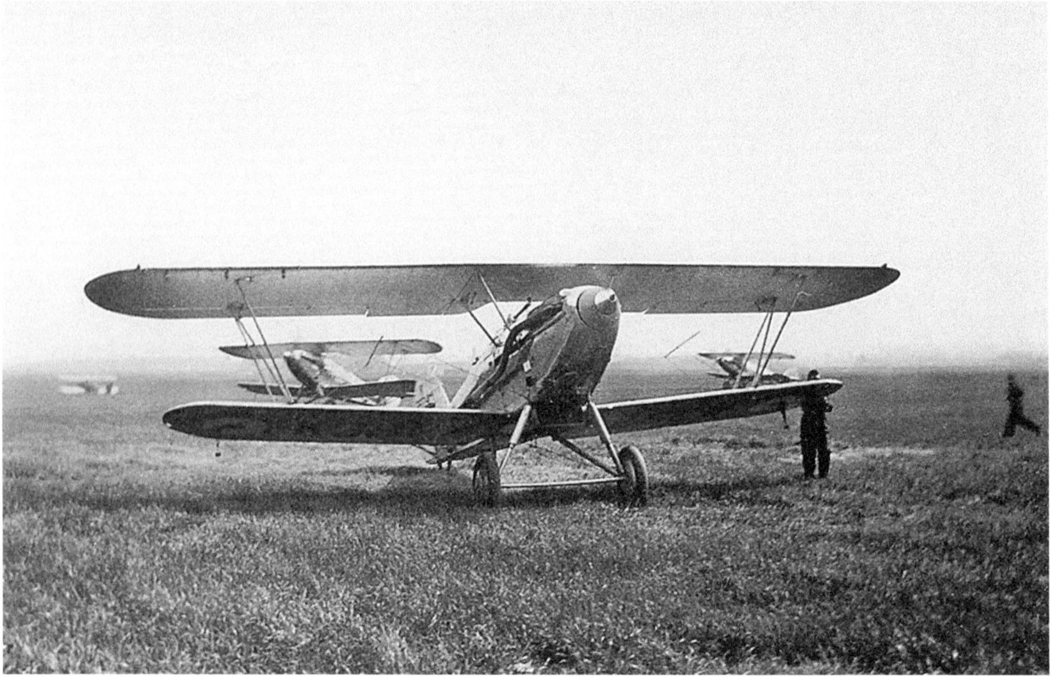

Three Hawker Demons from No. 41 Squadron at the Empire Day Flying Display laid on by Scottish Aviation Limited on 21 May 1938. It was the first airshow to be held at Prestwick. (James B. Aird)

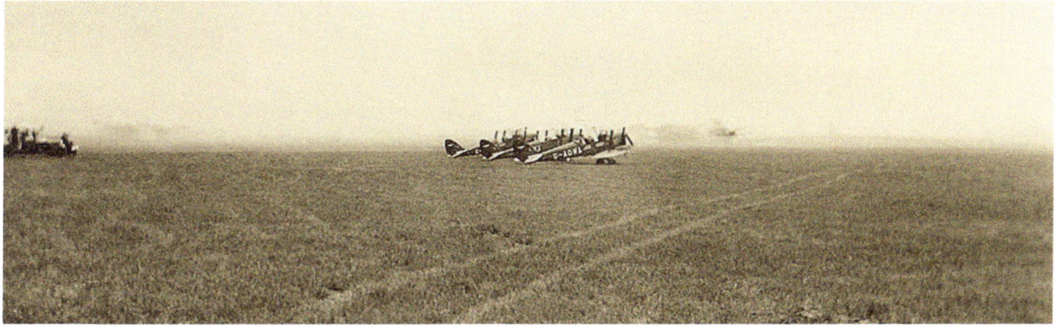

De Havilland DH.82A G-ADWA heads a line-up of three Tiger Moths at Monkton in 1934. (James B. Aird)

McIntyre and Douglas-Hamilton were two of the founding members of Scottish Aviation Limited and established a Reserve Flying School on the north side of the aerodrome. Operations began using de Havilland Tiger Moths a month after Prestwick opened as a civil airport on 17 February 1936, and the school was later re-equipped with Avro Anson and Fairey Battle aircraft. Ansons were also used by No. 1 Civil Air Navigation School (CANS), which opened on the site in August 1938, and No. 12 EFTS (Elementary Flying Training School) was formed a year later for pilot selection and training.

A hangar was constructed in 1935 to accommodate twenty-five aircraft, and an administrative block, built at the same time, contained lecture rooms, armament and photographic sections, and a parachute packing room, as well as quarters for the eight resident flying instructors, the ground instructor and for pupils.

Airshows

Scottish Aviation held a Coronation Air Display on Saturday 15 May 1937 in aid of the Royal Air Force Benevolent Fund. Four RAF squadrons took part as well as the school's own fleet of twelve de Havilland Tiger Moths, and three Hawker Hinds from No. 602 Squadron provided a dive-bombing exhibition to a crowd of around 5,000 people in the stands (some of the spectators were adversely affected by the stannic chloride from the practice bombs).

The first airshow to be held at Prestwick – an Empire Day Flying Display – took place on 21 May 1938. Organised by Scottish Aviation, it was the first time that pilots of the newly formed Royal Air Force Volunteer Reserve had appeared in public, flying Hawker Harts.

Prestwick Airport hosted the first bi-annual Scottish Airshow from 30 September 1967. It was relatively small in scale when compared to the shows at Farnborough or Fairford, and the event was eventually abandoned after 1992, primarily due to escalating overheads and insurance. In more recent times, reflecting the importance of Prestwick and its aerospace industries, and in order to create a compelling visitor attraction for South Ayrshire, the new 'Prestwick World Festival of Flight' was organised by International Arts Consultant Angela Wrapson, with George Kerevan and Lianne Hackett. The first annual spectacular (which included cinema, theatre, music, poetry, storytelling and visual arts on the theme of aviation and flight) took place between 30 August and 8 September 2013 to celebrate 100 years of aviation and aeronautical engineering at Prestwick.

Scottish Aviation built a factory at Prestwick in 1938, which included the original terminal building and hangars, to produce such aircraft as the Handley Page Jetstream and Beagle Bulldog. One part of the factory, the large white stone building, was the iconic Palace of Engineering that had been a part of the Empire Exhibition in Bellahouston Park in Glasgow in 1938. It was dismantled in 1940 and re-erected at Prestwick.

Olley Air Services Limited (of London) was granted a seven-year licence by the Air Transport Licensing Authority to carry passengers and goods by air between London (Croydon and/or Heston) during the racing season to seventeen destinations around the UK, including Ayr (Prestwick Airport and Ayr Racecourse), with daily services starting from 1 March 1939.

June 1939 saw Scottish Aviation increasing production of aircraft components after the completion of a new workshop, which enabled the company to double its output and treble employment for fitters, riggers and machine operators. The construction of a new hangar, large enough to accommodate forty aircraft, was also underway, and by August the company was employing ex-RAF aircraft engineers for de Havilland Tiger Moth, Hawker Hart Variant, Fairey Battle and Avro Anson airframes, and for the building and maintenance of Gipsy Major, Kestrel, Merlin and Cheetah engines.

Wartime

In 1940, Lord Beaverbrook, who was then Minister of Aircraft Production (MAP), took the decision to fly new aircraft across the Atlantic for delivery from the USA and Canada. The aircraft flown had not been built for trans-ocean flights although extra tanks were fitted to ensure adequate fuel reserve, and a loss of 8 to 10 per cent was anticipated. It will be remembered that up to June 1941 there was still a pretence of neutrality on the part of the USA. Prestwick became a major transatlantic ferry base, and it was then that the ferry service (Atlantic Ferry Organisation, or ATFERO, which was set up by MAP and administered by the British Overseas Airways Corporation) came into being, and as the ferrying commitment grew the expansion of the airport became essential.

It soon became evident, however, that BOAC was unable to recruit enough pilots to meet the demand despite a 'return ferry service' having being set up, whereby pilots and their crews were flown back to North America to make their next aircraft delivery to Britain. As a result, the induction operation passed under the control of RAF Ferry Command in July 1941, which employed a mix of civilians and military personnel to carry out most of the operations in order to maintain the high volume of traffic by day and night.

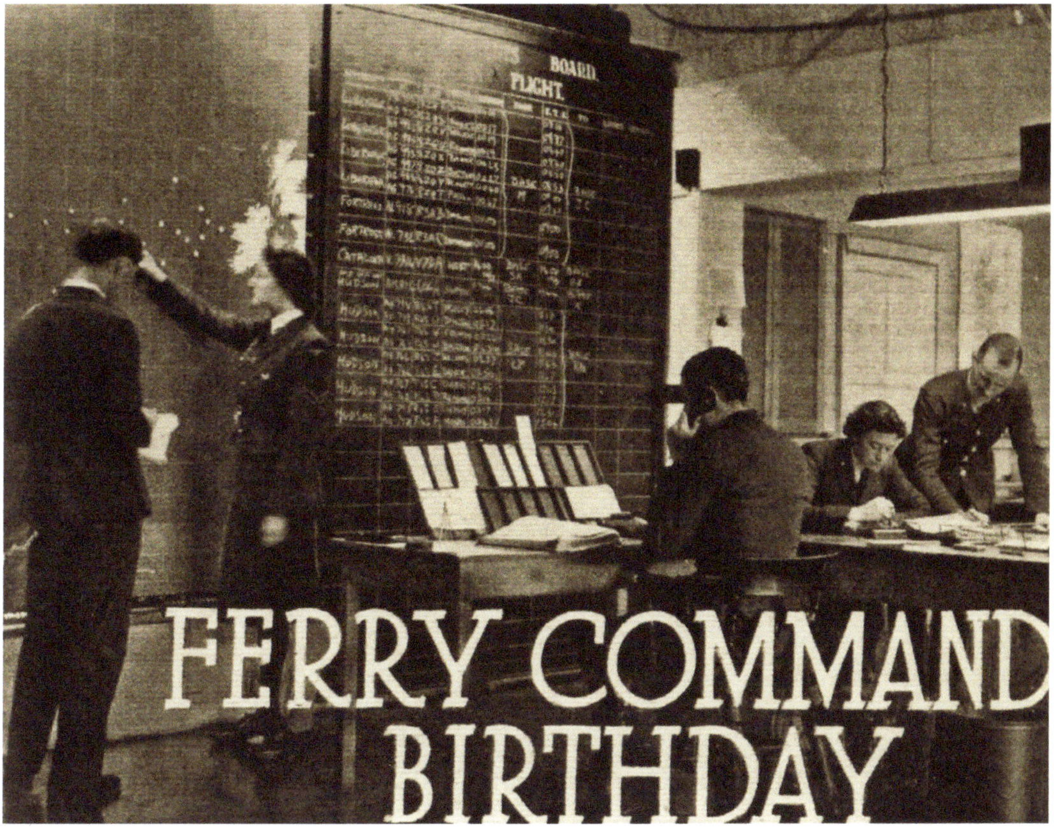

1940s

Inside the Terminal Operations Room of RAF Atlantic Ferry Command in 1942, a year after opening. (*Flight Magazine*, 23 July 1942)

Aldergrove, in Northern Ireland, was the original primary destination airfield, but early flights were soon switched to Prestwick following a number of diversions by lost pilots and the better weather conditions on the Ayrshire coast.

The construction of the two runways (6,600-foot (2,012 metre) runway 14/32 with 4,500-foot (1,372 metre) runway 08/26 crossing just west of its midpoint) and extensive new apron areas was undertaken in 1941 under Lord Beaverbrook's direction. Additional factory accommodation was also provided to keep up the pace of the assembly of Lend-Lease aircraft; on some days, 300 aircraft would arrive for onward delivery. The original factory was expanded when the Palace of Engineering, built in Bellahouston Park, Glasgow, for the 1938 Empire Exhibition, was taken down and rebuilt brick by brick on the north side of the airport, directly opposite the terminal at Prestwick. It survives today under the ownership of BAE Systems.

Orangefield House Hotel was developed into the 'Aerodrome Club' for the general public in 1941 and was first occupied by officers of the United States Army Air Force (USAAF) who were stationed at Prestwick as 'observers' while 'proving' flights from the US were taking place.

After an accidental fire destroyed the original control tower, the flying training school and watch office in February 1941, a new watch room was built on the roof of Orangefield House, from where all air traffic services were operated by the RAF. The RAF also requisitioned Redbrae House (a mock-Tudor mansion located along McNee Road on the perimeter of the aerodrome) as a control centre, with the USAAF 1403rd Base Unit taking over Westburn House (next door to Redbrae House) as a signals centre. Six seco-huts were also erected around the building in 1943, which were still in use in 1972 despite the prefabricated structures being clad with timber-framed units of flat asbestos facing sheets.

By late 1944 a flying control centre was also established at Redbrae House to provide area control for military flights operating in the UK in partnership with regional centres at Preston and Inverness. The centre, which included a search and rescue service for lost and distressed aircraft, was operated by a coalition of British, Canadian and American military personnel until the end of hostilities in 1945.

The Trans-Atlantic Air Control (TAC) was formed on 15 August 1941 to organise the vast numbers of aircraft ferried by ATFERO, initially taking up residence at Powbank Mill in November and then moving to Redbrae House a month later, from where it assumed overall control of all North Atlantic, Bermuda, Iceland and Russian flights east of 30 degrees west and north of 52 degrees 30 minutes north. Powbank Mill also housed an approach control unit for the airfield, together with a fighter command operations room located in the building's attic.

Transatlantic ATC remained at Redbrae House for thirty-one years, until 5 April 1972, when the oceanic control centre moved down the road to Atlantic House, the refurbished National Coal Board building.

Ferry Command was absorbed into RAF Transport Command in March 1943, and by the end of the Second World War some 37,000 aircraft had been ferried across the Atlantic via Prestwick to Allied fighter, bomber and maritime patrol and transportation squadrons. The major types were the Lockheed Hudson, Consolidated B-24 Liberator, Boeing B-17 Flying Fortress, Douglas C-47 Skytrain or Dakota, North American B-25 Mitchell, de Havilland Mosquito and Avro Lancaster. The American support units departed in September 1945 and Prestwick again became a civil airport in April 1946, with Scottish Aviation remaining in residence, although American military aircraft continued to stage at Prestwick en route to USAFE European bases.

The 'secrecy' surrounding the existence of a military airfield at Prestwick had been compromised in the summer of 1943 when the Biennial Report of the Chief of Staff of the US Army was published in the US. The 'stop' on the name and location of the base had been scrupulously obeyed by British newspapers, and the report not only contained a chart on which Prestwick was named, but the flying time to New York (20 hours) was noted for comparison with the time taken on passenger ships.

Trans-Canada Airlines (TCA, becoming Air Canada from 1965), which began a transatlantic service to Prestwick in 1943, became open to fare-paying passengers from September 1946, operating five times weekly in both directions using Avro Lancastrians (which were developed from the Lancaster heavy bomber). RAF Transport Command's 'Prestwick–Blackbushe Shuttle' flew a daily service, taking transatlantic passengers for London within a ninety-minute coach journey of their destination, and KLM

Royal Dutch Airlines operated Douglas C-54 Skymasters between Amsterdam and New York via Prestwick on a thrice-weekly schedule from 21 May 1946.

The airport was also used by services run under charter by Scottish Airlines, notably between Prestwick and Belfast, and a new service using converted Douglas C-47 Dakotas between Copenhagen and Reykjavik via Prestwick started at the beginning of June 1946. Air France started a direct thrice-weekly service schedule from Paris on 17 July, and BOAC stated their intention of routing two Lockheed Constellations a week through the airport, with *Balmoral* operating the first flight on the New York–Prestwick service.

By mid-1946, and despite controversy surrounding its suitability because of its pre-war layout, Prestwick was designated by the Minister of Civil Aviation as an international airport; it was well located with the main runway 6,600 feet long and the secondary runway 4,500 feet long for transatlantic flights to Canada and the USA, and the more northerly countries of Europe and Asia. Orangefield House had become the airport terminal and offered potential for expansion, and alongside the airfield an aircraft factory provided full services. Hotel accommodation was considerable at the airport itself, which was within easy distance of the industrial, commercial and more populated areas of Scotland around the Forth and the Clyde, and enjoyed an outstanding good weather record, closing on only two days during the year due to adverse conditions.

Scottish Aviation advertised their Prestwick factory in early 1947 as being equipped with the most modern machinery for aircraft conversion, overhaul and repairs, and were already working with Aer Lingus, American Overseas Airlines, British Aircraft Services, DDL (Danish Air Lines), KLM (Royal Dutch Airlines), Fred Olsen Aero Transport (Norway), Portuguese Airlines, Sabena, Scottish Airlines, Swissair and TWA (Trans World Airlines).

Irvin-Bell Helicopter Sales Ltd gave its first demonstration of the two-seater Bell 47B to a small but important gathering at Prestwick on 25 September 1947, the main purpose being to sell the Bell helicopter to the UK and to other countries, to train pilots and mechanics, and to explore the possibilities of commercial operation of helicopters for crop spraying, rescue and ambulance work, aerial survey and photography, mail carrying, traffic control and taxi work.

Prestwick took part in Operation 'New Horizon', the Ontario Government's Scheme of Air Immigration from Britain for 7,000 Britons seeking opportunity and a new way of life in Canada. In the early stages, three Skymasters were carrying forty passengers a week, but this was increased to forty-three aircraft per month, some of them departing from Prestwick Airport to take care of the many Scottish emigrants. By November 1947 just over 3,000 young British men and women had departed since the inauguration at the beginning of the year.

The Ground Controlled Approach (GCA), which had been installed and controlled by the RAF during the war, was 'borrowed' by the Ministry of Aviation in December 1947 in order to keep London Airport working. It had no reliable system to cope with poor weather (fog in particular), and if the existing wartime Standard Beam Approach was missed a pilot would have to catch sight of the white Very lights being fired by the runway control caravan. Its more effective Instrument Landing System (ILS) was in its infancy and was temperamental, over-sensitive and could easily be disabled by interference (not that many aeroplanes at the time were fitted with ILS receivers). Prestwick No. 12 GCA unit was chosen because the airport had an excellent weather record and could afford to lose the sophisticated approach aid.

The work of strengthening the runways, aprons and taxi tracks to withstand landings by aircraft of Stratocruiser weight began on 12 April 1948, starting with runway 14/32. Pilots were requested to use the subsidiary 08/26 crossing just west of its midpoint when wind considerations were favourable, or to use the airfield at Heathfield, close to the end of runway 21, so that the work at Prestwick could continue uninterrupted. During the Second World War, RAF Heathfield (which also served the Royal Navy as HMS *Wagtail*) was used for the servicing of American Consolidated B-24 Liberator heavy bombers, and as a training ground for aircrews, and is now covered by the Heathfield Retail Park together with housing and a golf course to the west.

The robust, high-wing A4/45 monoplane used for military communications was being built by Scottish Aviation under the name of 'Prestwick Pioneer' and intended to begin civil duties from September 1948. The first two of four prototypes (VL515 and VL516) were fitted with 240 hp de Havilland Gipsy Queen engines, but were considered underpowered by the RAF, and so during their conversion these were replaced with 520 hp Alvis Leonides engines. Registered as G-AKBF and G-ANAZ, the Pioneer II first flew on 5 May 1950, and the type was subsequently ordered by the RAF as the Pioneer CC.1.

On 5 May 1949, the inaugural flight of the Iceland Airways Reykjavik to London service reached Northolt. Operating with forty-seat Douglas Skymasters, the company made one return flight each week, calling at Prestwick, and on 13 June Air France started a service between Belfast and Paris – the first service to link Northern Ireland and the French capital – operating three times a week with thirty-three-seat Languedoc aircraft. Air France had already been operating a thrice-weekly service from Prestwick to Le Bourget (with some flights operated via Edinburgh Turnhouse) since 23 June 1947.

1950s

By 1950, Prestwick had also become well established as one of the outstanding holiday attractions of the Ayrshire coast, and figures for the busiest airfields in the UK in December 1949, which were published in April, showed Prestwick was placed fourth in the table, with 6,148 passengers arriving and departing on scheduled services. Northolt, London and Glasgow (Renfrew) airports came top.

During the season from April to October, over 43,000 visitors used the public enclosure to enjoy watching the spectacle of airliner arrivals and departures, but it was only the arrival of HRH Princess Margaret at Prestwick by air on 10 August, which drew nearly 3,500 visitors who paid for admission, that prompted plans to provide more amenities for future seasonal visitors. Subsequently, many of the airport buildings were floodlit and the approach roads were decorated with international flags. By the end of 1951, the airport was visited by 75,000 members of the public; one visit alone on 18 August by the Bristol Brabazon prototype airliner G-AGPW drew 19,000 spectators in three days.

Caledonia, the flagship of BOAC's new fleet of double-decked sixty-seat Boeing Stratocruisers, was officially named by the Minister of Civil Aviation, Lord Pakenham, at Prestwick amidst a ceremony with pipers and drummers playing Scottish airs on Saturday 7 January 1950. Stratocruisers began to operate two of the four weekly flights from Prestwick to Montreal, and on 6 November a BOAC Stratocruiser broke the (unofficial) record for a transatlantic crossing from Montreal to Prestwick, making the trip in eight hours and three minutes. Previously the best time by a Stratocruiser on this route was eight hours and forty-five minutes, although a Constellation had made the crossing in eight hours and fourteen minutes.

David F. McIntyre (Managing Director of Scottish Aviation) assured the Ayr Chamber of Commerce, which was continuing to press for the full development of Prestwick, that if the recommendations of the Clydesmuir Committee (set up by Scottish Council under Lord Clydesmuir to consider the future of Prestwick Airport), which looked ahead and visualised the immense development (with an emphasis on the need for adequate feeder services) that Prestwick was entitled to, were carried out, Scotland would have an international airport capable of meeting not only its own needs, but those of northern England and Northern Ireland as well.

The Committee had recommended that the Government should get on with the job of improving the runways and the aerodrome instead of waiting until 1953, which was the earliest date prescribed under the Ministry of Civil Aviation's (MCA) development policy. The Committee also suggested that a Scottish Public Utilities Corporation should be set up, which could then be placed in complete control administratively and technically of Prestwick Airport, and as such would be able to co-ordinate its efforts and its future with the general interests of Scottish trade and industry.

The MCA granted permission for Scottish Aviation Ltd to run charter services from February 1951 to provide links between Prestwick and seven English cities. The agreement stipulated daily feeder services from the Scottish airport to Brough, Exeter, Birmingham, Blackpool, Liverpool, Leeds and Newcastle, and thrice-daily flights between Prestwick and Ronaldsway, Isle of Man, to begin in June.

The United States Air Force (USAF) Military Air Transport Service (MATS) 1631st Air Base Squadron opened a base in 1952 on the site of the original airport using former RAF facilities, and in 1953 expanded to the Monkton side of the airport, where it remained until 1966.

Two USAF Air Rescue Sikorsky H-19 helicopters landed at Prestwick on 31 July 1952, completing the first transatlantic helicopter flight in aviation history. The two Sikorskys made the cross-ocean flight as part of a journey that took them from Westover Air Force Base, Massachusetts, to Wiesbaden, Germany. The mission was undertaken by the USAF to investigate the problems of the long-range ferrying of helicopters. The total distance covered by the two helicopters in their flight from Westover to Prestwick was 3,535 miles with an air time of forty-two hours and twenty-five minutes, but adverse weather conditions at several stops en route

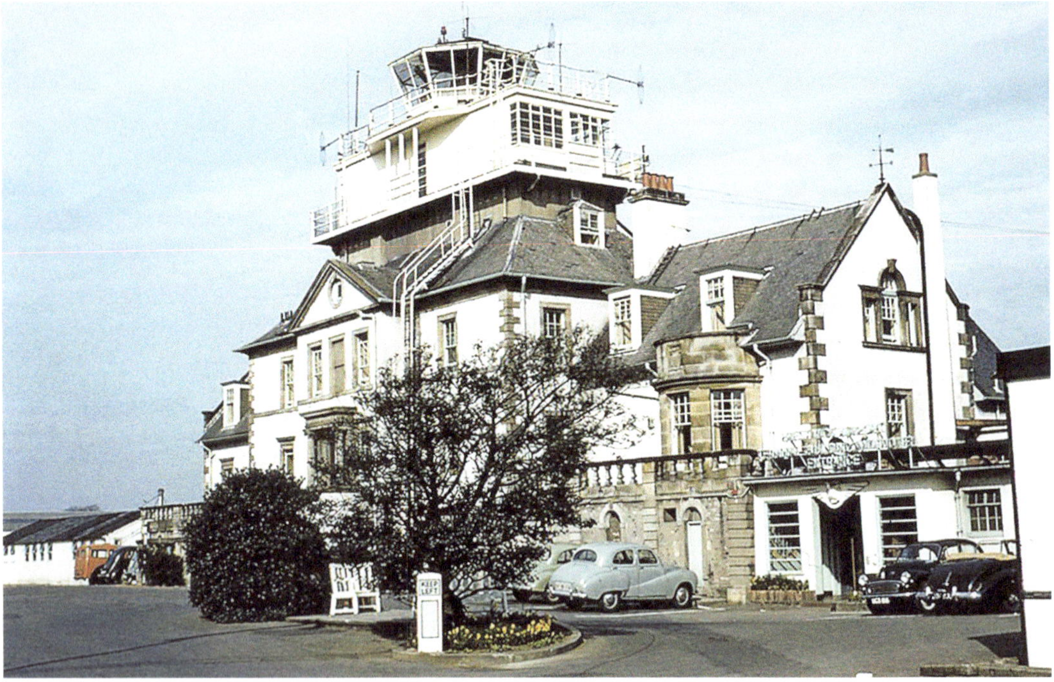

1950s

Orangefield House was used by the RAF and USAAF during the Second World War, and a control tower was built through the roof in 1943. The building was demolished in February 1966 when Prestwick Airport was expanded. This photograph was taken in April 1958. (Author's Collection)

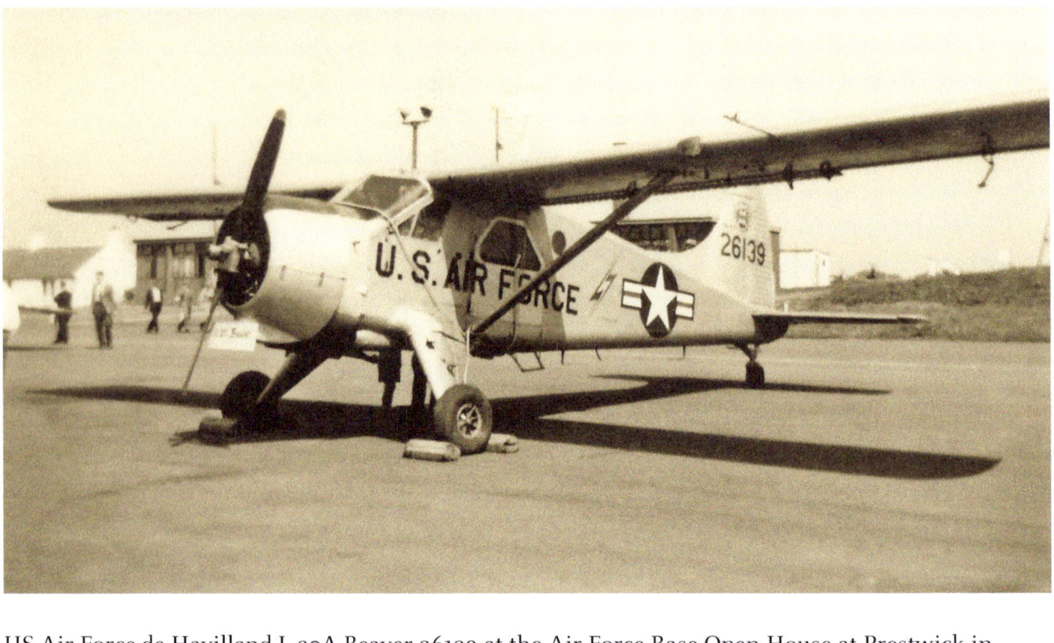

US Air Force de Havilland L-20A Beaver 26139 at the Air Force Base Open House at Prestwick in May 1959. It was mainly used in night landing training for Dakota pilots and for personnel and mail transport, and spent eleven years in service. (Author's Collection)

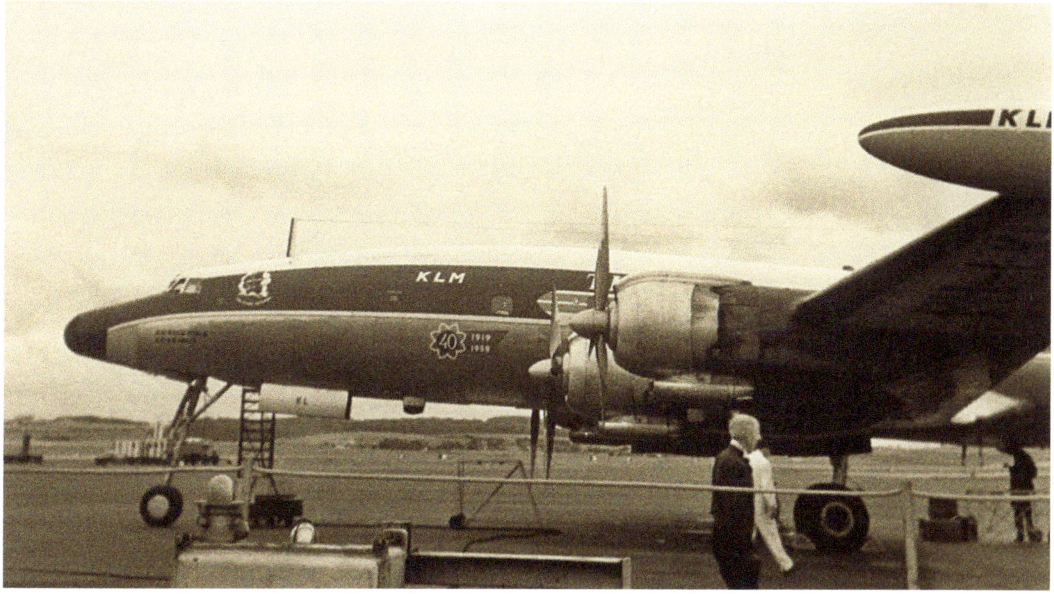

KLM Lockheed L-1049H Super Constellation PH-LKL *Desiderius Erasmus* wearing her 40th anniversary decals. Sadly, this aircraft crashed on take-off from Mesa-Falcon Field, Arizona, on 11 May 1975 after a complete power loss on all four engines. (James B. Aird)

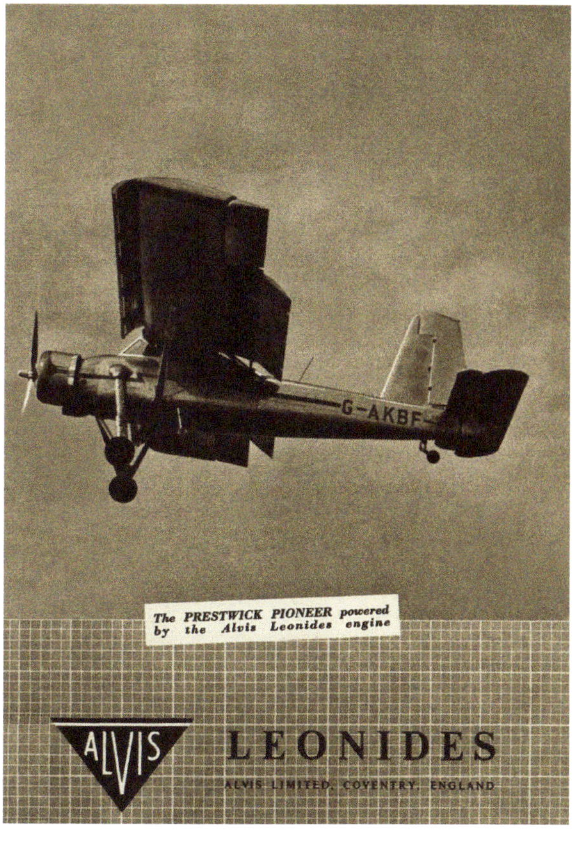

The 'Prestwick Pioneer' G-AKBF was powered by the Alvis Leonides 501/4M engine, as advertised in 1951. (Author's Collection)

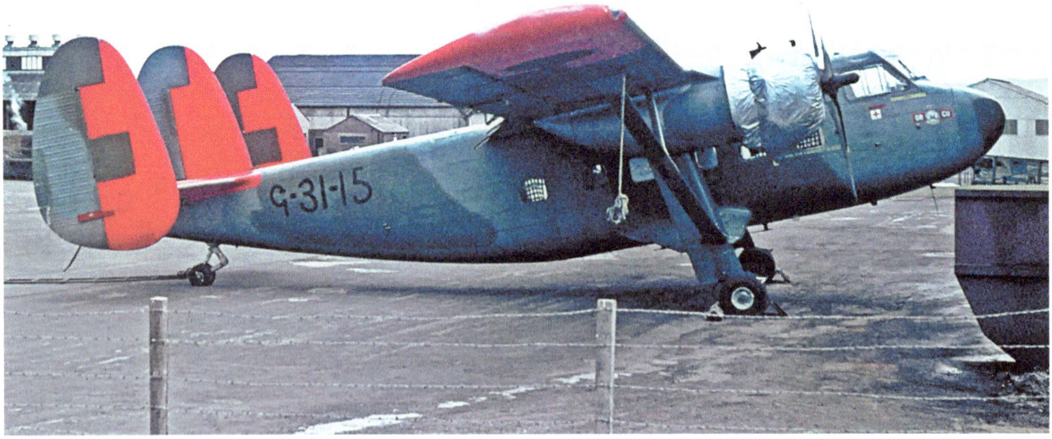

Scottish Aviation Twin Pioneer CC.2 G-31-15, seen on 19 July 1958. Scrapped in 1992, the cockpit is displayed at the Dumfries and Galloway Aviation Museum. (Malcolm Nason)

stretched the elapsed time for the Atlantic crossing to fifteen days, eight hours. The test was conducted to raise the potential value of helicopters by showing how large helicopters of the future could be stationed at a few strategic spots in various parts of the world and could, on short notice, fly to virtually any place on the globe within a few hours.

Two new Scandinavian Airlines System (SAS) services over the North Atlantic were inaugurated on 26 October 1952 with the 'Royal Viking' luxury flights and 'Globetrotter' reduced-fare services. The former, operated by thirty-four-seat Douglas DC-6Bs, flew non-stop between Prestwick and New York, while the sixty-seat 'Globetrotter' DC-6s made a short refuelling stop at Gander. Between them the two services provided seven weekly flights to New York from Stockholm and Oslo, and twice-weekly flights from Helsinki.

One of Scottish Airlines' first overseas engagements was its participation in the 1948–49 Berlin Airlift, where two of its Douglas DC-3 Dakotas and three Consolidated B-24 Liberators took part in Operation 'Plainfare', during which it delivered over 2,700 tons of supplies and carried over 15,000 East German refugees to Hanover and Hamburg. The company's fleet of Avro Yorks also operated troop flights from airports in the London area to Australia, Canada, Southern Rhodesia, Cairo, Sudan, Aden and Singapore. The aircraft, which were maintained at Prestwick, were fitted with backward-facing seats and carried fifty troops or their wives and families.

By mid-May 1953, work had started on a contract worth several million dollars for the construction of Greensite, a vast new American air force base covering 40 acres on the Monkton side of the airport. The USAF personnel who had occupied the heart of the airport terminal area subsequently moved to the new camp, leaving only operations, traffic signals and weather staff in the main buildings. No. 1602 Military Air Transport Service Wing transferred to Greensite from its base near Munich on 15 September 1956 to fulfil its role of controlling by air all movements of American military personnel in Europe and the Near East.

As a result of discussions between the Ministry of Civil Aviation and representatives of local authorities in the Prestwick area in March 1949, the new 6,000 foot runway (13/31) came into operation on 30 September

1955, although due to associated ongoing construction work (including the new taxiway) it was restricted for use only in VFR (Visual Flight Rules – under which pilots have sufficient visibility to fly the aircraft maintaining visual separation from terrain and other aircraft) conditions as there were no approach aids until April 1956. Most of the remains of Fail Monastery, which was situated on the bank of the Water of Fail in the Parish of Tarbolton, South Ayrshire, had been removed in 1952 and were used for the foundations for the runway and building. The first 'official' landing was made on it by a Ministry of Transport & Civil Aviation (MTCA) de Havilland Dove carrying Sir Alfred Le Maitre, Controller of Ground Services, and Air Commodore J. G. Murray, Scottish Divisional Controller. The official party was greeted by the airport commandant, J. Jeffs, who joined them aboard the Scottish Aviation Twin Pioneer prototype to make the first take-off from the new runway.

Scottish Aviation Ltd's prototype STOL (Short Take Off and Landing) Twin Pioneer G-ANTP first flew on 25 June 1955, with the first production aircraft following on 28 April 1956. By the end of 1958, the company had no fewer than sixty-nine Twin Pioneers and fifty-two Prestwick Pioneers either in service or the subject of firm orders, and demonstration visits had been made to Lebanon, Jordan, Sudan, Italy, Abadan, Mexico, Central America and the Caribbean. Production of the Prestwick Pioneer ceased in November 1961.

David McIntyre, Managing Director and co-founder of both Scottish Aviation and Prestwick Airport, was killed on Sunday 8 December 1957 when the Twin Pioneer he was flying, G-AOEO, crashed on a demonstration flight in Tripolitania, Libya, after a wing had broken off. He was forty-two years old. The senior test pilot, engineer and three passengers were also killed. A memorial to his name was unveiled at Prestwick Airport in 1958, and a new VIP suite for visiting dignitaries was named the McIntyre Suite in memory of him. A plaque was commissioned in 1965 to hang in the new terminal, and in 2006 a lounge bearing his name and a marker reflecting the event were unveiled.

A new terminal building was a part of development plans drawn up in 1958, which included a three-storey block (which would house offices, telecommunications, restaurant, cafeteria, passenger waiting areas, and a rooftop observation gallery), a freight building, a control tower and an extension to 7,000 feet (2,134 m) of the 13/31 runway. It was also decided that a loop road around the airport was required because the main road out of Prestwick towards Monkton crossed the runway. Prestwick also became the first British airport to sell duty-free whisky – something already commonplace in Europe – after a license was granted by the Ayr District Licensing Court in March 1959.

1960s

Several big names from the screen and stage have used Prestwick airport over the years, such as Danny Kaye (1949), Frank Sinatra (6 July 1953), Roy Rogers and his horse Trigger (14 February 1954), Bing Crosby (5 August 1970) and US astronauts David Scott and Neil Armstrong (January 1972), but probably the most memorable visit was on 3 March 1960, when the airport became the only piece of British territory that Elvis Presley, having just finished his military service, ever set foot on when his US Army transport plane stopped to refuel while en route from Germany. The brief visit was made due to the fact that aircraft in the 1950s were unable to carry sufficient fuel to go all the way to London or Europe from the US, so they would refuel at Prestwick.

Runway 13/31 was opened on 17 May 1960, with construction work for a new parking apron with stands for twelve aircraft starting in December. The work on the runway extension, elongating it to 9,800 feet (2,987 metres), caused considerable disruption to road users as the main road from Monkton into Prestwick crossed the tarmac of the runway and was controlled by a level crossing system, which remained in place until the new perimeter road was completed in 1964.

The summer peak of 1961 saw ninety-nine scheduled transatlantic flights passing through Prestwick each week: forty-seven BOAC (twenty-one Bristol Britannias and twenty-six Boeing 707s); fifteen TCA (Douglas DC-8); fourteen SAS (Douglas DC-8); nine Pan American World Airways (Pan Am) (three Douglas DC-8 and six Douglas DC-7C); and fourteen KLM (ten Douglas DC-8 and four Douglas DC-7C).

The new ATC tower, built at the intersection of runways 13/31 and 03/21, was opened on 24 April 1962 by Sir Thomas Moore, MP for Ayr, and it was used for the first time immediately after the ceremony by a BOAC Scottish Monarch Boeing 707 flight, for which the accompanying new thistle and crown symbol had been adopted. The Scottish Monarch flights were the first daily all-year-round transatlantic jet services to be operated through Prestwick by any airline.

John Laing Construction Ltd was awarded the contract by the Ministry of Aviation for the construction of the new terminal – the last phase of the redevelopment at Prestwick Airport – and work was under way in August 1962. The new terminal building (which was described in the 24 January 1963 edition of *Flight International* as 'a finger-shaped building, partly underground with gates at the head and along each side') was officially opened by Queen Elizabeth the Queen Mother in 1964.

BAC/Vickers Standard VC10 G-ARVF *Victor Foxtrot* made its debut at Prestwick Airport in October 1963, making a series of circuits and bumps at Prestwick as part of route proving and crew-training flights as part of their VC-10 test fleet, until it was delivered to BOAC in September 1964.

The first Learjet 23 to arrive in Europe landed at Prestwick on 16 April 1965, en route to Frankfurt, Germany. The six-to-eight-seat twin-engine high-speed business jet was the seventh to be built by American inventor and businessman Bill Lear's Swiss American Aviation Corporation (SAAC). Lockheed-Georgia placed an £890,000 order with Scottish Aviation in late 1965 to fabricate forty-eight fuselage sections for the RAF C-130K Hercules programme. The finished sections were shipped to Lockheed for final assembly.

Airport statistics published in 1964 showed that Prestwick, despite being Scotland's 'Transatlantic Gateway', had been on a slow but steady decline in the number of passengers handled and aircraft movements during the previous year, a trend that had become more apparent since the late 1950s. When Roy Jenkins MP (Labour Minister for Aviation) promoted the Airports Authority Bill in 1965, his key argument was that the nation's airports could be more flexible and better able to generate profits by remaining responsible to Parliament. The Bill was passed and the British Airports Authority (BAA) was established, and subsequently assumed ownership and responsibility for Heathrow, Gatwick, Stansted and Prestwick airports in April 1966. However, in light of the current financial situation, both the BAA and British Rail reluctantly 'dropped' the idea of a

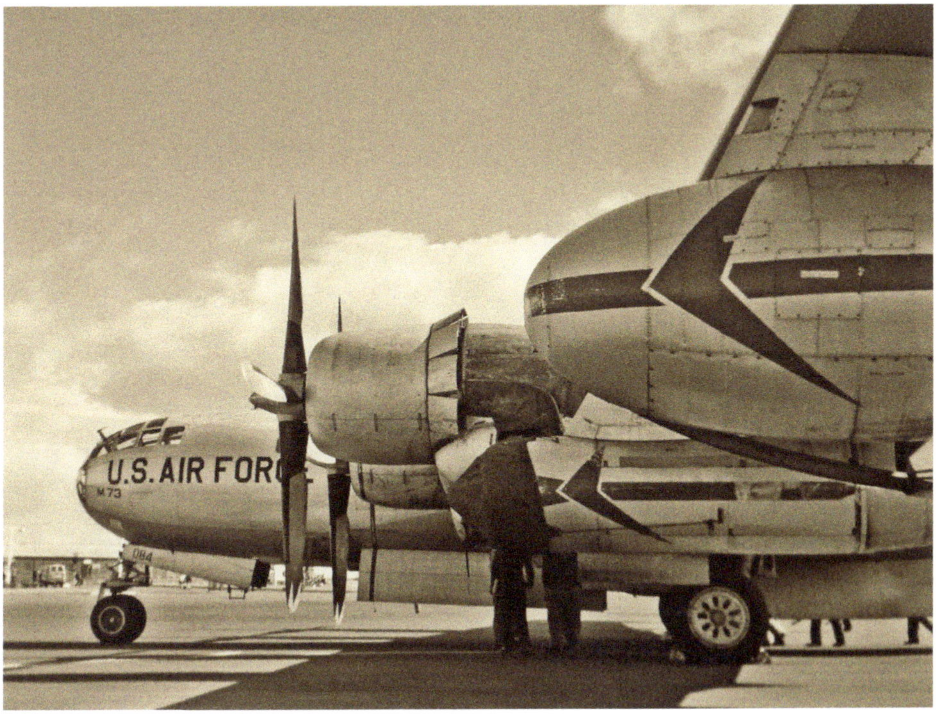

1960s

One of the larger exhibits at the 1960 Armed Forces Display on 28 May, visiting from 420th ARS, RAF Sculthorpe, was 0-80084/M73, a superb Boeing KB-50J Superfortress. (James B. Aird)

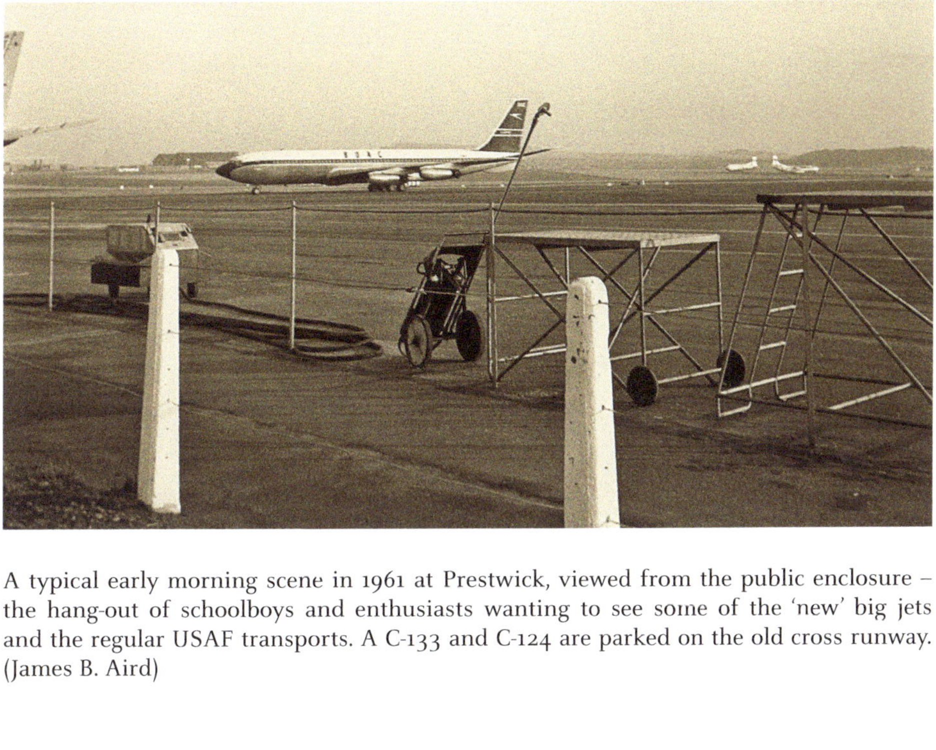

A typical early morning scene in 1961 at Prestwick, viewed from the public enclosure – the hang-out of schoolboys and enthusiasts wanting to see some of the 'new' big jets and the regular USAF transports. A C-133 and C-124 are parked on the old cross runway. (James B. Aird)

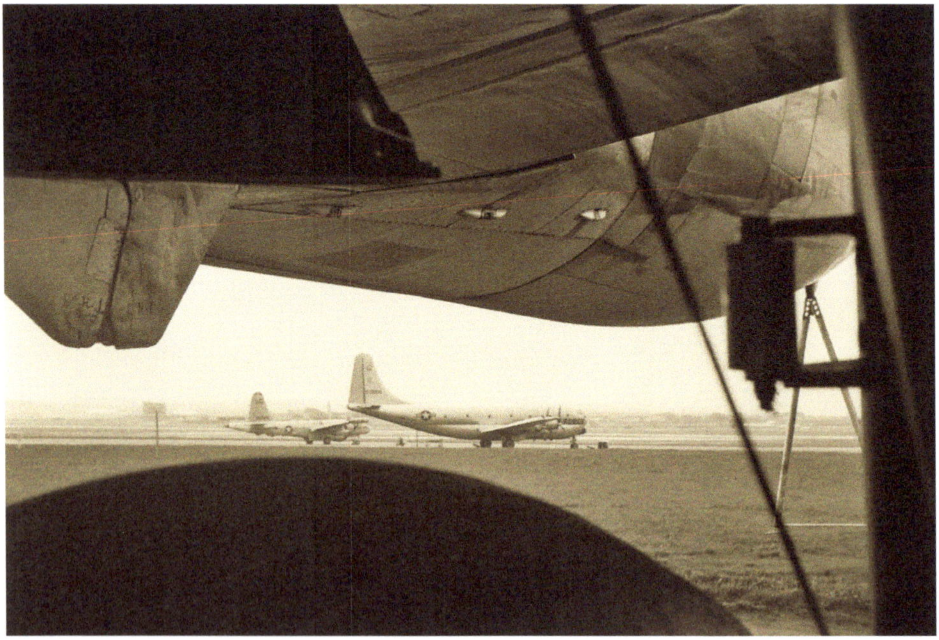

A photograph taken from under a Douglas C-124 Globemaster of a Boeing C-97 Stratofreighter of the New York ANG and a Lockheed SP-2 Neptune of VP-56, USN, which are parked on the old runway on 22 May 1965. (James B. Aird)

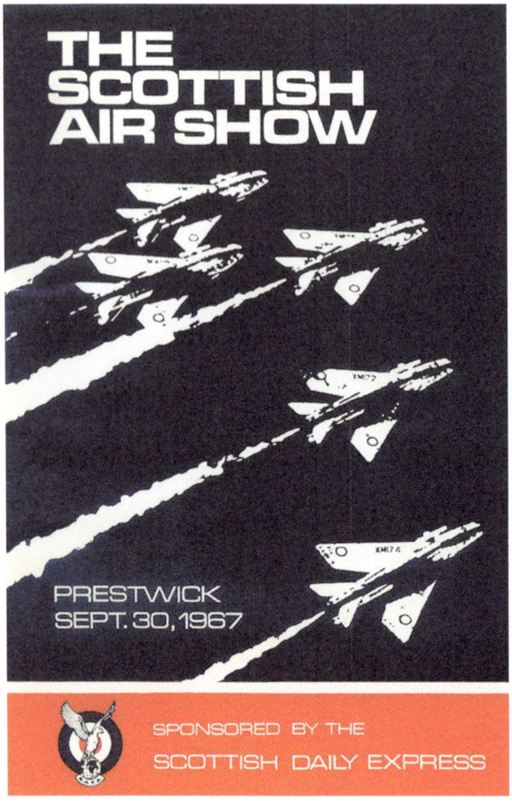

Prestwick airshow programme cover, 1967. (Author's Collection)

FLYING PROGRAMME

1. HAWKER HURRICANE and SUPERMARINE SPITFIRE
A ten-minute display by the last survivors of the R.A.F.'s Battle of Britain Fighter Force. A remarkable demonstration by two veteran aircraft, designed almost 30 years ago.

2. R.A.F. LIGHTNING
From the age of the piston aircraft straight into the era of the Supersonics. Built by English Electric Ltd., the Lightning demonstrates the qualities required by the fighters—men and machines—of today.

3. SCOTTISH AVIATION LTD.—TWIN PIONEER
Designed and built by Scots at Prestwick, the "Twin" shows that speed is not everything—by landing and taking off at bicycle speed.

4. R.A.F. WESTLAND WHIRLWIND HELICOPTER DEMONSTRATION
This impressive helicopter shows her manoeuverability—then stages a rescue drama, by men of one of the R.A.F.'s crack Air Rescue units.

5. R.A.F. SHACKLETON
Long range sea patrol and rescue aircraft, powered by Rolls-Royce Griffon engines. Its role—to guard the Air routes used by the giant passenger-carrying Jet Airliners.

6. R.A.F. ANDOVER
As a troop and cargo carrier, the Andover is one of the R.A.F.'s "workhorses". And today it will give an extra demonstration after the Show—by flying the Dog Team back to their home base in Essex.

7. SUPERMARINE SPITFIRE
A five-minute display by a privately owned Spitfire—proudly preserved by Rolls-Royce Ltd., who supplied the engines for the war-time Spitfire air fleet.

8. THE GIN TEAM
Led by Hawick-born Fl. Lt. Jim Burns, the team show that their B.A.C. Jet Provost aircraft may be a basic trainer—but their performance takes them right to the top of the bill.

9. HANDLEY PAGE JETSTREAM
Brand new Executive Jet—being partly built by Scottish Aviation Ltd. at Prestwick. It has already won over 150 orders from Britain and abroad.

10. BRITTEN-NORMAN ISLANDER
Designed and built on the Isle of Wight, the Islander, owned by Loganair, is opening up new areas to freight and passenger operations.

11. R.A.F. DOMINIE
Built by Hawker Siddeley, the Dominie is a familiar sight at Prestwick Airport. For, under their Civil name—HS-125—a number have flown the Atlantic to operate as Executive jets throughout North America.

12. ROYAL NAVAL BUCCANEER
Representing the R.N.A.S. at Lossiemouth, the demonstration will show the Buccaneer's very high performance in range, speed and climb. Equipped to carry bombs, rockets or missiles—or any combination of these weapons—they carried out the strikes against the wrecked *Torrey Canyon* oil tanker.

13. R.A.F. GNAT
This advanced trainer is developed from the Gnat fighter in service in India and Finland. A very fast, agile aircraft it has a maximum speed of 650 m.p.h. at sea level.

14. THE WRIGHT JUBILEE TROPHY COMPETITION RUNNER-UP
Awarded by the R.A.F.A. to commemorate the 50th Anniversary of powered flight, this year's runner-up Fl. Lt. J. E. Howton, puts his Jet Provost through its prize-winning routines.

15. ROYAL NORWEGIAN AIR FORCE ALBATROSS
These Grumman-built long range aircraft have flown specially from Norway to Scotland for the Air Show. They represent Norway's 303 and 333 Squadrons, which were based in Scotland during World War II, manned by Norwegians who escaped after the Occupation.

16. ROYAL NETHERLANDS AIR FORCE NEPTUNE
This item, too, has its war-time links with Scotland. The aircraft represents the Netherlands 320 Squadron, which—like the Norwegians—found a home base in Scotland after escaping from Occupied Holland.

17. DE HAVILLAND TIGER MOTH
Owned by Mr. W. P. Meynell, a business-farmer, it has a special place in any show at Prestwick. For it was the wood-and-fabric Moths which pioneered flying at Prestwick.

18. AIRWORK CESSNA 310 AIRCRAFT
Based at Perth, the Cessna show off their paces in the hands of senior flying instructors.

19. THE RED ARROWS
The R.A.F. crack aerobatic display team perform their fantastic ballet in the sky. All pilots are top instructors at the Central Flying School at Little Rissington. Flying red-painted Gnats, they are the only team which can roll swept-wing aircraft in formation.

20. THE FALCONS
The curtain falls—from probably 12,000 feet up (cloud permitting). A breath-taking display of sky-diving by the R.A.F.'s wonder Falcon team—top instructors from the Parachute Training School.

Special Note
To avoid interruption—and possible danger—to large passenger-carrying Jet Airliners operating Trans-Atlantic and European scheduled services through Prestwick (Scotland) Airport during the Display, the sequence and nature of aerobatic demonstrations is subject to alteration.

0 21

Prestwick airshow programme interior, 1967. (Author's Collection)

fast rail link between Prestwick and Glasgow as it would incur a continuing annual deficit until well into the 1980s.

Orangefield House, which had served as the main terminal building for the airport in the post-war era, was demolished in February 1966 to make way for an extension to the parallel taxiway; the only known items to still exist are the aviation murals that once decorated the main lounge and the maple floor, which was re-laid in the 'Aviator Suite' function room in the terminal building.

1970s

The huge hangar that fronted onto the airfield was converted into a production shed in 1965 for Lockheed Hercules components. Initially Scottish Aviation (now the principle tenant of the BAA at Prestwick) was contracted to supply centre fuselage panels and pylons for sixty-six Hercules C-130Ks for the RAF with subsequent re-orders dramatically increasing that number to 771 sets. The requirement of the contract was that all materials were to be supplied from the USA, and even allowing for the shipping of the completed items back to Georgia, the cost of the Scottish product was less than that of local manufacture.

The Royal Canadian Air Force (RCAF) occupied a substantial part of Prestwick for its aircraft operating in Europe to be brought to Scottish Aviation for overhauls, maintenance, upgrades and, if operational commitments so dictated, for storage. The airfield's long runways and good weather record played a part in this particular contract because not many overhaul specialists in the UK had the facilities necessary to handle the variety of aircraft such as the Lockheed T-33, Beechcraft C-45 and, in more recent years, Lockheed F-104 Starfighters.

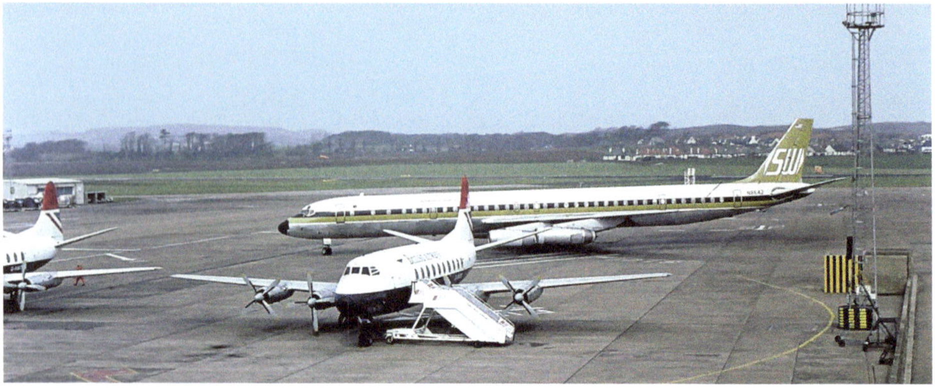

1970s

Seaboard World Douglas DC-8 and two British Airways Viscounts in March 1976. (Author's Collection)

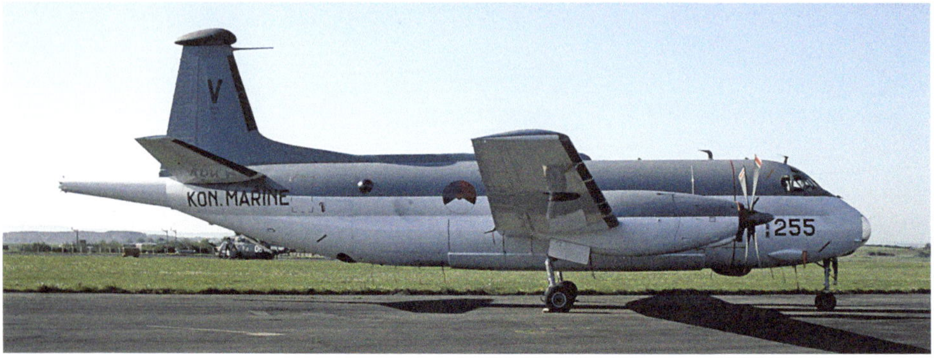

Breguet Br. 1150 Atlantic 1 'V-255' of No. 321 Squadron, Koninklijke Marine (Royal Netherlands Navy), a long-distance scout and submarine fighter, in 1979. The aircraft was ditched in the Irish Sea on 15 January 1981 with the loss of three of the twelve crew after a hydraulics failure. (Author's Collection)

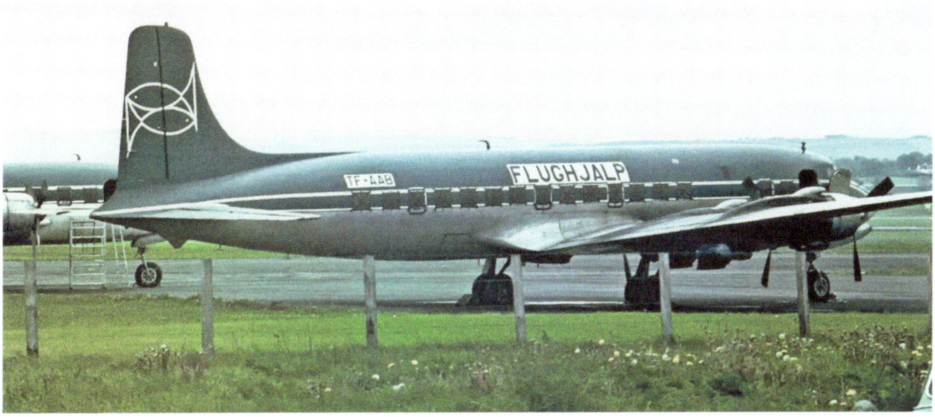

Douglas DC6B TF-AAB of Flughjalp (Joint Church Aid), seen parked in May 1970 after the Biafran airlift. (Malcolm Nason)

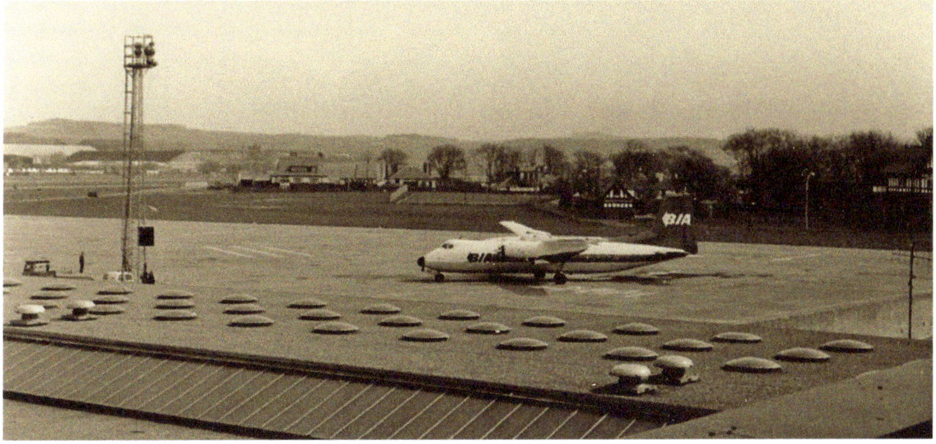

British Island (Channel Island) Airways' 1963-built Handley-Page HPR-7 Dart Herald 201 G-APWG, a turboprop, fifty-eight-seat passenger aircraft, is seen on 10 April 1971. It is now on display at the Imperial War Museum, Duxford. (Bill Johnston)

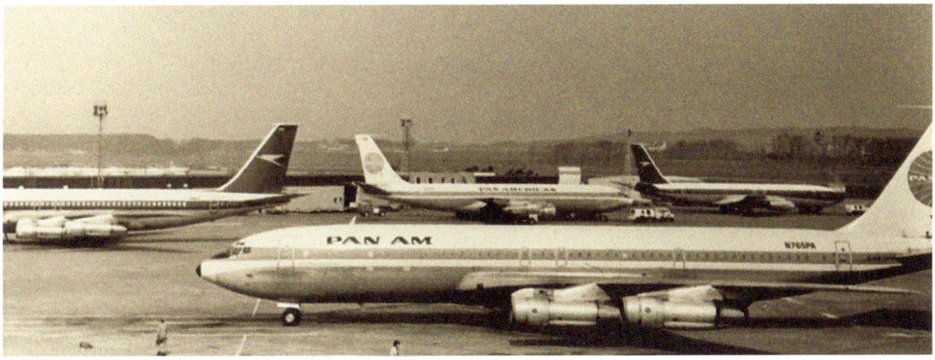

Pan American World Airways (Pan Am) Boeing 707-321Bs, photographed at Prestwick Airport on 10 April 1971. (Bill Johnston)

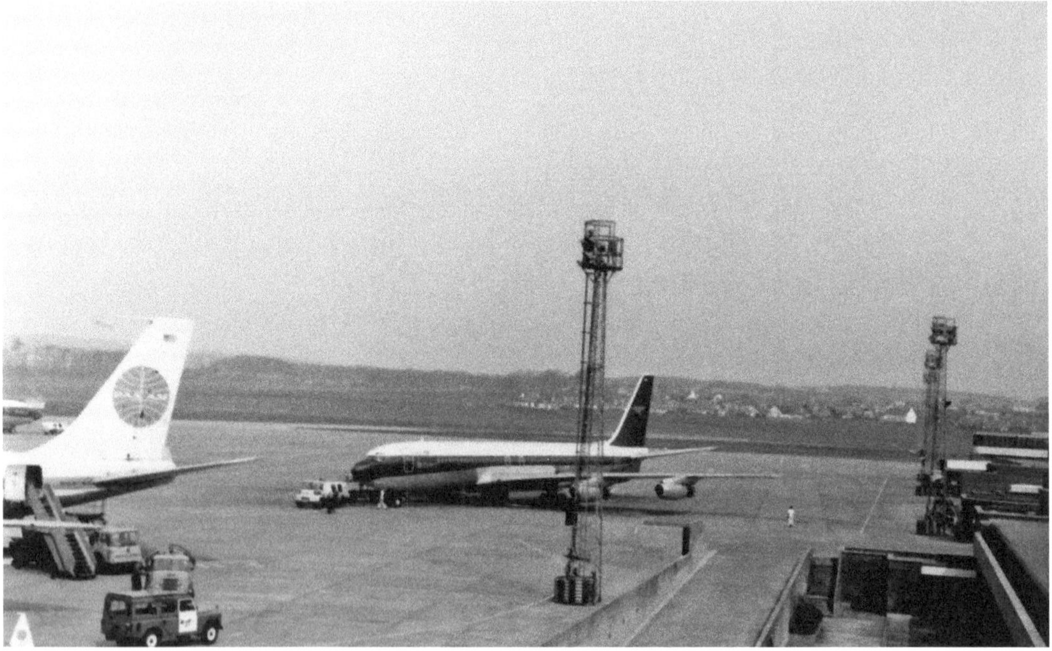

British Overseas Airways Corporation (BOAC) Boeing 707-465 G-ARWD on 10 April 1971. Previously registered VR-BBW, it also saw service with BEA Airtours, British Airtours and Air Mauritius, and was scrapped in 1981. (Bill Johnston)

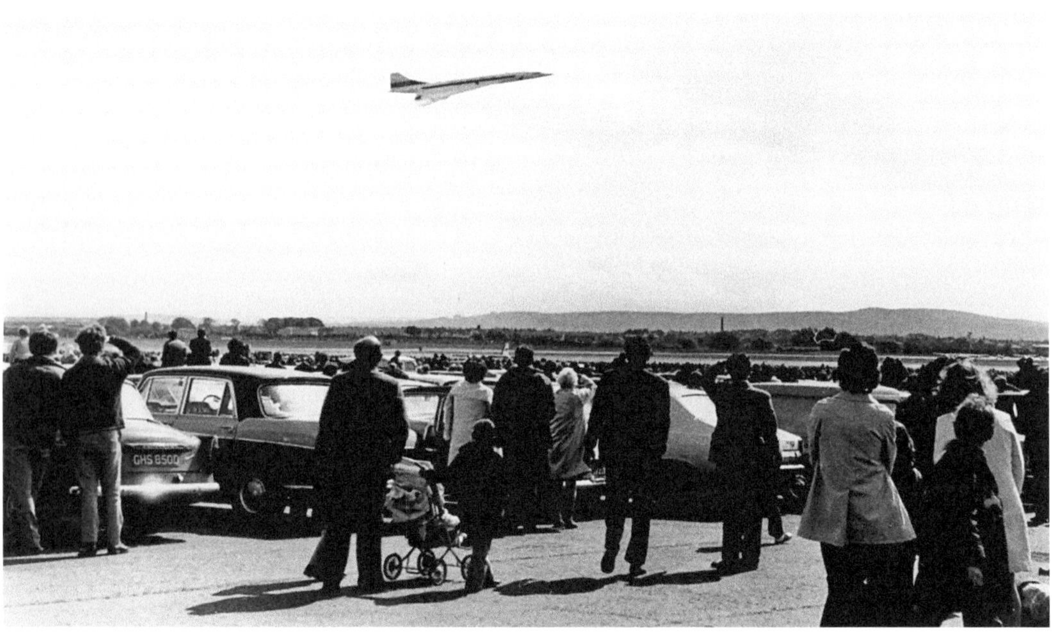

Concorde 002 G-BSST at Prestwick Airshow on 3 June 1972. This was the second prototype of this Anglo-French aircraft and made 438 flights (836 hours), of which 196 flights were supersonic, between 9 April 1969 and 4 March 1976, when it was delivered to its final resting place at Yeovilton Air Museum. (Bill Johnston)

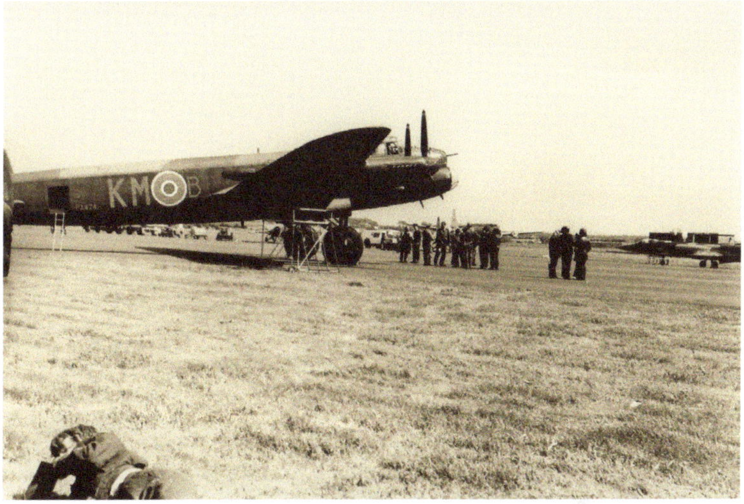

Avro Lancaster PA474 at the Prestwick Airshow on 3 June 1972. It is one of only two Lancaster aircraft that remain in airworthy condition out of the 7,377 that were built. (Bill Johnston)

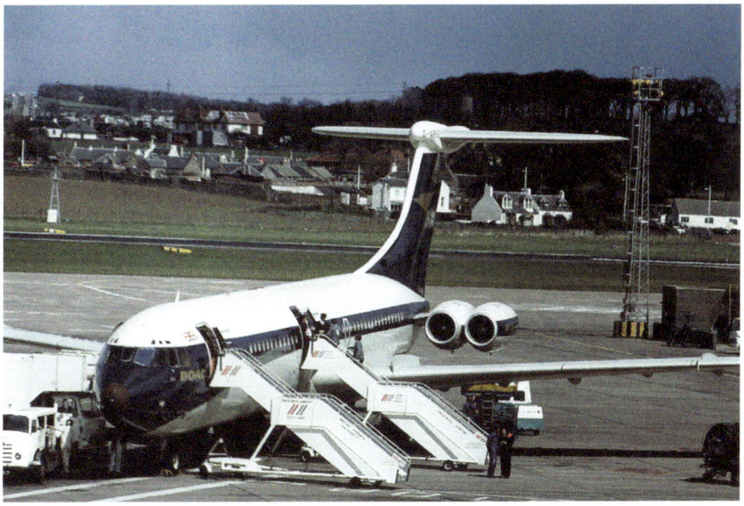

BOAC Vickers Standard VC-10 G-ARVG on 27 April 1973. 'Swift and silent' and 'A little VC10derness' were the catchphrases used by BOAC to advertise the two-class layout for its capacity of 135 passengers. (Trevor Hall)

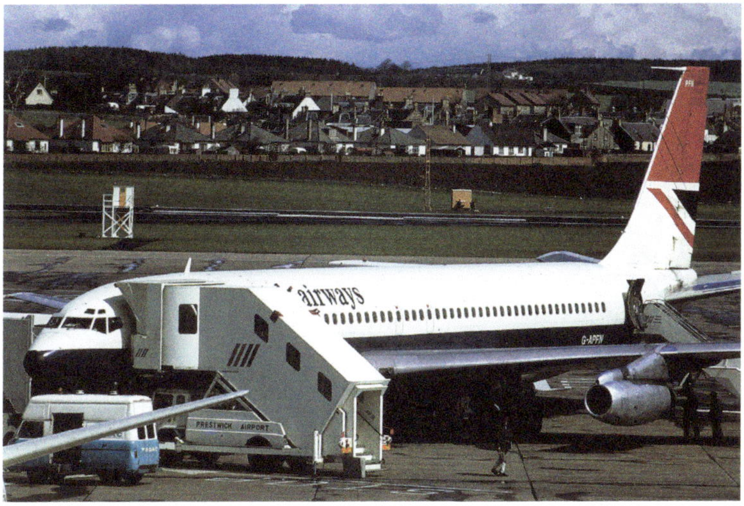

British Airways Boeing 707-436 G-APFN at Prestwick Airport in 1975. This aircraft underwent extensive repair after it ran off the end of runway 23 at London Heathrow Airport on 24 December 1960, causing its landing gear to collapse. The aircraft was broken up in 1988. (Trevor Hall)

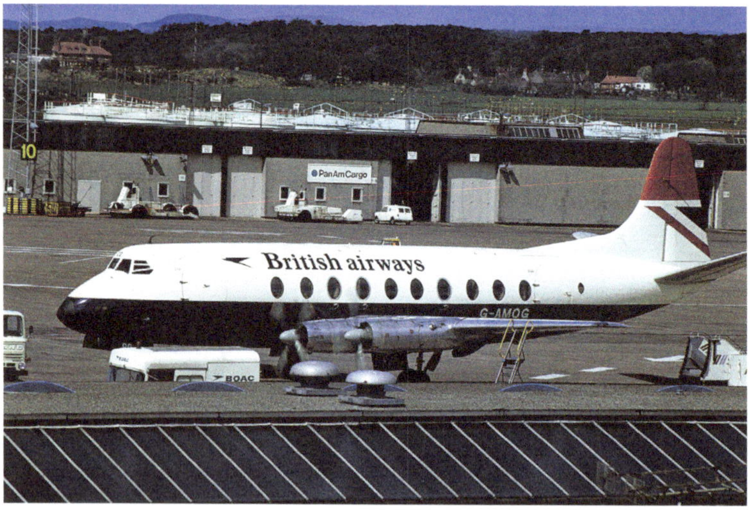

British Airways Vickers Viscount V.701 G-AMOG *RMA Robert Falcon Scott* is seen on 1 May 1975. It is now at the Scottish Museum of Flight at East Fortune. (Trevor Hall)

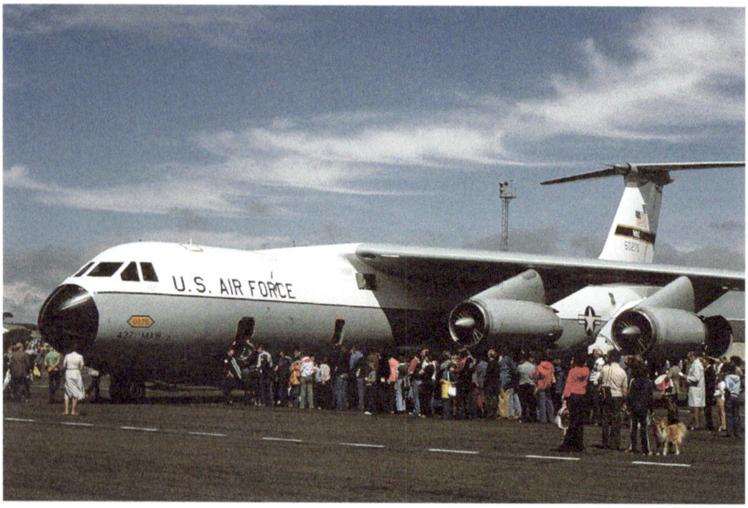

USAF Lockheed C-141A Starlifter 50275 of the 437th Military Airlift Wing (MAW) at Charleston AFB, South Carolina, is seen at HMS *Gannet* on 26 July 1978. (Trevor Hall)

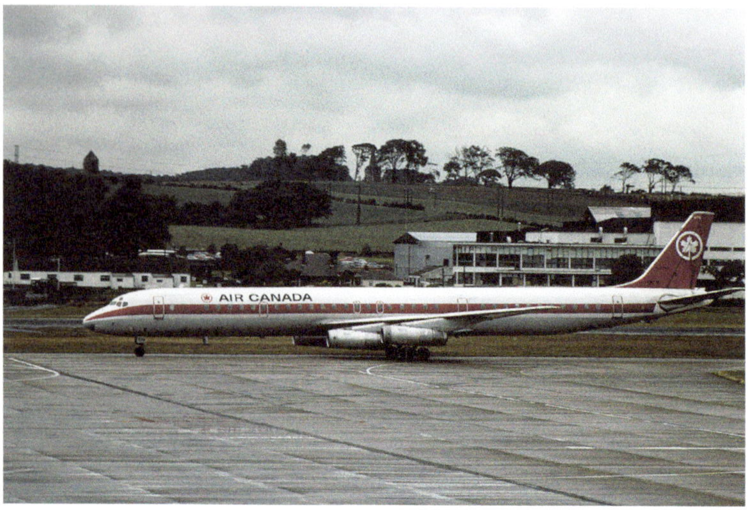

Air Canada McDonnell Douglas DC-8-73(F) C-FTIR, photographed on 26 July 1978. It was operated by DHL Airways as N804DH from 1994 until it was sold to ASTAR Air Cargo in 2003. It was retired to Kingman in 2012 and was subsequently scrapped. (Trevor Hall)

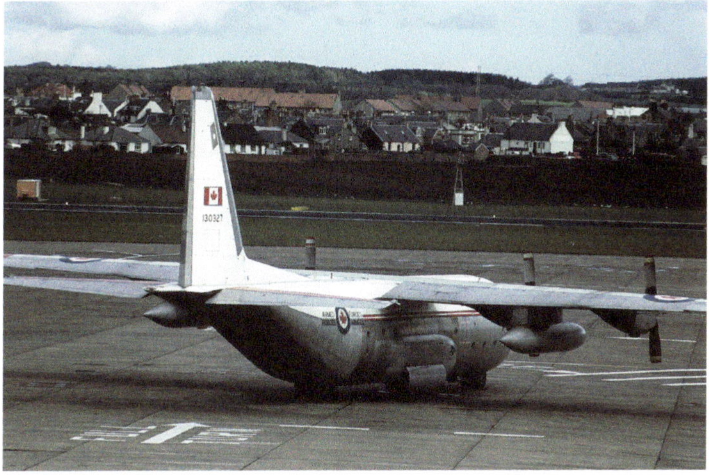

Canadian Armed Forces Lockheed CC-130E (L- 382) Hercules 130327, seen on 1 May 1975. It is still in service today. (Trevor Hall)

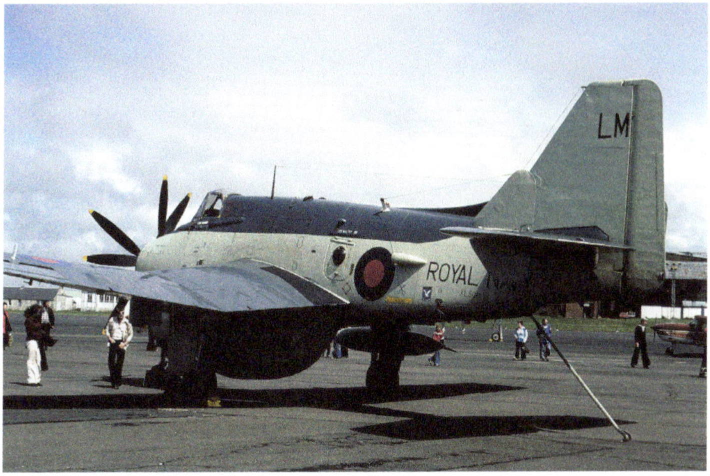

Royal Navy Gannet AEW.3 XL500 at HMS *Gannet* on 26 July 1978. Now with civil registration G-KAEW, it is still undergoing comprehensive restoration to return it to airworthy condition by Hunter Flying Ltd at their new base at St Athan. (Trevor Hall)

When Handley Page went into voluntary liquidation and finally collapsed in March 1970, the production of wings by Scottish Aviation for the HP Jetstream was thrown into turmoil, but the company secured an order from the Royal Swedish Air Force for the manufacture of fifty-eight two-seat side-by-side Bulldog trainers, the first of which, G-AXEH, was converted from a Beagle Pup, and the prototype for which first flew from Shoreham airport on 19 May 1969. New jigs and tooling were bought along with the design and manufacturing rights, and this took priority over existing airframe overhauls, which included Loftleidir CL-44s, Dakotas, Viscounts, Herons, DC-6s and Twin Pioneers, and existing customers' Pups and 206s. 320 Trainers were built. The second prototype Scottish Aviation Bulldog made its first and second flights at Prestwick on 14 February 1971. Scottish Aviation Limited built a further thirty-two Bulldogs for the Swedish Air Force and this was followed by an order by the RAF for another 132 to replace the Chipmunk basic trainer. Further orders were received for Bulldogs for the civilian market.

HMS *Gannet*

Part of the site occupied by RNAS Prestwick (more popularly remembered as HMS *Gannet*, which was established in 1971) was home to a detachment of No. 771 Naval Air Squadron. The squadron was disbanded on 1 December 1964 upon being absorbed into No. 819 Naval Air Squadron and operated three HAS6 Sea King helicopters. HMS *Gannet* was decommissioned in November 2001, and with effect from 1 January 2016 the SAR Flight was transferred to Bristow Helicopters, acting on behalf of HM Coastguard, part of the UK's Maritime and Coastguard Agency. It became the busiest unit in the UK from 2005 to 2010, with a record-breaking 447 rescues being made in 2009, and at that time the crews were regularly featured as part of the Channel 5 documentary series *Highland Emergency*.

From the 1970s to the mid-1990s, Scottish Aviation Limited (which became part of British Aerospace (BAe) in 1977) built the Jetstream multi-engine trainers for the RAF and observer trainers for the Royal Navy, and aircraft such as the Bulldog *ab initio* trainer and the improved eighteen-seat Jetstream 31/32 mini-airliner, of which 386 were built, found worldwide acceptance. This was followed by the bigger twenty-nine-seat Jetstream 41, of which 104 were produced. The first production Scottish Aviation Jetstream T Mk 1 for the RAF, XX475, made its maiden flight from Prestwick on 13 April 1973 before it underwent about fifty hours of test flying prior to being delivered to the Aeroplane & Armament Experimental Establishment (A&AEE) at Boscombe Down, Wiltshire, in mid-May. The RAF ordered twenty-six Series 200 Jetstreams to serve as the standard multi-engined pilot trainer, replacing the Vickers Varsity.

Scottish Aviation's prototype Bullfinch, G-BDOG, a four-seat, retractable version of the Bulldog primary trainer, made its first flight at Prestwick on 20 August 1976, and plans were in hand to produce a military counterpart called the Bulldog 200.

The manufacture of turbo-props at Prestwick, which totalled almost 1,000, came to an end in 1995 as orders dwindled. It also marked the end of BAe's troubled regional commercial involvement with Scottish Aviation, but it continued to back expansion plans for the site in support of retaining 1,000 jobs at Prestwick for work in aerostructures.

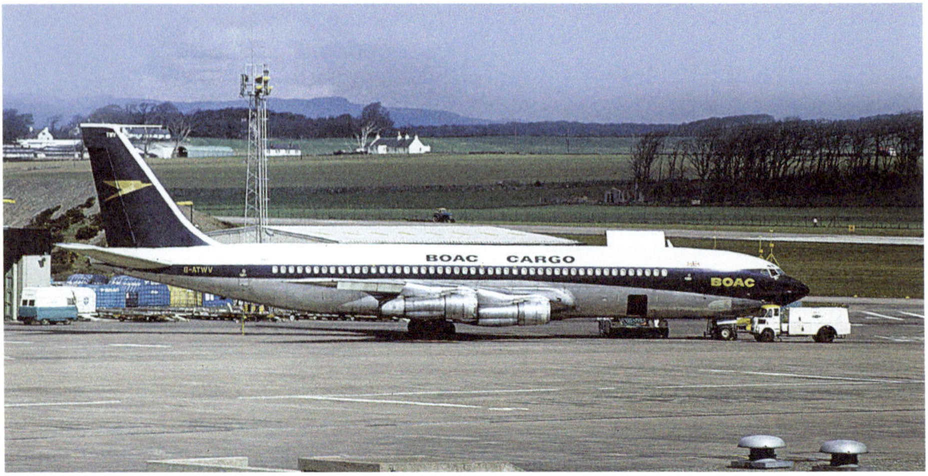

Pictured from one of the best viewing terraces around Prestwick Airport in the 1970s is BOAC Cargo Boeing 707-336C G-ATWV. It was withdrawn from use in 2000 after thirty-three years of service and was stored for spares at Pietersburg, South Africa. (Trevor Hall)

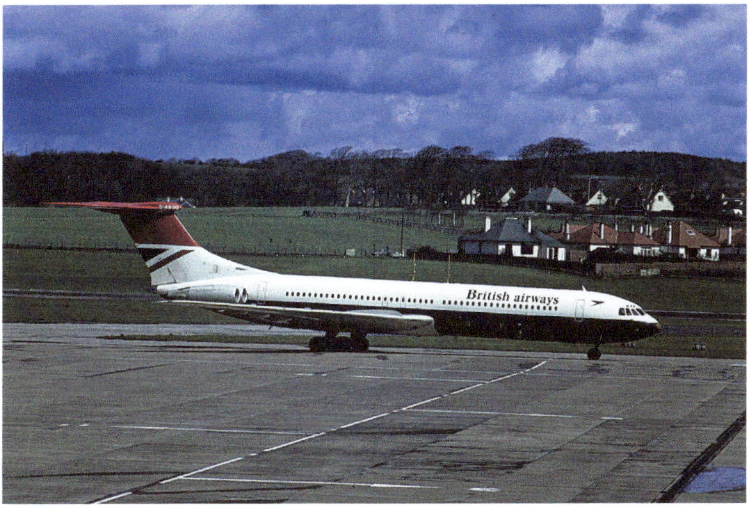

Pictured from the viewing terrace on 1 May 1975 is British Airways Vickers Super VC10-1151 G-ASGG. Converted to a K4 tanker and re-registered ZD235 in 1995, it spent the rest of its operational life with the RAF (No. 101 Squadron), and was finally scrapped at St Athan in 2004. (Trevor Hall)

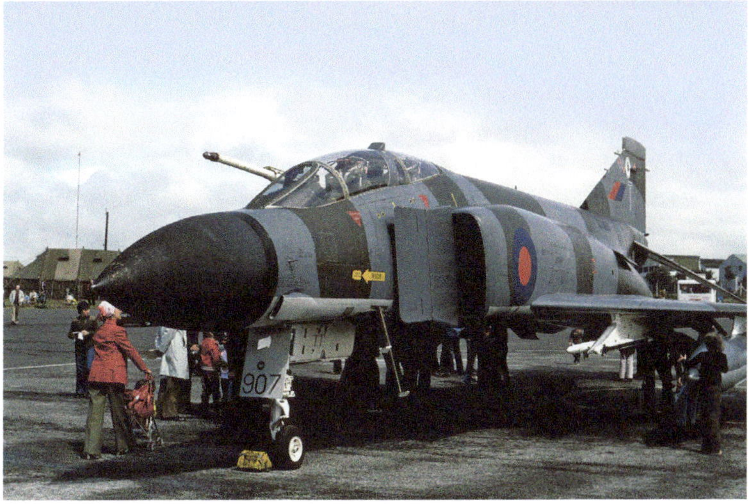

RAF No. 228 Operational Conversion Unit McDonnell Douglas F-4M Phantom FGR.2 XT907 at HMS *Gannet* on 26 July 1978. As of August 2017, XT-907 resides at Brentwaters Airfield, Suffolk. (Trevor Hall)

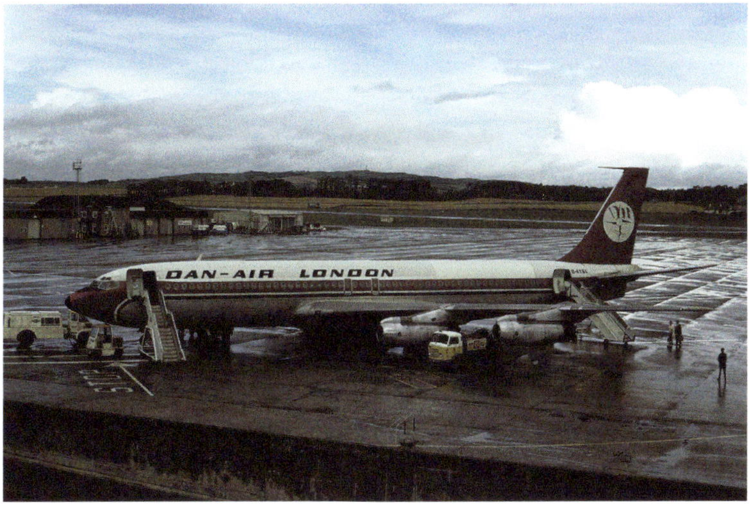

Former Pan Am Boeing 707-321 G-AYSL in the colours of Dan-Air London at Prestwick Airport on 25 August 1974. (Trevor Hall)

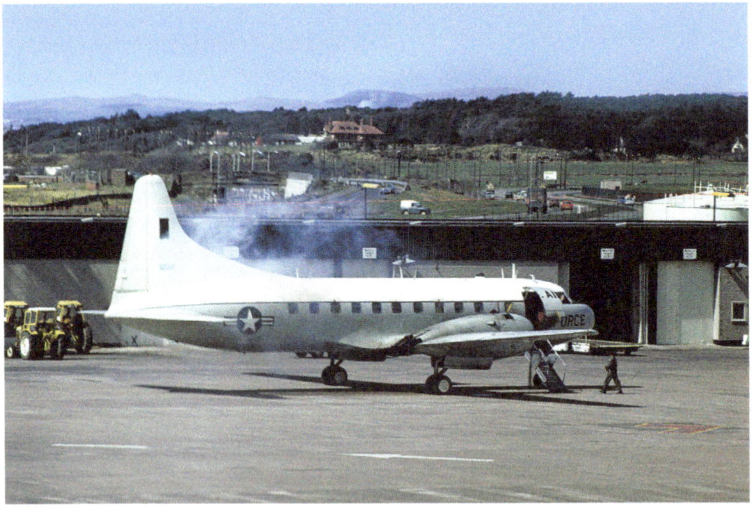

USAF Convair T-29B 13816 is seen starting up its starboard engine on 27 April 1973. A pressurised trainer, the aircraft was based on the Convair 240 with room for up to ten student navigators and four student radio operators. (Trevor Hall)

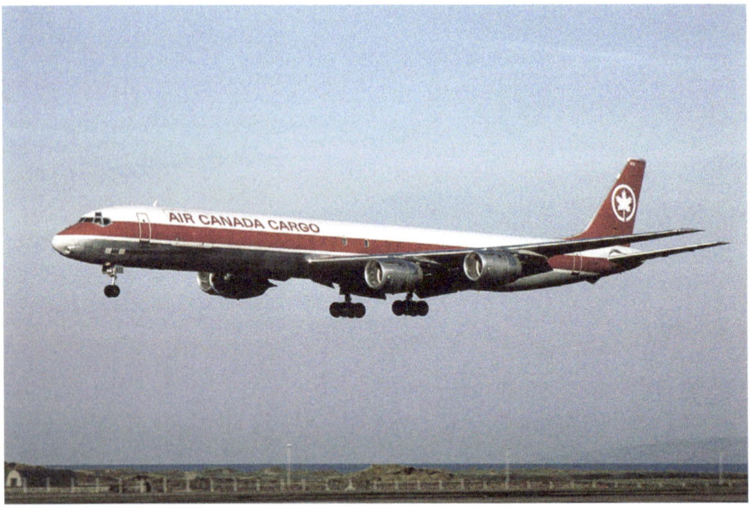

Air Canada Cargo McDonnell Douglas DC-8 CF-TIP in 1977. Air Canada Cargo is part of the flag carrier and largest airline of Canada. (Author's Collection)

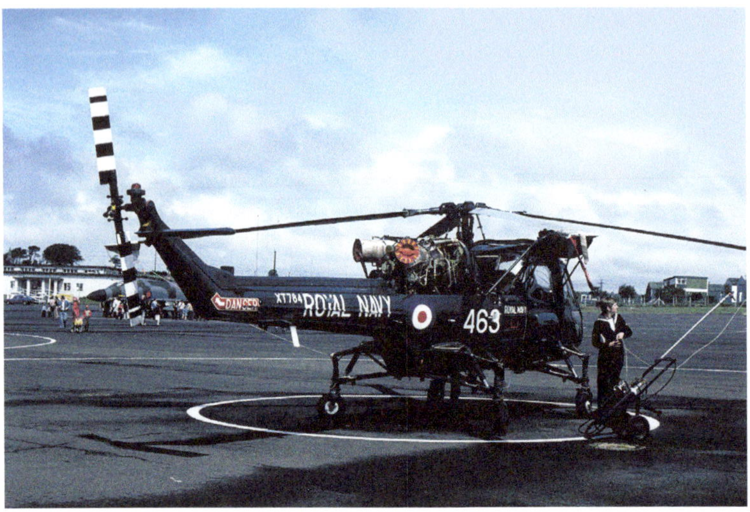

Royal Navy Westland Wasp HAS.1 XT784 of No. 829 Squadron at HMS *Gannet* on 26 July 1978. Representing the first generation of British helicopters purpose-designed to operate from frigates at sea, it was placed in preservation at the Malaysian Air Force Museum in Kuala Lumpur on 29 November 2002. (Trevor Hall)

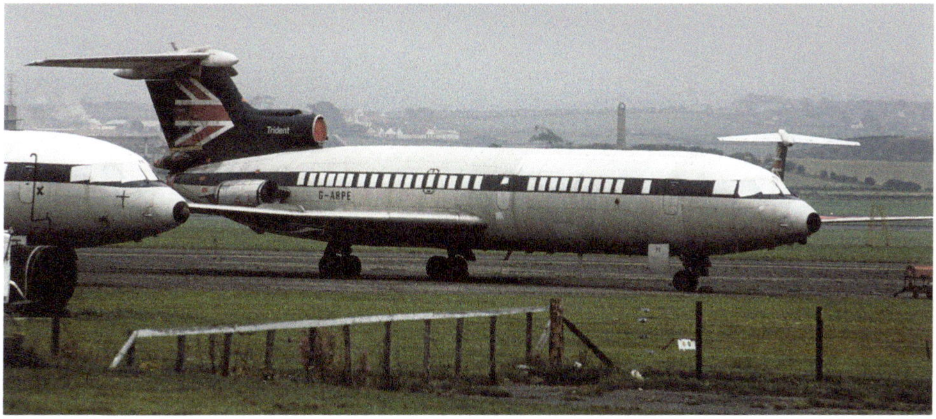

Former BEA/British Airways ninety-six-seat Hawker Siddeley HS-121 Trident 1C G-ARPE is seen stored at Prestwick on 27 August 1975. It was broken up there in May 1976. (Trevor Hall)

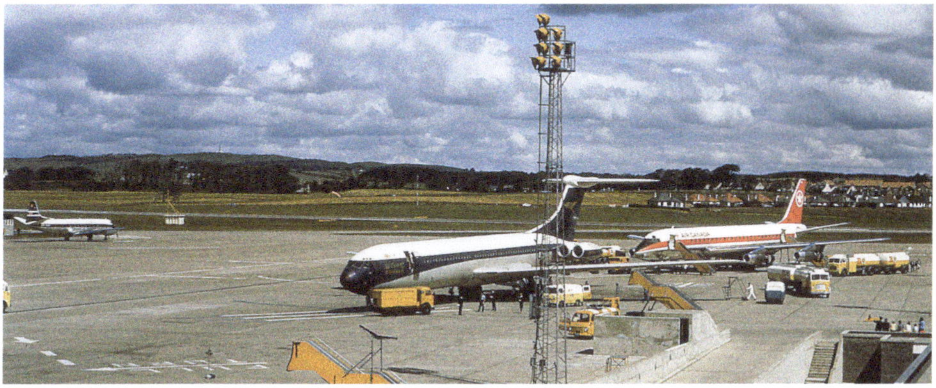

This shot from the terrace in 1972 depicts BOAC Vickers V.701 G-AMOG, Trans International Douglas DC-8-61 N8962T wearing Universal Airlines colours and Donaldson International Boeing 707-321 G-AYVG. (John Exton)

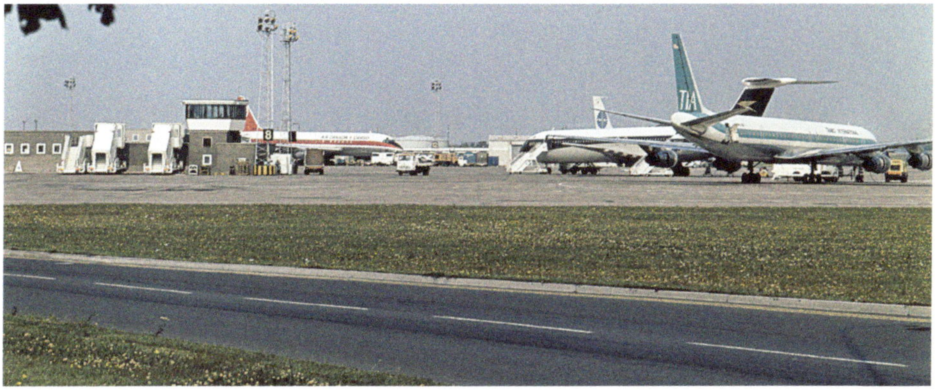

Seen here from the old apron area are Douglas DC-8F-54 CF-TJP, Air Canada Cargo N457PA, Boeing 707-321C Pan American Cargo G-ASGF, a BOAC Vickers Super VC-10 and a Trans International Douglas DC-8-61CF. (John Exton)

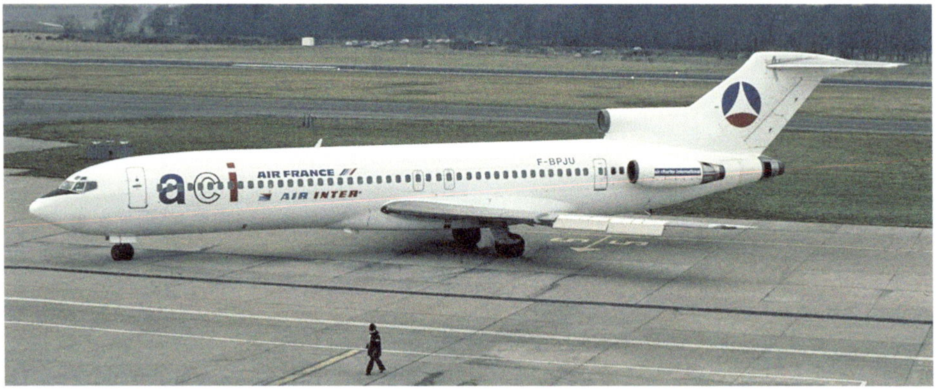

Air Charter International (Air France/Air Inter) Boeing 727-214 F-BPJU. First registered as N5228PS with Pacific Southwest Airlines in 1967, it was re-registered F-BPJU and spent just a short time with Air Charter from May 1972 before being leased to Tunisair for three months. It was then scrapped in the September. (Author's Collection)

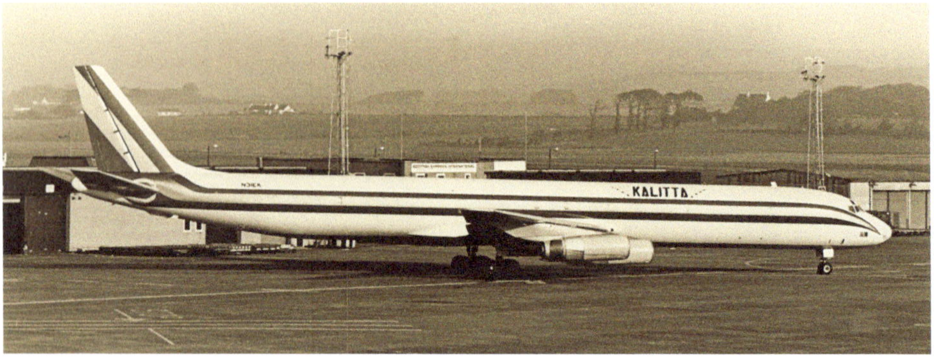

1980s

Kalitta Air Douglas DC-8-63CF N31EK in 1984. This aircraft went into storage with United Parcel Service (UPS) after being re-registered N852UP in 1985. (Alan Lord)

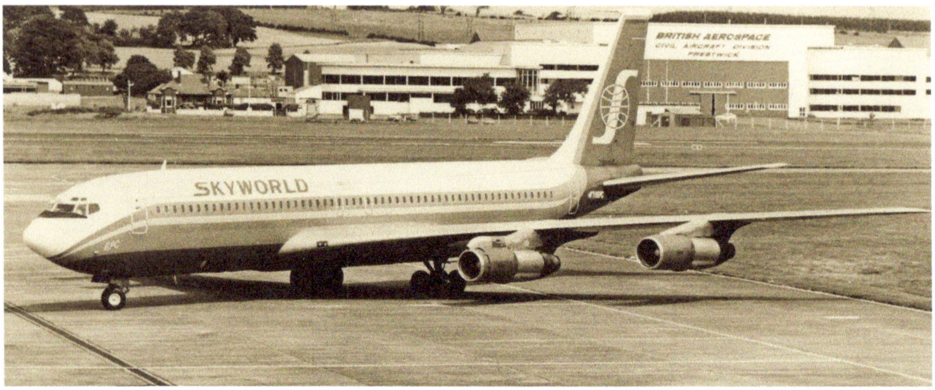

Skyworld Airlines' 1969-built Boeing 707-323B N706PC at Prestwick in the 1980s. This aircraft went to Omega Air and then Ports of Call before being placed into storage at Mojave, California. (Alan Lord)

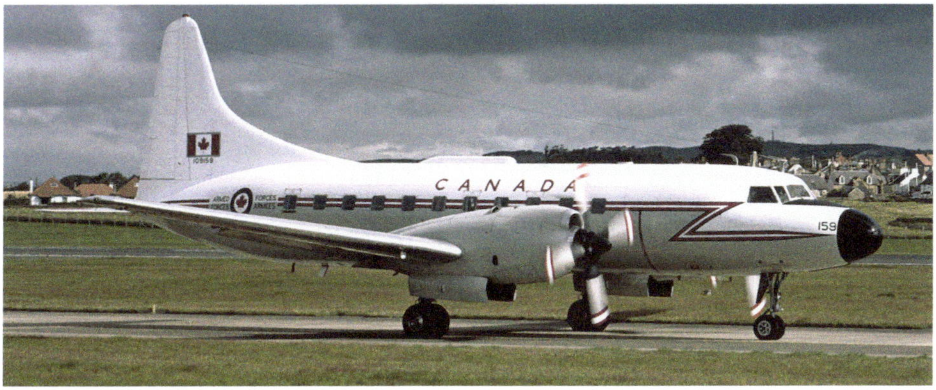

Canadian Armed Forces' No. 412 Squadron (Ottawa) Canadair CC-109 Cosmopolitan 109159 is seen taxiing at Prestwick in 1985. (Author's Collection)

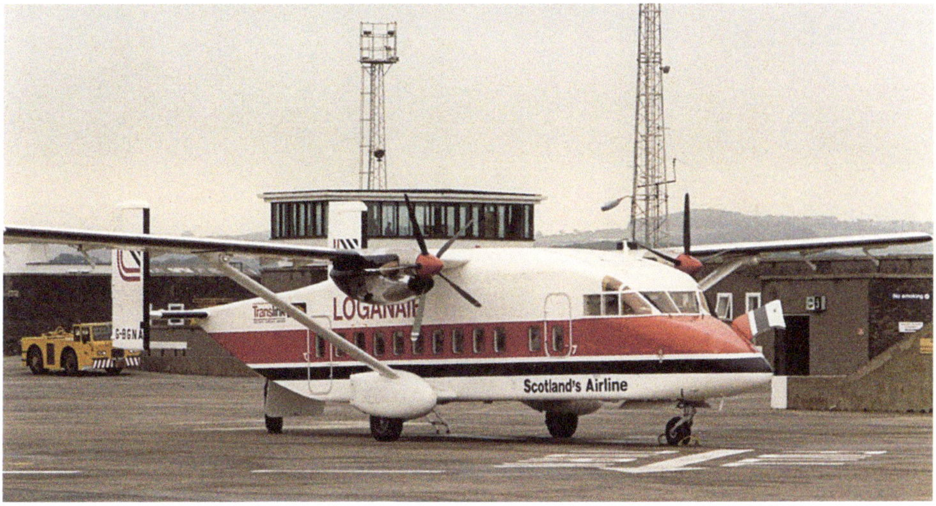

Loganair Short 330-200 cargo plane G-BGNA is seen parked on Apron A. (Bob Smith)

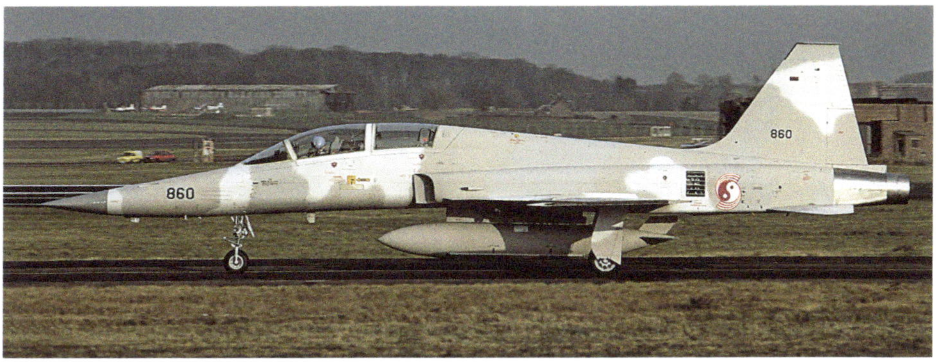

The Singapore Air Force's delivery flight of Northrop Grumman F-5E Tiger 860 in 1985. The aircraft proved to be a successful combat aircraft for US allies and served with the US Air Force from 1975 to 1990. (Author's Collection)

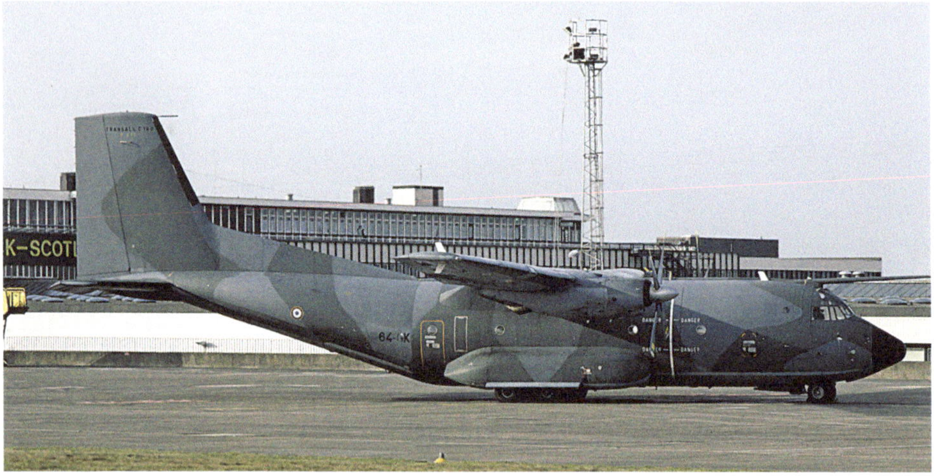

Armée De L'Air (French Air Force) Transall C-160 medium-lift tactical transport 64-GK at Prestwick in 1985. (Author's Collection)

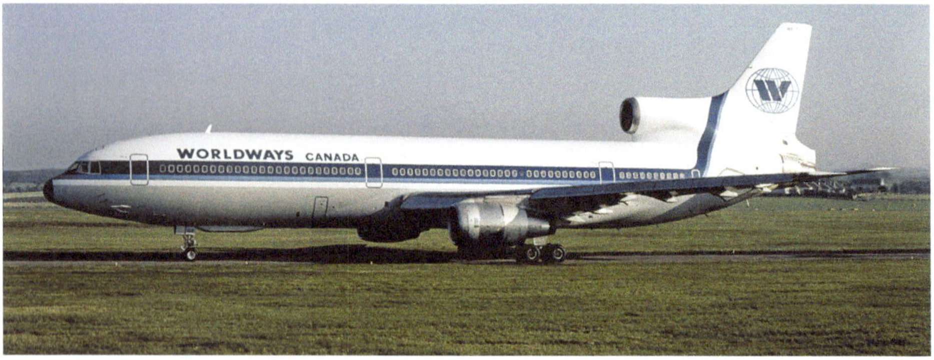

Worldways Canada Lockheed Tristar L-1011-1 C-GIFE at Prestwick in 1985. The aircraft was broken up as N125DT at Opa Locka Airport, Miami, in October 1997. (Author's Collection)

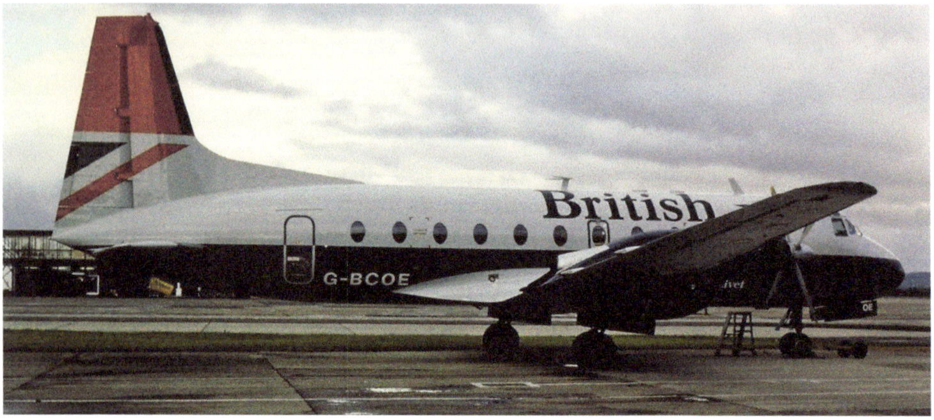

British Airways' Hawker Siddeley HS-748 medium-sized turboprop airliner Srs2B/287 G-BCOE at Prestwick in October 1984. (Author's Collection)

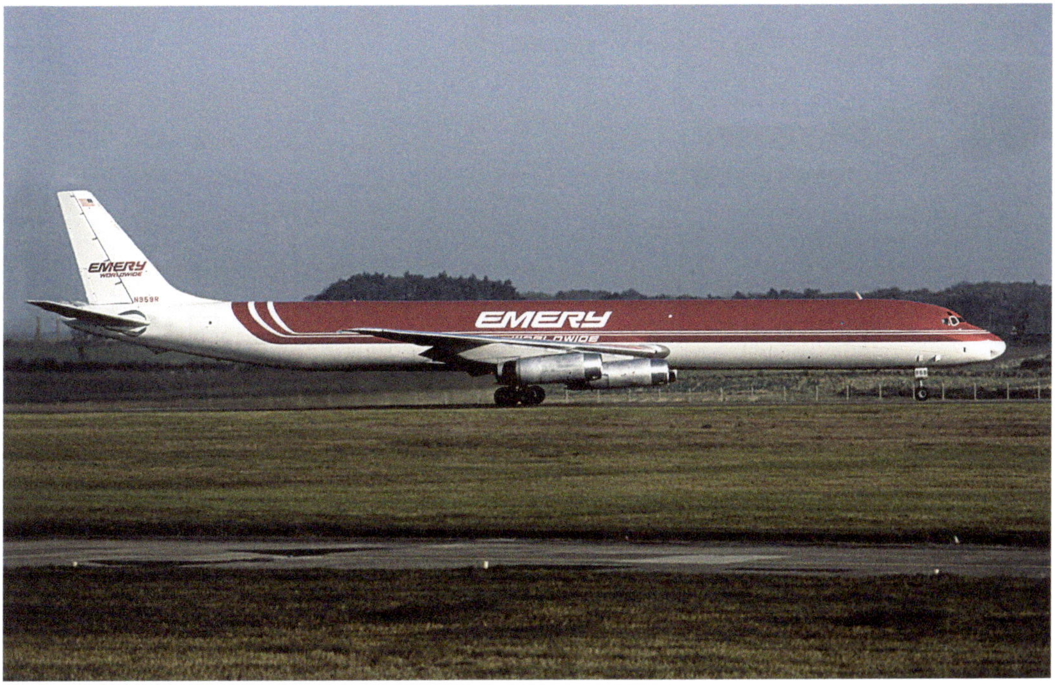

McDonnell Douglas DC-8-63CF N959R at Prestwick during its first year of service with Emery Worldwide Airlines in 1985. It went to Skymaster Airlines on 22 April 2002 and was placed into storage. (Author's Collection)

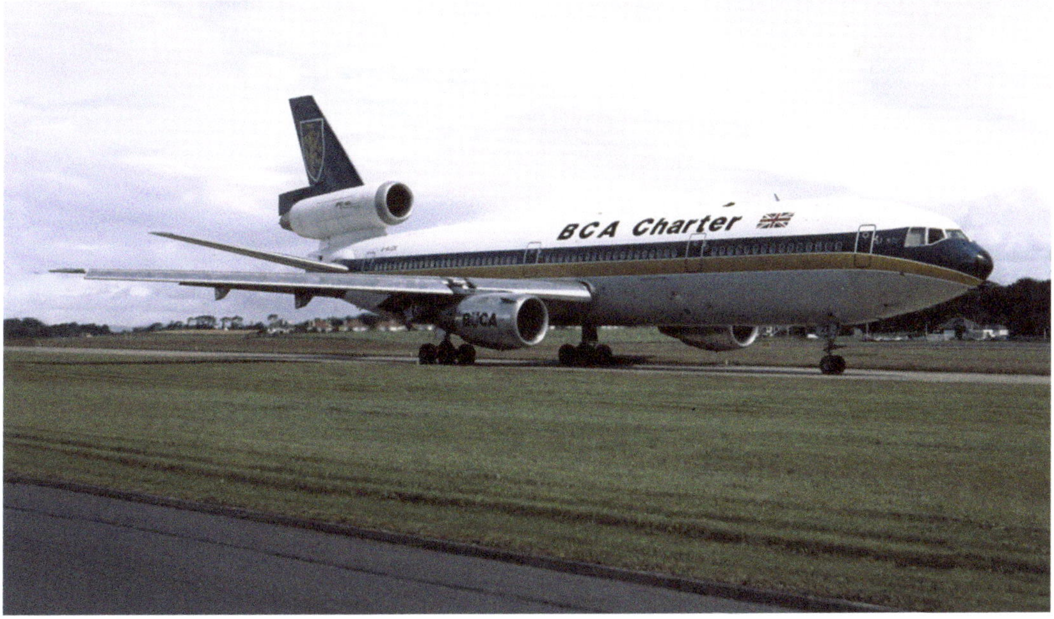

BCA Charter McDonnell Douglas DC-10-10 G-BJZE, in British Caledonian Airways colours, is seen taxiing for departure in the summer of 1985. The aircraft underwent an M-10 conversion (a retrofit cockpit upgrade) in 2008, and is still in service as of November 2017. (Author's Collection)

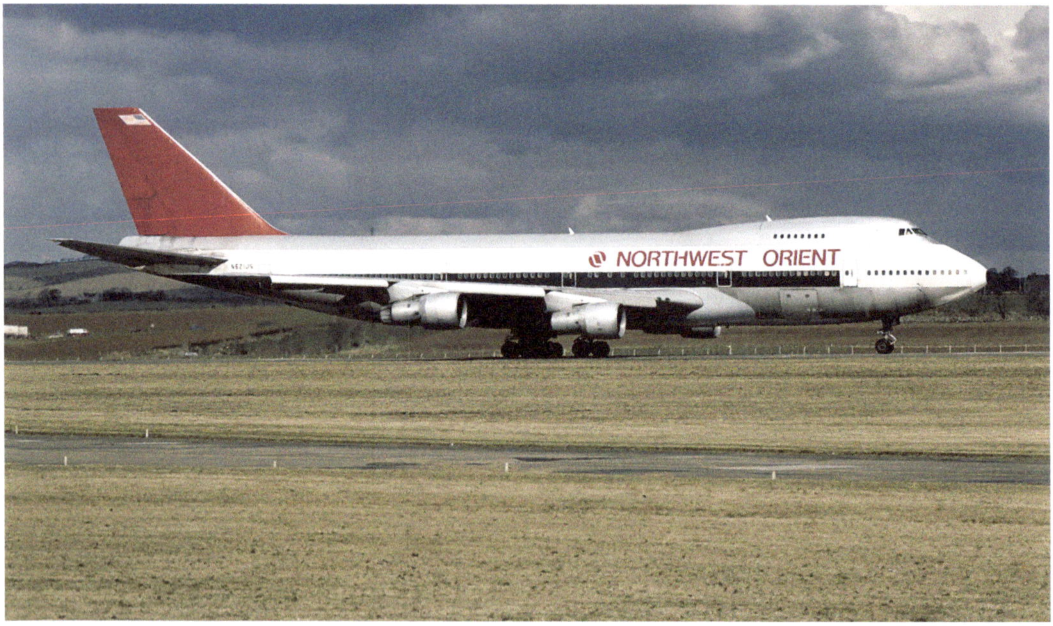

Northwest Orient Airlines Boeing 747-135 N621US is seen ready to depart Prestwick in 1985. It was withdrawn from service by 1998 and scrapped in 2009, a year before National Airlines merged with Delta Air Lines. (Author's Collection)

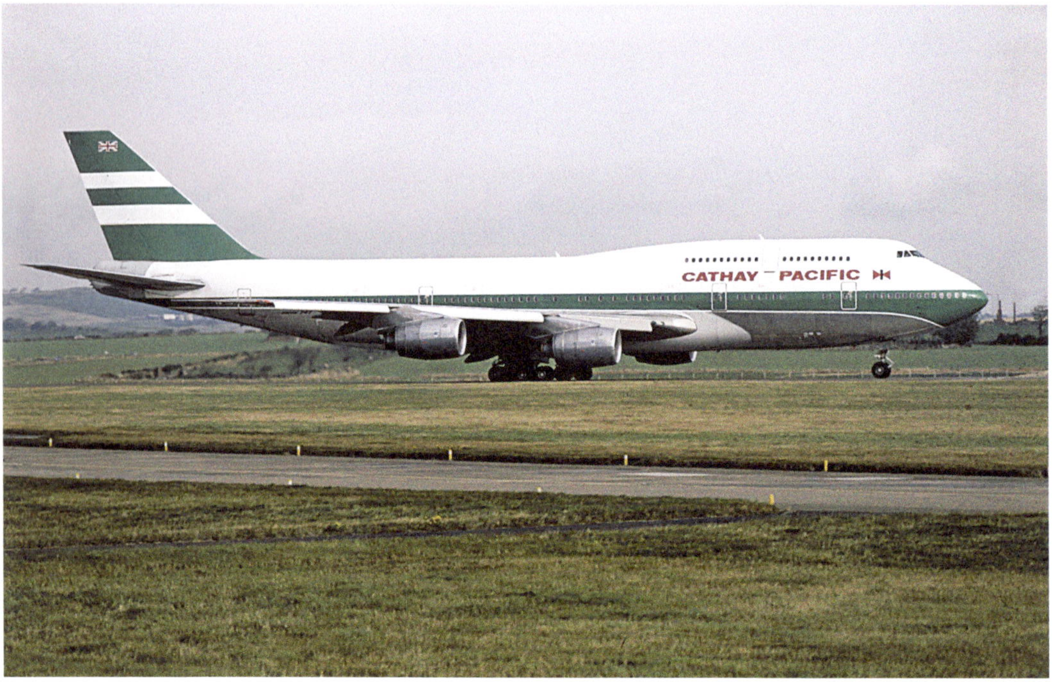

Cathy Pacific Airways Boeing 747-367 VR-HII in 1986. It was last owned by Pakistan International Airlines as AP-BFW and went into storage in Karachi from November 2012. It was scrapped in August 2013. (Author's Collection)

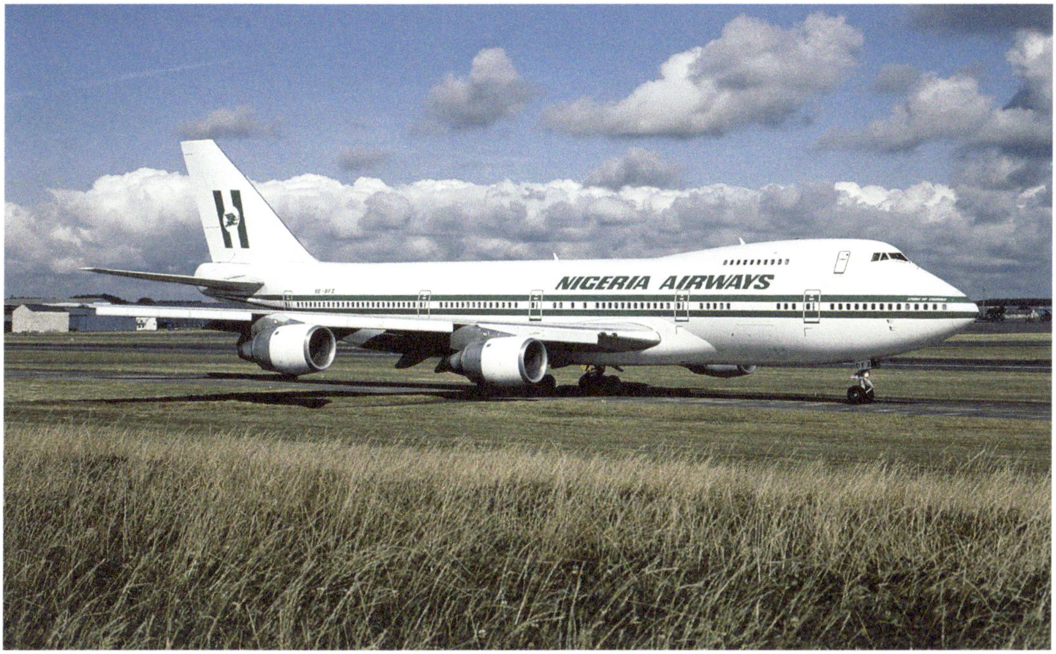

Nigeria Airways Boeing 747-283BM ZA367 *Spirit of Courage* at Prestwick in 1986. It was leased to several airlines during its lifespan until it was finally stored at Châteauroux-Centre 'Marcel Dassault' Airport in August 2007 before it was scrapped. (Author's Collection)

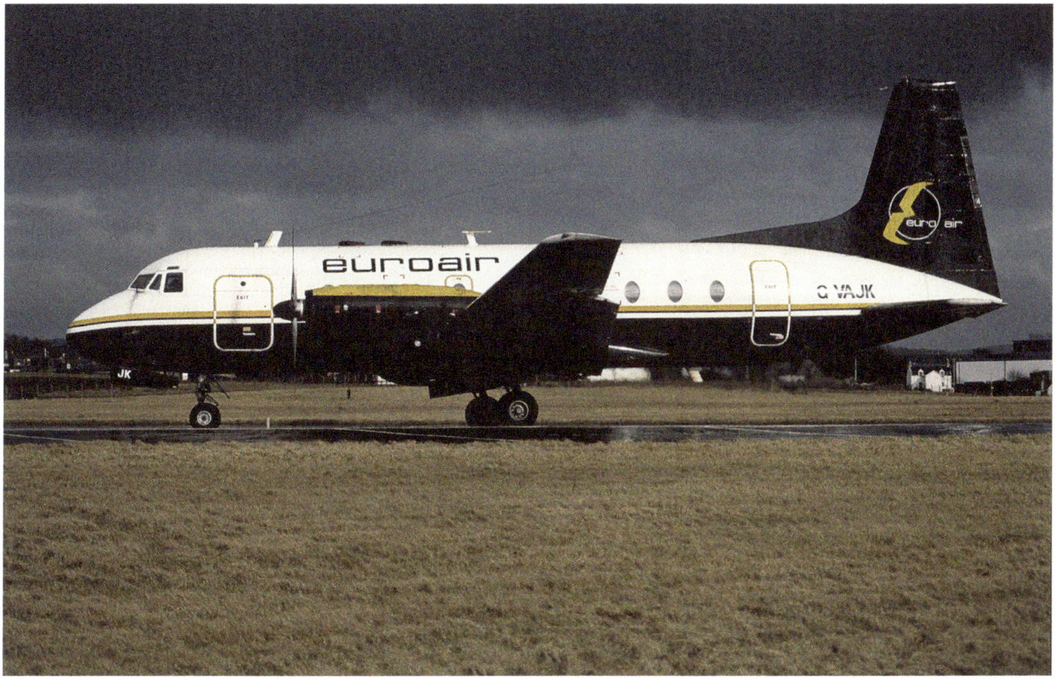

EuroAir Hawker Siddeley HS-748 Srs1/105 G-VAJK in 1986. The HS-748 was designed as a replacement for the Douglas DC-3 in the medium-range airliner market. (Author's Collection)

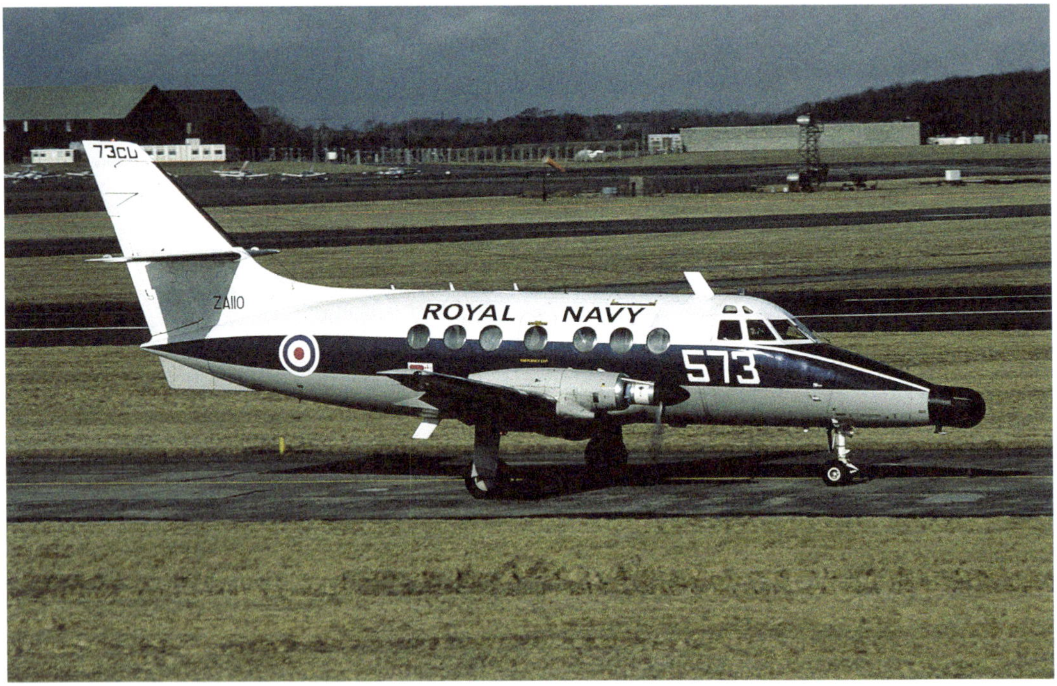

Royal Navy BAe Jetstream T2 ZA110 (573/CU) is seen taxiing at Prestwick in 1986. (Author's Collection)

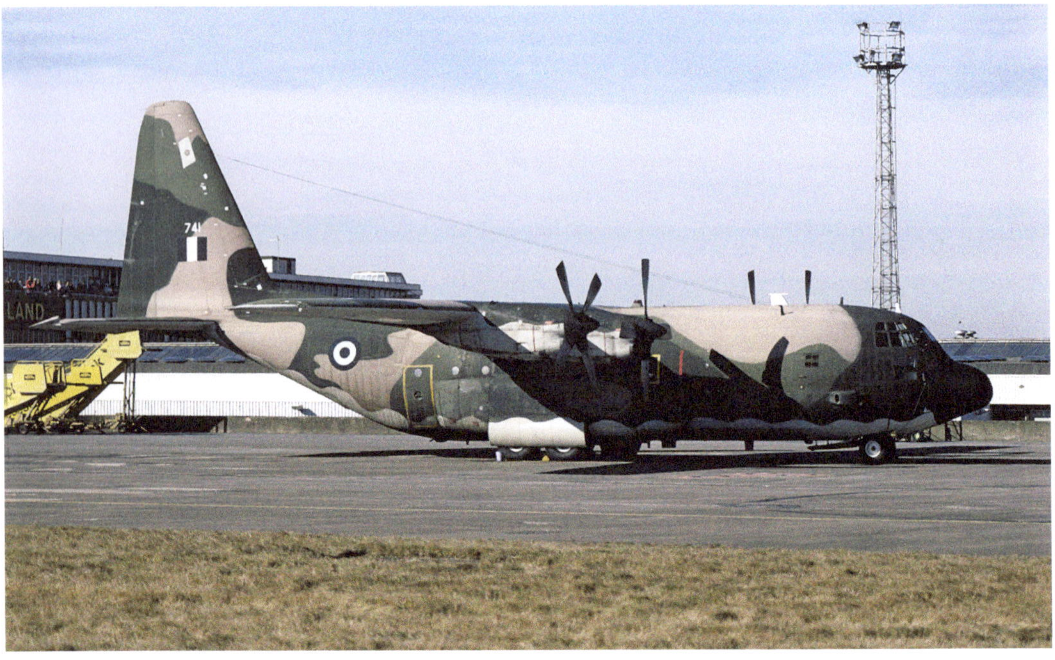

A Hellenic Air Force (HAS) Lockheed Hercules C-130H (741) in 1986. The Hercules had been in service with No. 356 Squadron of the 112 Combat Wing (HAS), based at Elefsis Airport, since 1975. (Author's Collection)

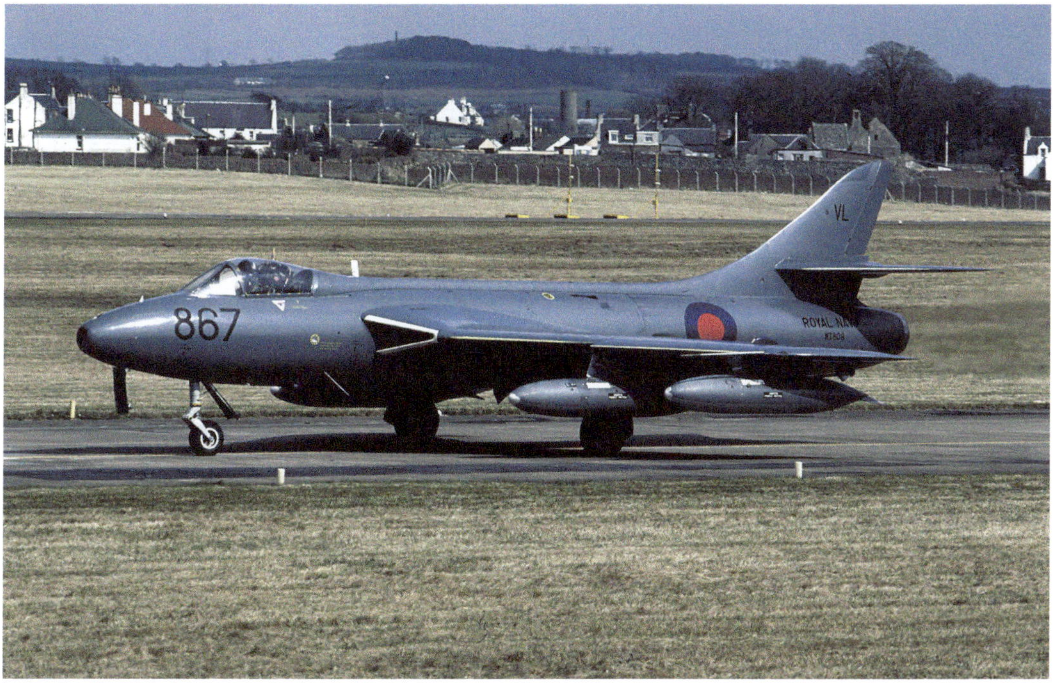

Royal Navy Hawker Hunter GA.11 WT809 (867/VL) of the Fleet Requirements and Air Direction Unit (FRADU) in 1986. (Author's Collection)

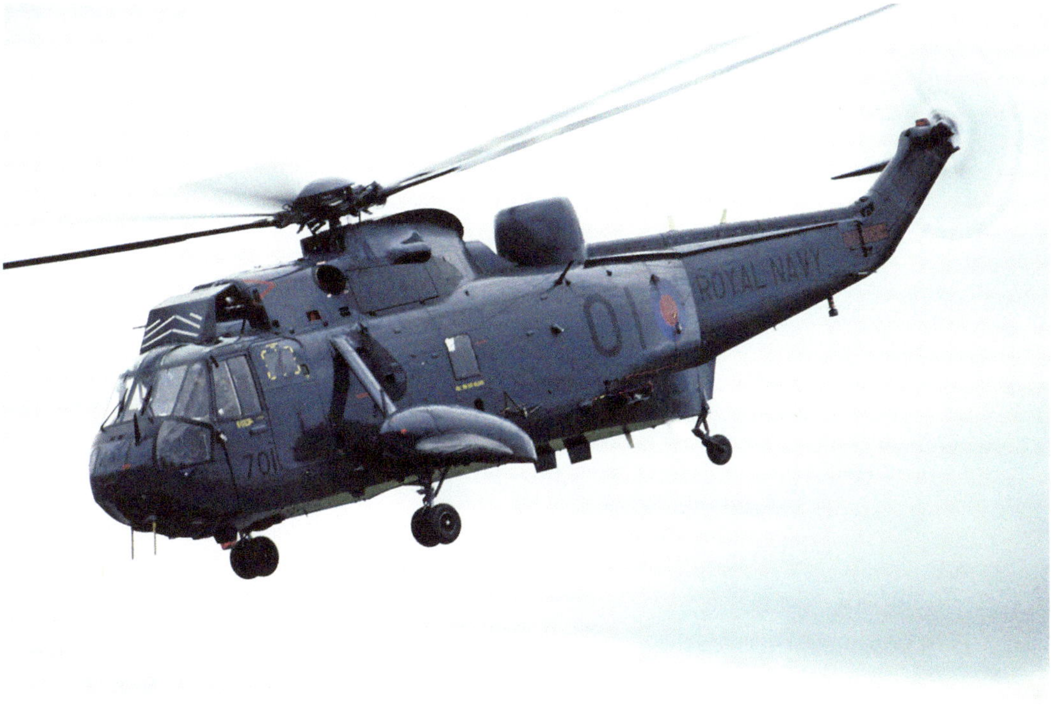

Royal Navy Sea King HAS-5 ZD636 (701) at Prestwick, 1986. (Author's Collection)

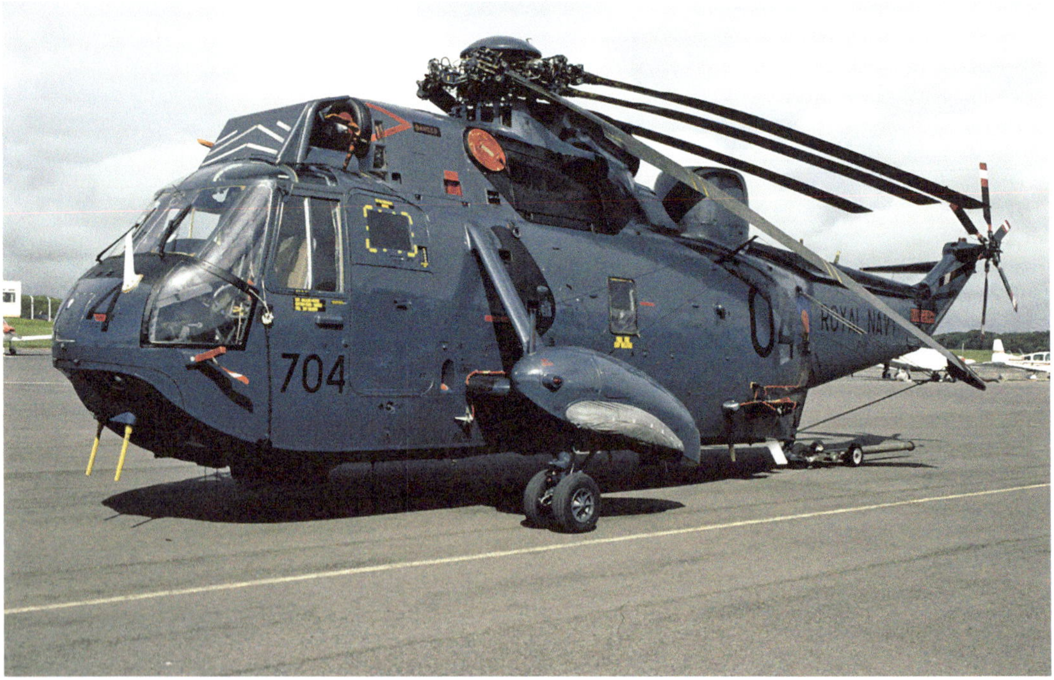

Royal Navy Sea King HAS-5 ZD637 (704) at Prestwick, 1986. (Author's Collection)

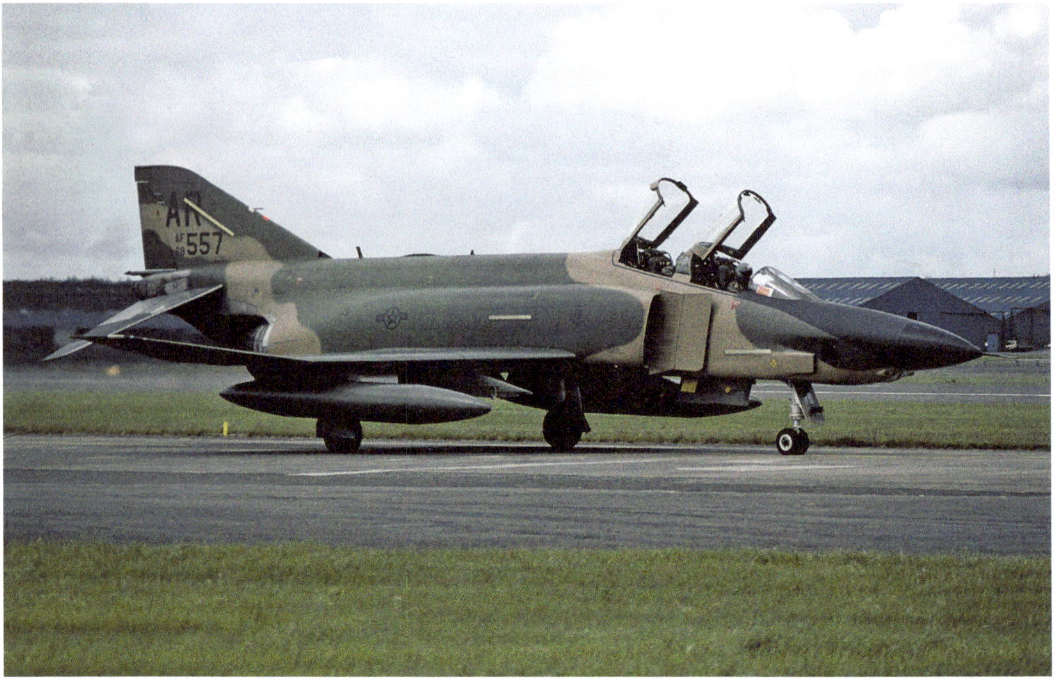

USAF McDonnell Douglas RF-4C Phantom 68-557 AR, 1st Tactical Reconnaissance Squadron (TRS)/10th Tactical Reconnaissance Wing (TRW Alconbury), taxiing at Prestwick in 1985. (Author's Collection)

Flying Schools

Two companies at Prestwick offer fixed wing flying training courses for the Joint Aviation Regulations Private Pilot's Licence and National Private Pilot's Licence as routes for pupils to obtain their licences for private flying or to go on to train towards a Commercial Pilot's Licence if aiming to be a pilot as a career. Prestwick Flying Club was established in 1975 at New Dykes Farm, Shawfarm Road, Prestwick, and, through the support of successive management at the airport and the efforts of the voluntary work of members, still exists in its non-profit making format today, as does the Prestwick Flight Centre, a CAA-approved flight training organisation, which is currently based in Hangar 22.

In May 1988, a British Aerospace Flying College began operations with a fleet of twelve aircraft from the pre-war Fokker Hangar, but with the increase of commercial flights training circuits became more and more restrictive, resulting in the college closing and moving out of Prestwick in 1999, with most of the instructors moving to Flyglobespan, Loganair or Flybe, based at Glasgow and Edinburgh.

British Airways (BA) began to run regular passenger services to Europe during the 1960s, but ceased in the late 1970s, giving rise to speculation that the loss would spell the end of Prestwick Airport. The airport kept going by drawing on the financial benefits of its other operators, and despite withdrawing its regular services, BA continued to run occasional flights from it, and also used the long runway to train pilots for the Concorde (the prototype of which made an appearance at the 1972 airshow) as well as a series of weather research flights in order to assess the effects of supersonic transport operations in the upper atmosphere.

Prestwick's ATC Centre became the first in the UK to use fully synthetic displays as part of the Marconi-developed Locus 16 mini-computer system that was installed during May 1977. Twenty-eight of the thirty-four computers were fitted with display screens, and three operated purely as radar data-processors. Secondary radar data was 'piped-in' from six remote sites scattered around the mainland and the Hebrides, with provision for four further sites. The Scottish Area Control Centre (ScATCC) moved into Atlantic House on 2 November 1978 after the completion of the purpose extension.

Despite being officially designated in 1977 as the 'Gateway for Scotland' for all scheduled and chartered flights from the United States, Prestwick was at the beginning of a downwards trend in business. It had lost transatlantic services by KLM, SAS, British Caledonian and Pan Am during the following year, and by October 1979 it was in danger of becoming a ghost airport with both BA and Air Canada planning to transfer a number of its Atlantic services from Prestwick to Glasgow.

It was the start of a period of problems mixed with successes, with the airport manager of the day, George Giles, stating in 1985 that Prestwick (now in its Golden Jubilee year) was a national asset that was vital to the development of civil aviation in this country.

1990s

Prestwick had been scraping by throughout the 1980s with freight work and a few charter flights operating regularly, and the hard times continued into the early 1990s, with passenger numbers continuing to slide. With the loss of its 'Transatlantic Gateway' status, it faced the real threat of going out of business. The crisis peaked in 1991, and the British Airports Authority (BAA) plc (which had privatised by the Conservative government in 1987) placed Prestwick Airport for sale to the private sector after consolidated their portfolio of UK airports, a part of which resulted in moving all transatlantic traffic departing Scotland to Glasgow Airport.

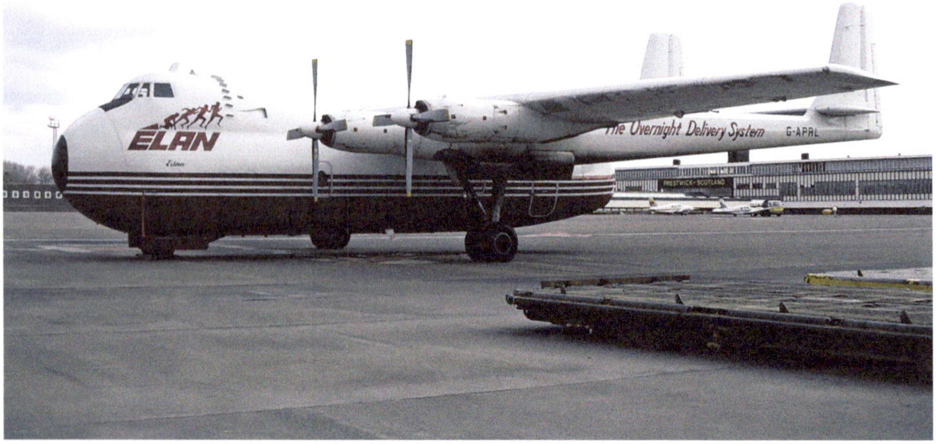

Elan Overnight Delivery System Armstrong-Whitworth AW 650 Argosy 101 G-APRL *Edna* in 1986. It is preserved at the Midland Air Museum. (Author's Collection)

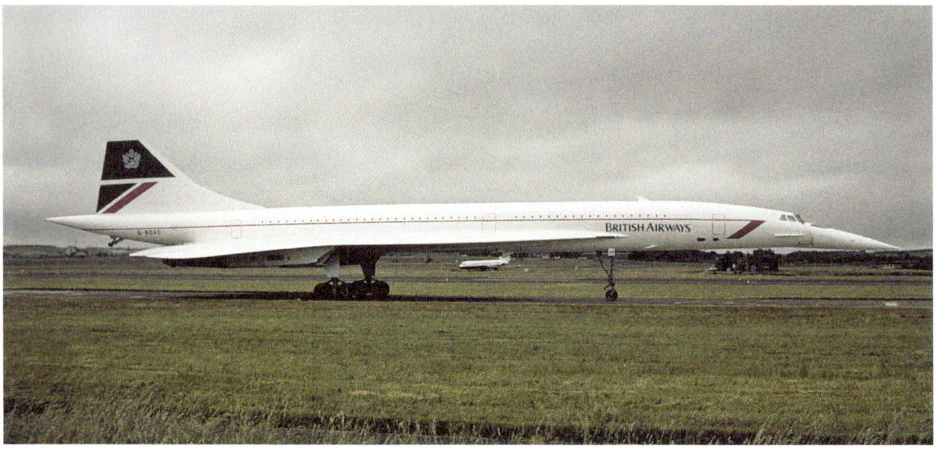

British Airways Aérospatiale/BAC Concorde 102 G-BOAD on 21 January 1986. The supersonic passenger jet airliner became a fairly regular visitor to the airport for pilot training. (Author's Collection)

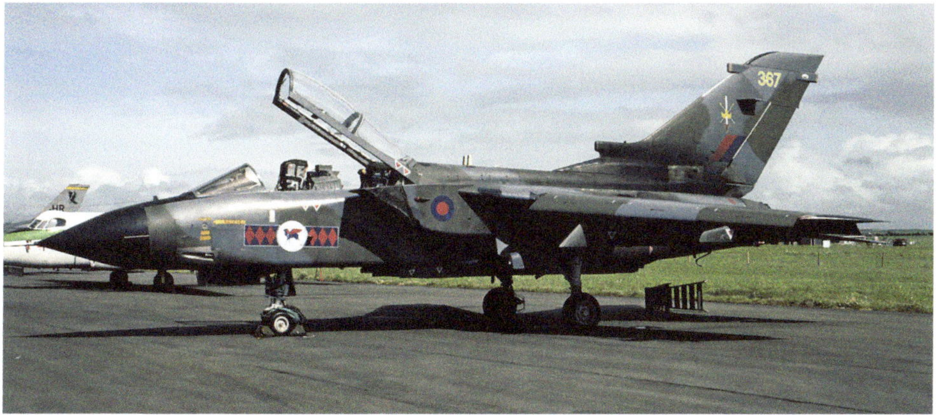

A Royal Air Force Panavia Tornado GR.1 of No. 45 Squadron Tornado Weapons Conversion Unit (TWCU) on display on 30 May 1987. (Author's Collection)

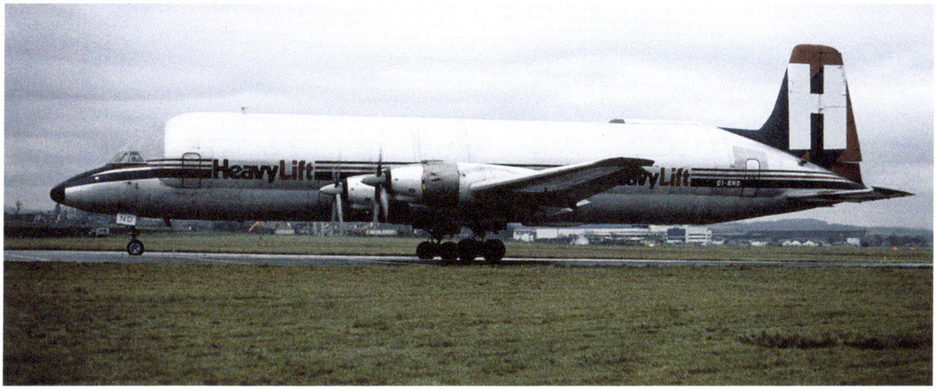

Licenced to Heavylift Cargo Airlines is this Conroy standard Guppy Conversion CL44-0, EI-BND, which is seen at Prestwick in 1986. As of August 2017 it has spent more than thirteen years in storage. (Author's Collection)

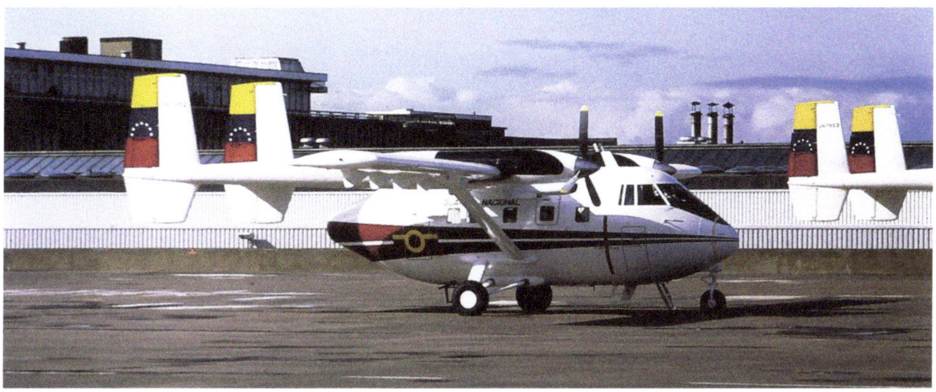

Venezuela National Guard Israeli Aircraft Industries Arava 201 GN-7952 is seen at Prestwick in 1980. This military variant of the Arava could also be equipped with a range of weapons in order to act in anti-submarine or gunship roles. (Author's Collection)

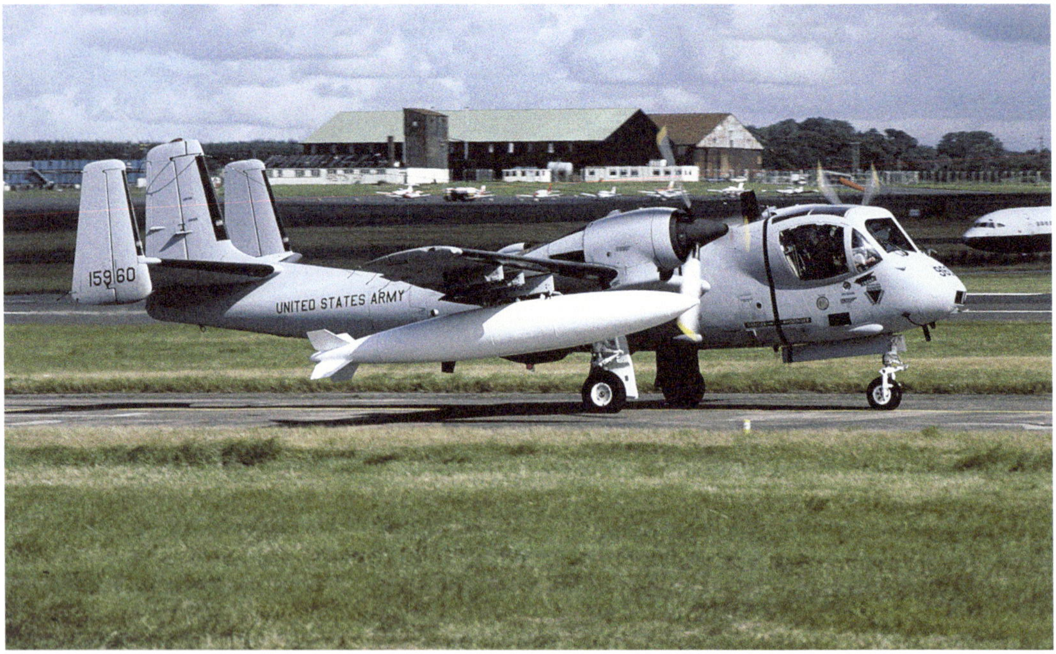

US Army Grumman OV-1 Mohawk 68-15960 is photographed taxiing at Prestwick in 1986. The OV-1 was designed to meet a joint Marine Corps/Army requirement for a short take-off and landing (STOL) battlefield surveillance aircraft. (Author's Collection)

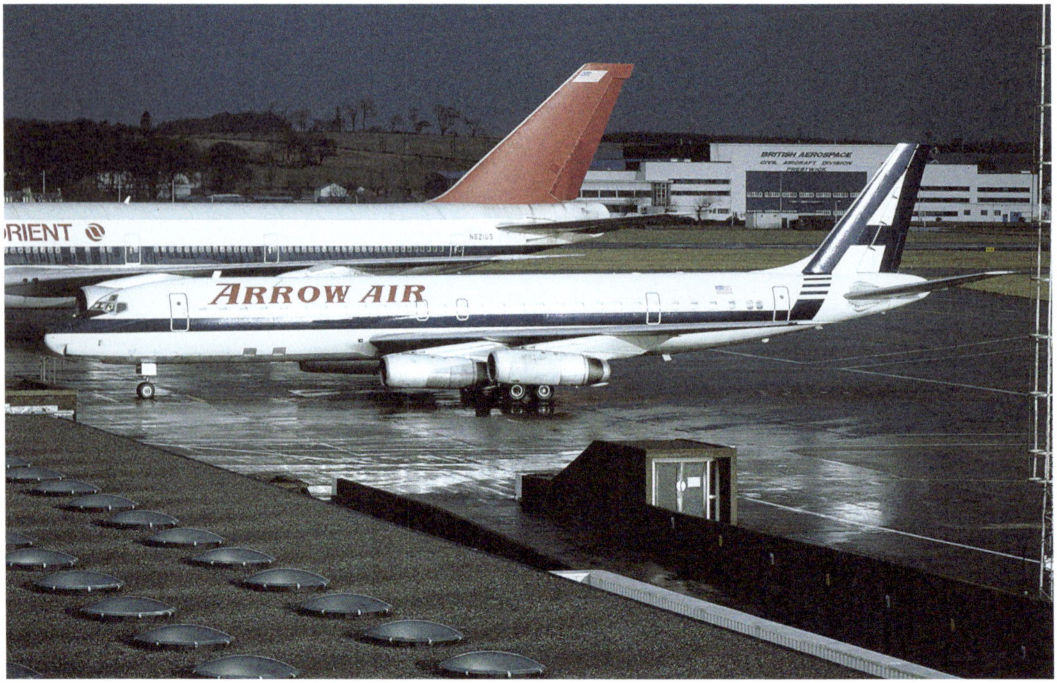

Leased from United Airlines in 1982, this Miami-based Arrow Air Douglas DC-8-60, N8968U, is pictured at Prestwick in 1986. (Author's Collection)

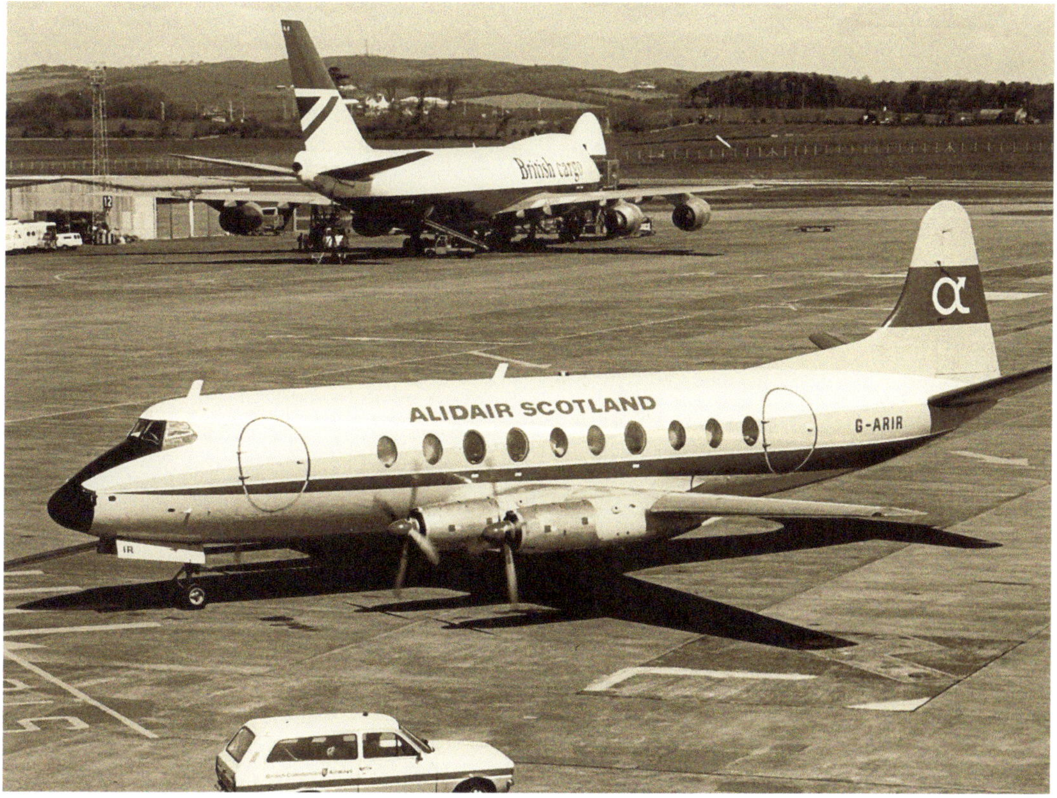

Alidair Scotland Vickers Viscount G-ARIR (708) at Prestwick *c.* 1981. Purchased from Air Inter (Lignes Aériennes Intérieures) in November 1975, and re-registered from F-BLHI, it was leased to Dan Air in December. (Author's Collection)

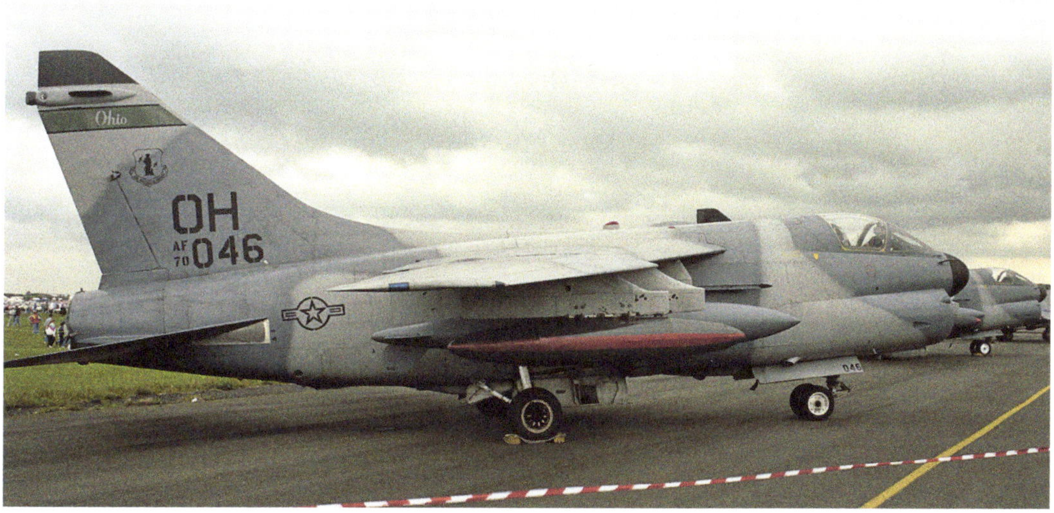

Ohio Air National Guard Ling-Temco-Vought (LTV) A-7D Corsair 70-046 of No. 112 Tactical Fighter Squadron (TFS) of Toledo is seen at the Prestwick Airshow on 10 June 1989. (Trevor Hall)

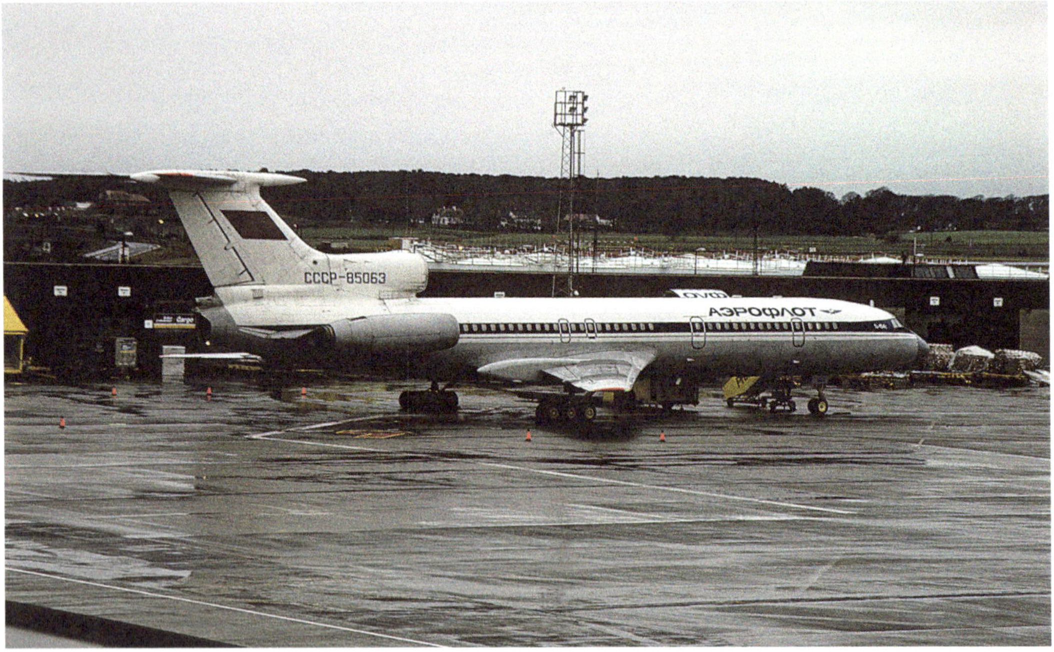

A rare visitor in the 1980s was this Aeroflot Tupolev Tu-154B, CCCP-85063. It was converted to a TU-154A (freighter) in 1984, was withdrawn from use at Sheremetyevo in 1993, and was scrapped in 1995. (Trevor Hall)

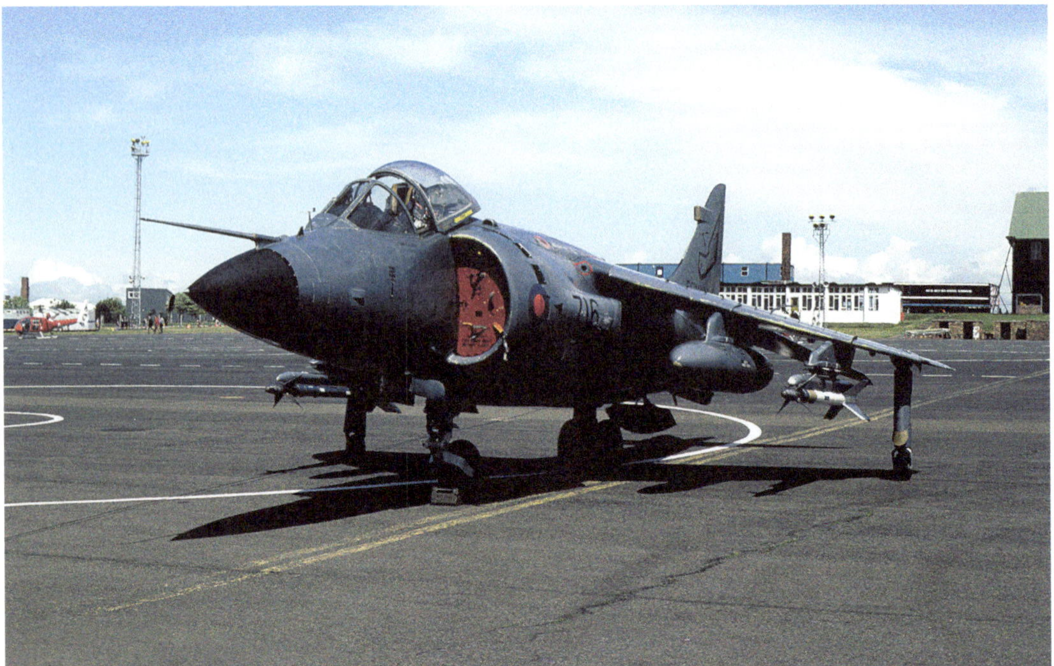

Royal Navy British Aerospace Sea Harrier FRS.1 XZ494 (716) on the ramp at HMS *Gannet*, the Royal Navy's shore facility at Prestwick Airport, on 2 June 1984. (Trevor Hall)

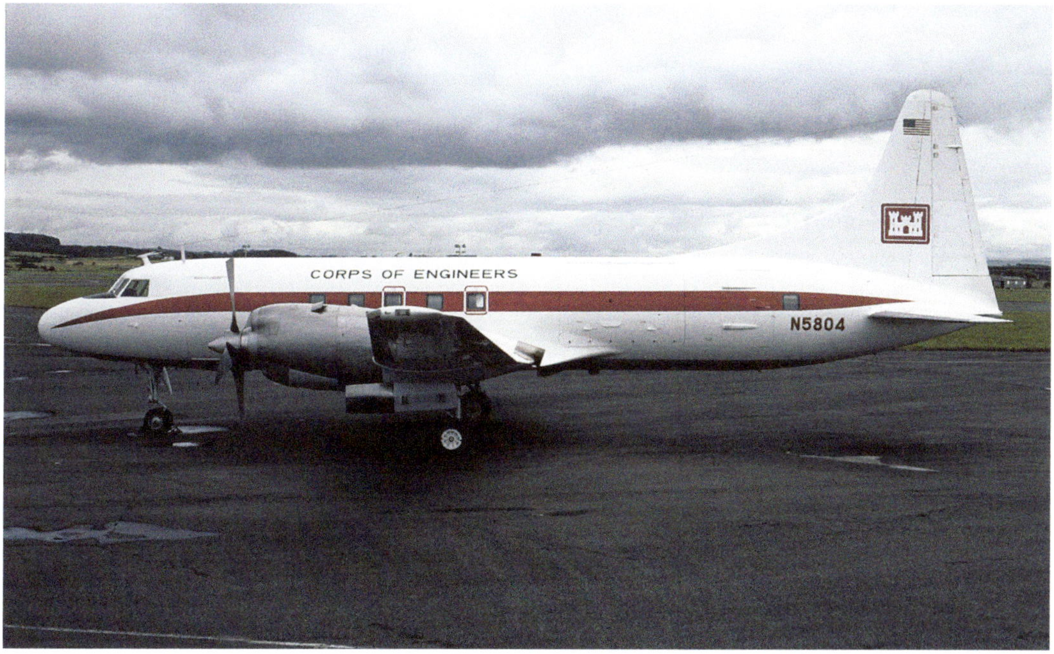

US Army Corps of Engineers 1954 Convair CV-580 N5804, a conversion from a CV-340, is seen at Prestwick in 1985. (Author's Collection)

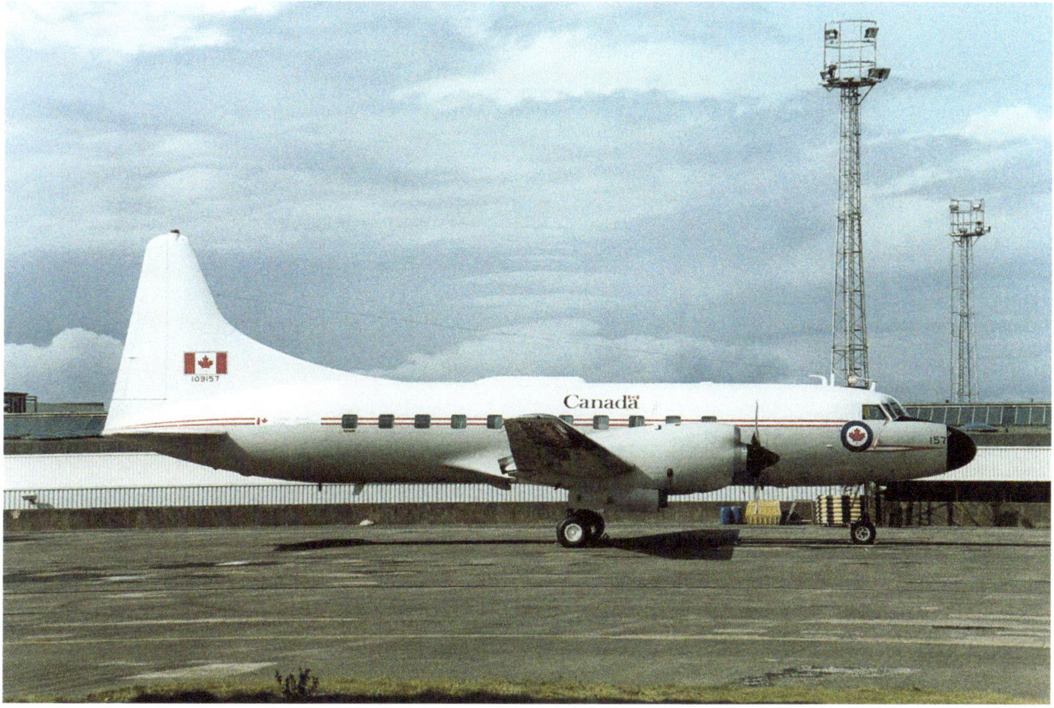

RCAF/CAF Canadair-built CC-109 Cosmopolitan 109157 is captured at Prestwick in 1986. Based on the Convair 440, this type served the RCAF from 1960 to 1994. (Gerry Rudman)

Shanwick is the ATC call sign for the control of all air traffic routing across the Atlantic up to 30 degrees west. The Prestwick part issues route clearance to westbound aircraft and co-ordinates with the Irish centre at Ballygirreen near Shannon Airport. As there is no radar over the Atlantic, Ballygirreen uses HF frequencies to communicate with aircraft. The aircraft would call in on VHF requesting clearance, and the Clearance Delivery Officer (CDO) would input the request on the green computer screens. These were updated in the 1990s, but in the early 2000s a new Operations Room was bought online with brand-new, state-of-the-art equipment.

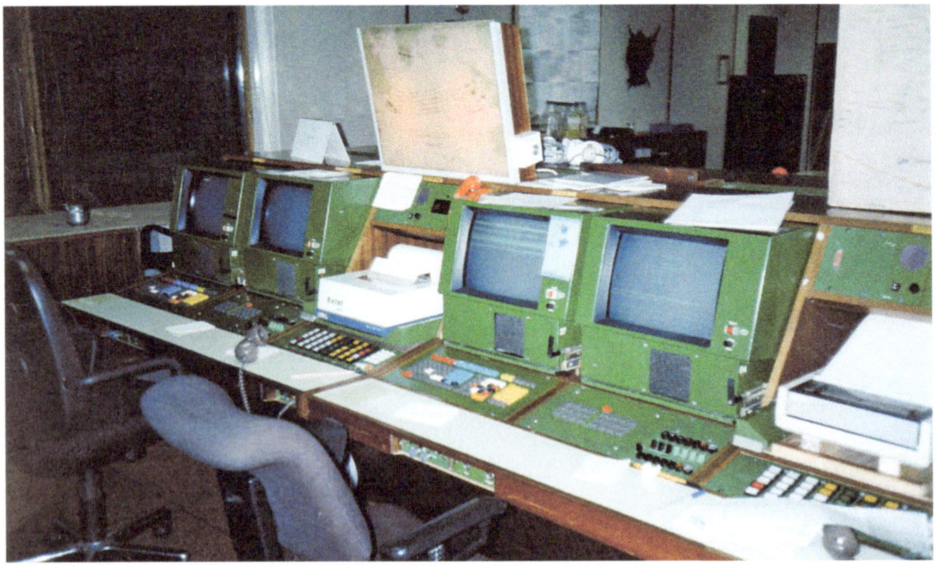

Shanwick Oceanic Control in 1989. The old green boxes were used to input flight plans. (Norman Henderson)

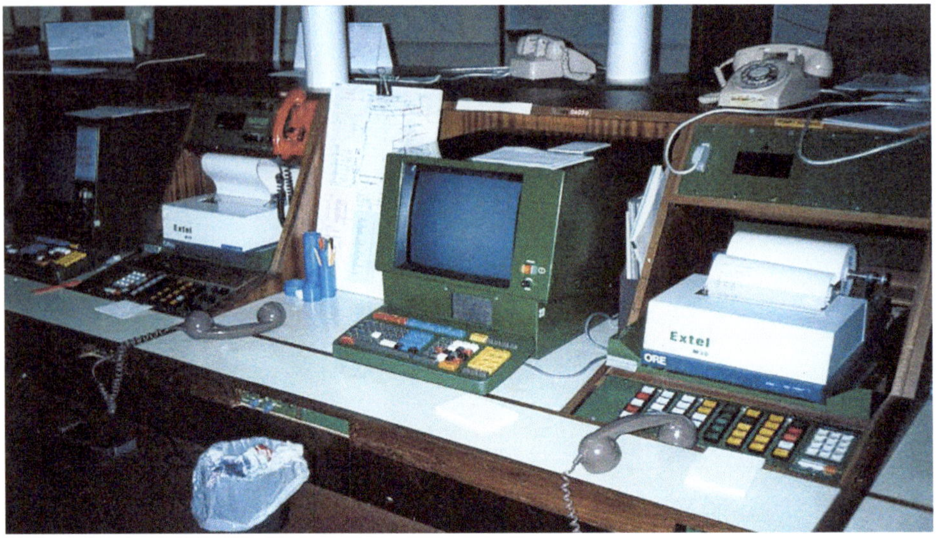

Shanwick Oceanic Control Room's CDO input screens in 1989, with the transmission foot switch at the bottom of the photograph. The phone lines were to Canada, Spain, Iceland, New York, Portugal, France and Ireland. (Norman Henderson)

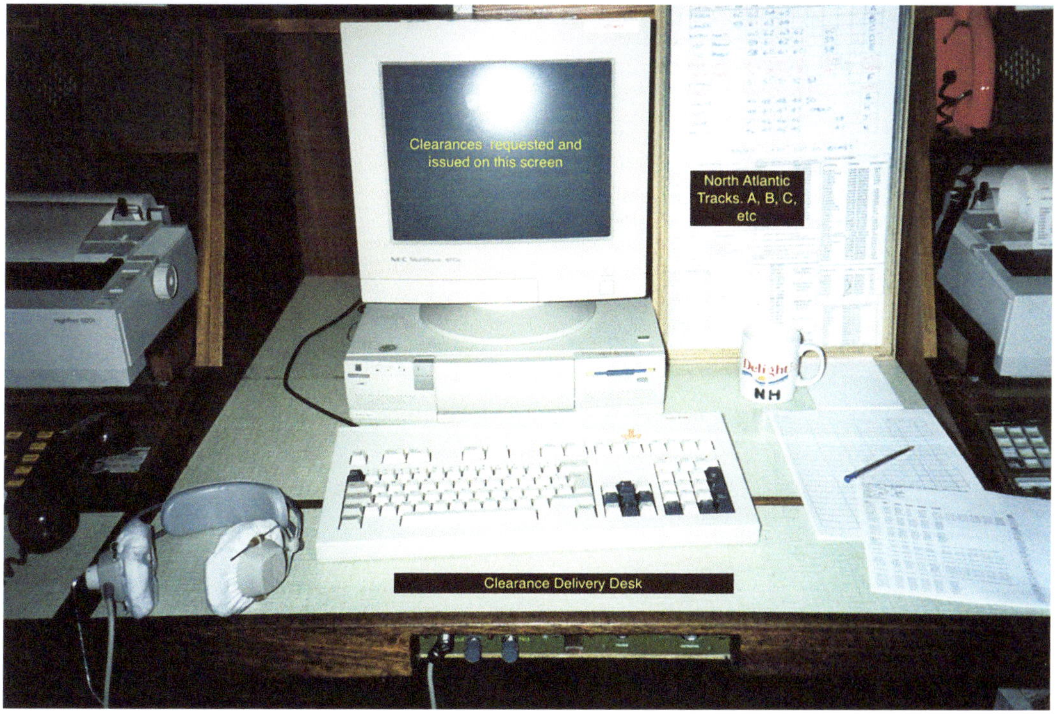

CDO position, 1990s. (Norman Henderson)

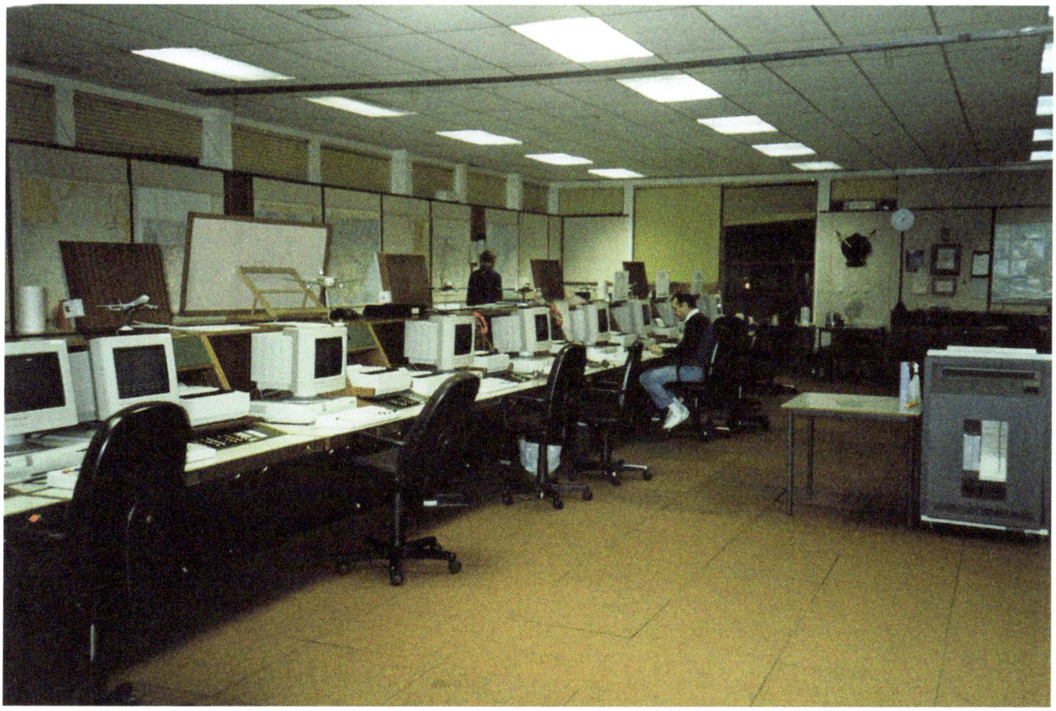

Shanwick Operations Room, 1990s. (Norman Henderson)

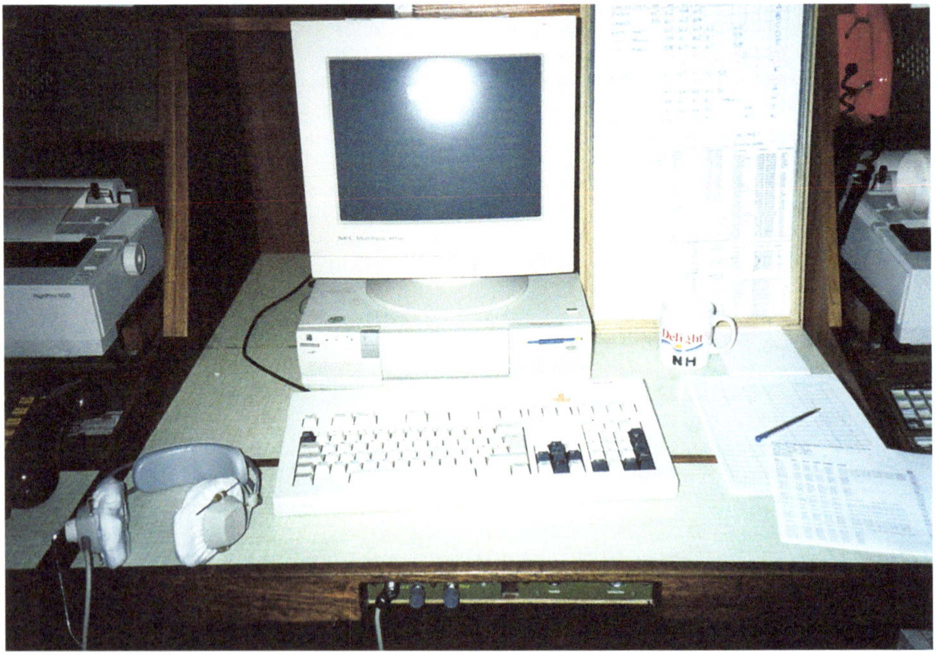

Shanwick Oceanic Control, 1993, with the new boxes. This is one of the three Clearance Delivery Officers' positions. (Norman Henderson)

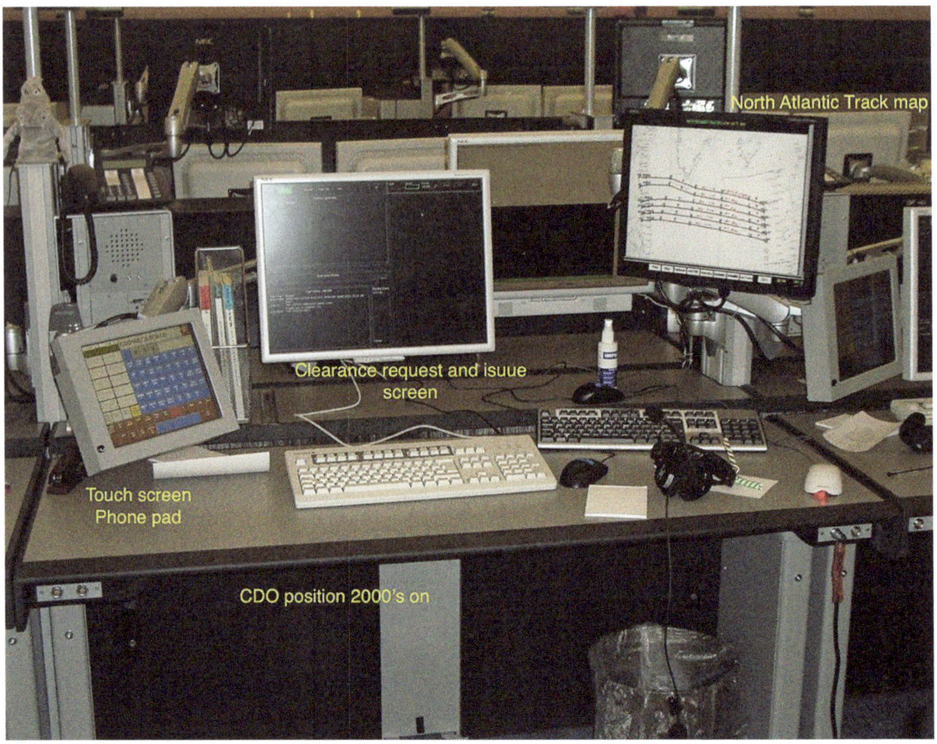

Shanwick Operations Room, between 2000 and 2010. (Norman Henderson)

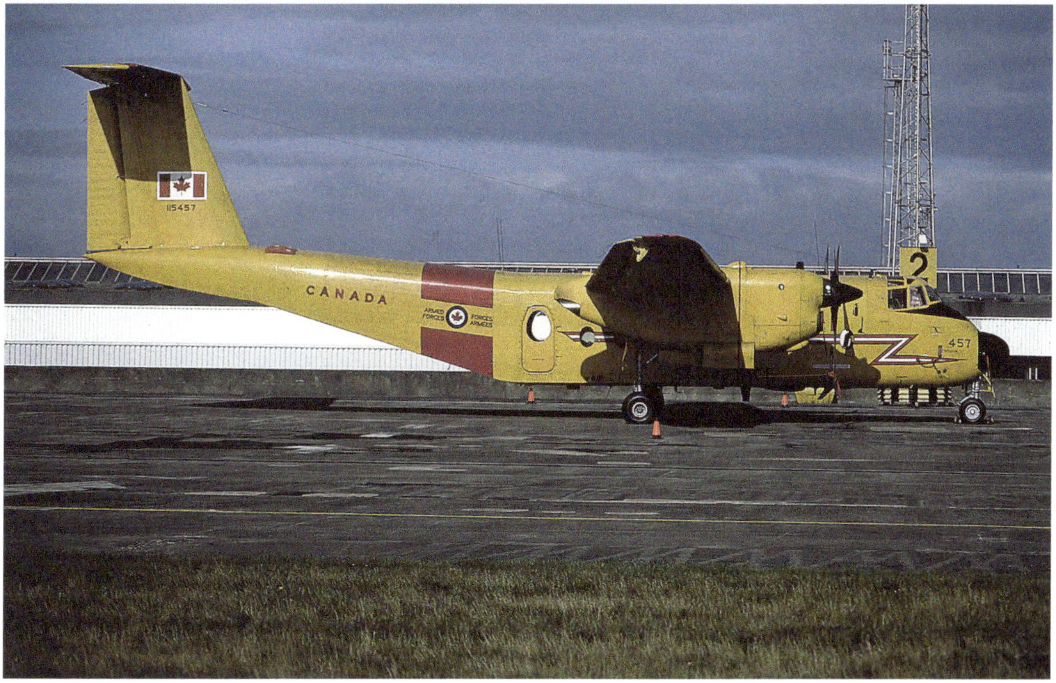

De Havilland Canada DHC-5 Buffalo 115457 Sauvetage (Rescue) of the Royal Canadian Air Force on the old bay 2 at the main terminal in the 1980s. (Leslie A. Rodger)

In 1992 a lifeline was provided by Winnipeg-based entrepreneur and millionaire Matthew Chance Hudson, who led a consortium of businessmen in the purchase of the airport in a deal clinched by the intervention of BAe. Hudson set out his vision for south-west Scotland as an international transit hub, creating thousands of jobs, and the renaissance began with the construction of a railway station on the existing Ayrshire Coast Line, which had been electrified in 1986, and which runs past the airfield (accessed via a covered air-bridge from the airport). This was a move that turned out to be perfectly timed for the beginning of liberalised markets in air transport that spawned the budget airlines boom from the late 1980s, and in 1994 an ambitious little airline called Ryanair, attracted by the new direct rail link to the airport, started offering flights to Dublin, soon after adding flights to London and Continental Europe. By the late 1990s Prestwick had grown larger in terms of traffic than it had ever been when it was under state ownership.

Hudson, who had bought the airport for under £3 million and formed Prestwick Aviation Holdings, sold a 75 per cent share to Stagecoach Aviation (a newly formed division of the Scottish transport company) in 1998 for £41 million. Stagecoach invested a further £10 million refurbishing the passenger terminal, upgrading the second runway and building a 61,000 square foot maintenance hangar, which was leased to Polar Air Cargo of California as a maintenance and repair base for its fleet of fourteen Boeing 747 freighters for an initial period of ten years. A new cargo terminal was also built south of the parallel taxiway, which offered nose-in parking for the range of wide-bodied aircraft, with the added facility of direct on-site transfer to road transport in anticipation of a significant increase in freight over the next few years.

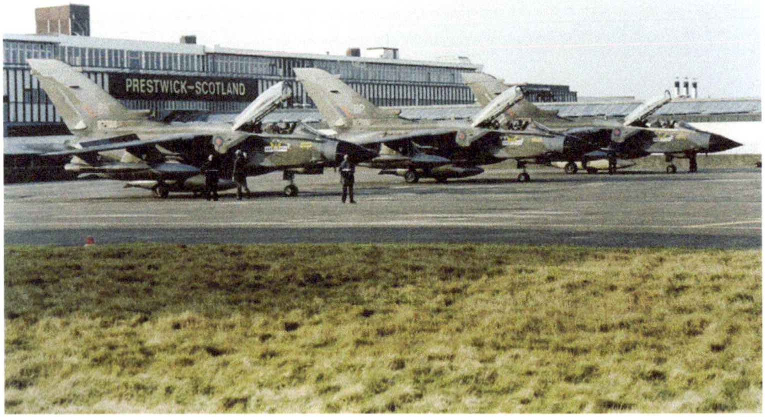

1990s

A trio of Panavia Tornado GR.1s from No. 14 Squadron, RAF Lossiemouth, at Prestwick Airport sometime in 1990. (Gerry Rudman)

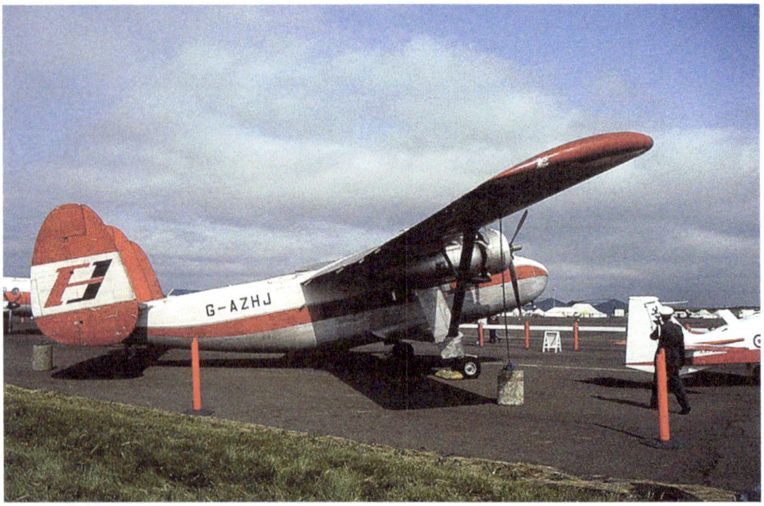

Scottish Aviation's 1959-built Twin Pioneer 3 G-AZHJ at the Prestwick Airshow on 6 June 1992. It was de-registered on 23 July 1997 and was later purchased by Air Atlantique for spares. (Author's Collection)

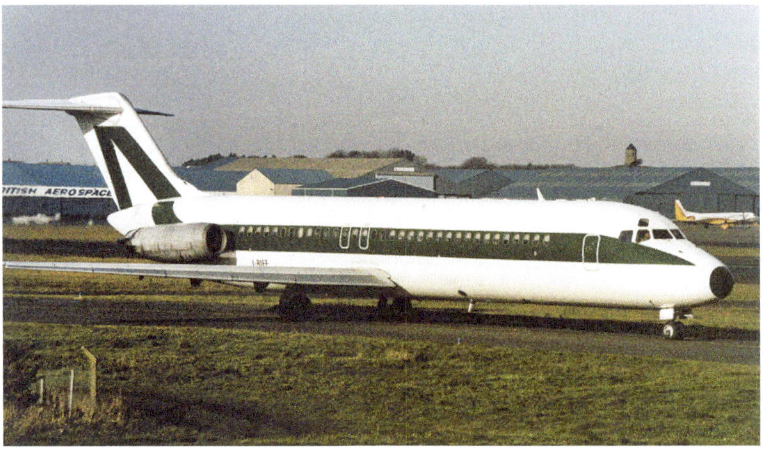

Formerly I-DIZO, Alitalia Douglas DC-9-32 I-RIFE is seen on its ferry flight to the USA on 11 November 1996. (Jim Fulton)

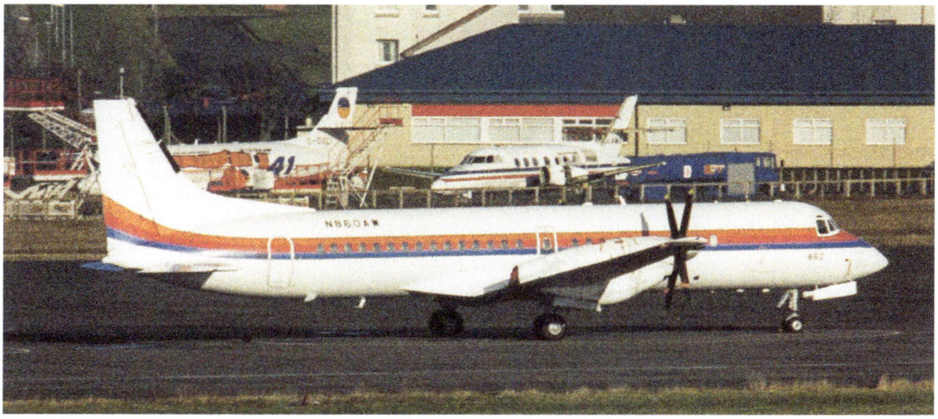

United Express/Air Wisconsin British Aerospace Advanced Turbo-Prop (BAe ATP) N860AW on 4 November 1996. (Jim Fulton)

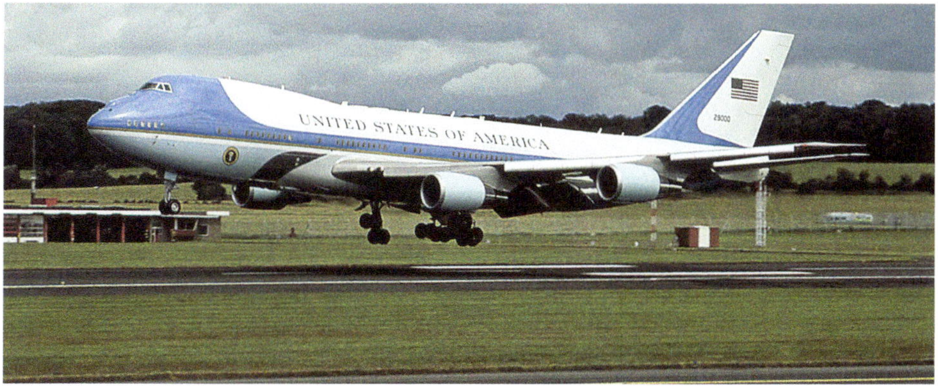

2005

Boeing 747 VC-25A 'Air Force One' arriving for the G8 Summit on 6 July 2005. (Paul Thallon)

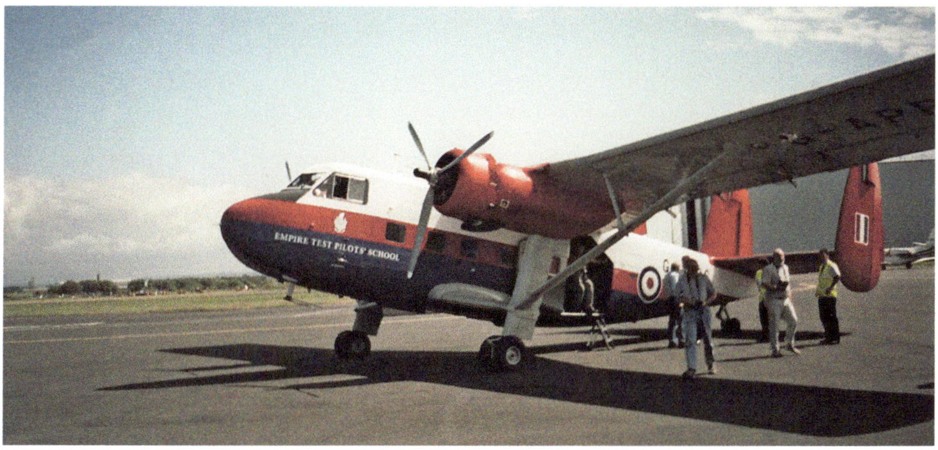

The last airworthy Twin Pioneer Srs.3 in the northern hemisphere, G-APRS revisits Prestwick to celebrate the 50th anniversary of the type on 25 June 2005. (Alexander Cunningham)

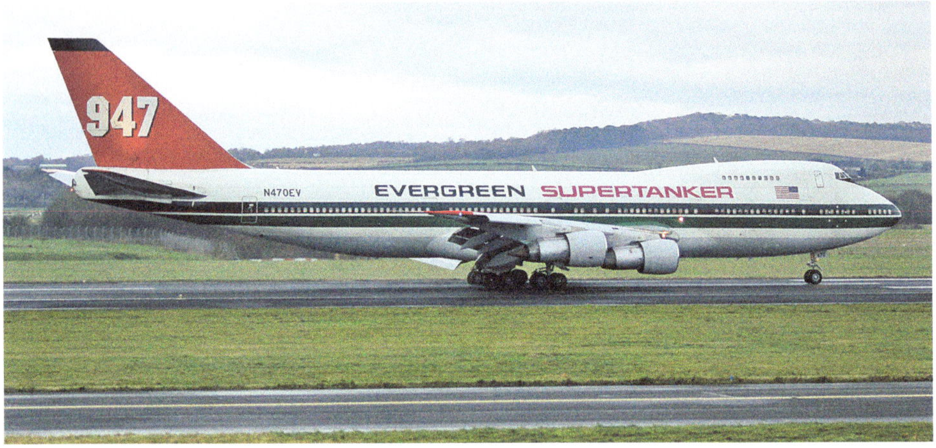

2007

Evergreen International Aviation 747-273C Supertanker N470EV/947 on 18 November 2007. The company intended to convert up to four 747 cargo planes into aerial firefighting assets, but ceased all aviation-related operations on 29 November 2013. (Scott Wright)

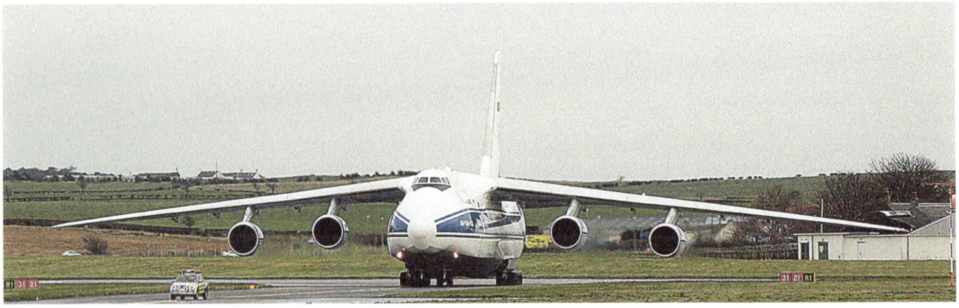

Volga-Dnepr Airlines Antonov An-124-100 RA-82044 on 18 November 2007. Based on the Ruslan heavy military transport aircraft, it is currently the biggest series heavy lifter in the world. (Scott Wright)

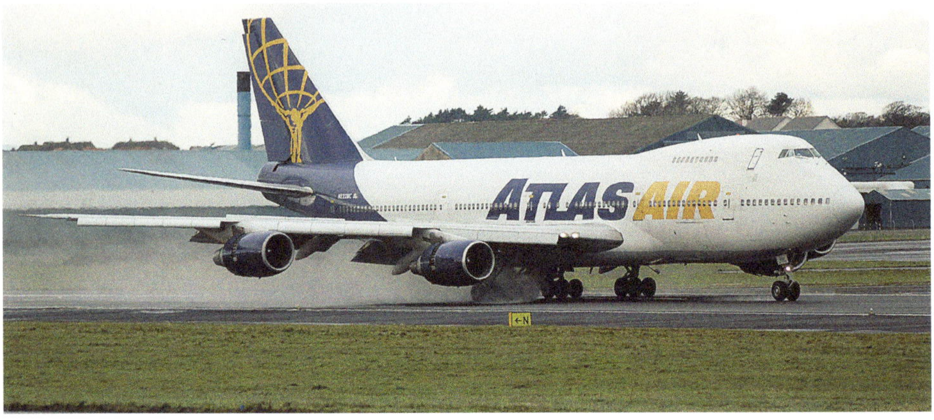

Atlas Air Boeing 747-2D7B/F N522MC on 18 November 2007. It is currently stored at the Mojave Air & Space Port, California. (Scott Wright)

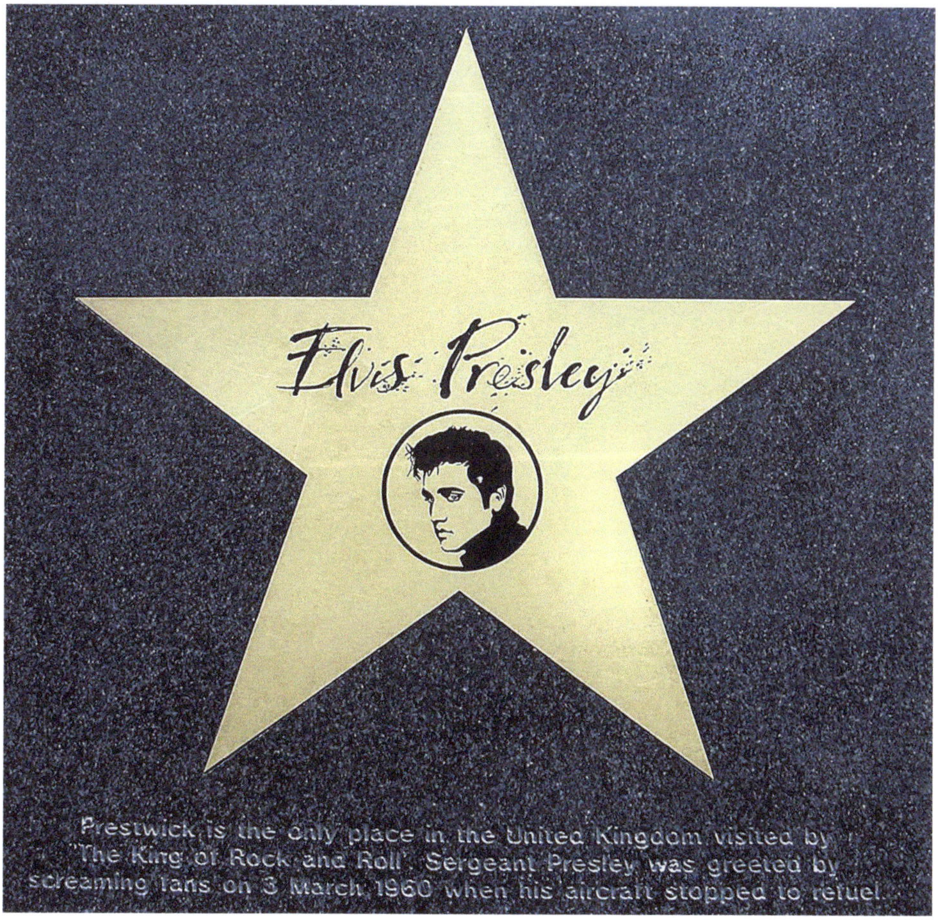

A plaque commemorating Elvis Presley's memorable visit to Prestwick Airport on 3 March 1960 is set, Sunset Boulevard-fashion, in the concourse floor. (Author's Collection)

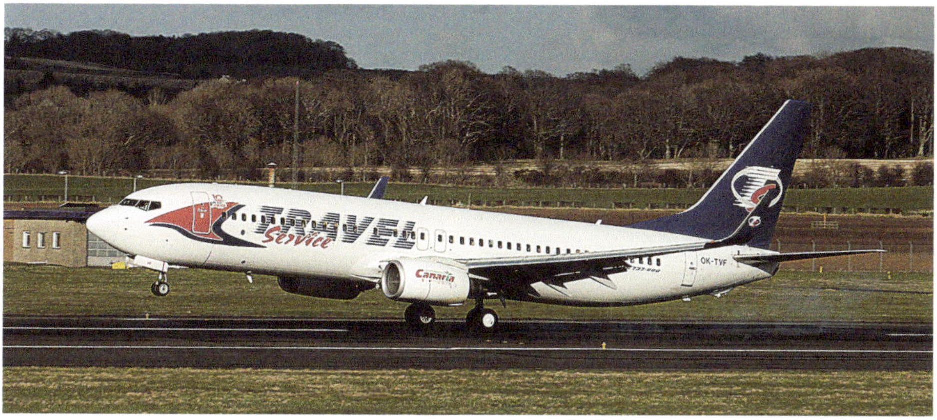

2008
Travel Service Boeing 737-8FH OK-TVF on 30 March 2008. The aircraft went on a regular seasonal lease to Sunwing Airlines from October 2011. (Scott Wright)

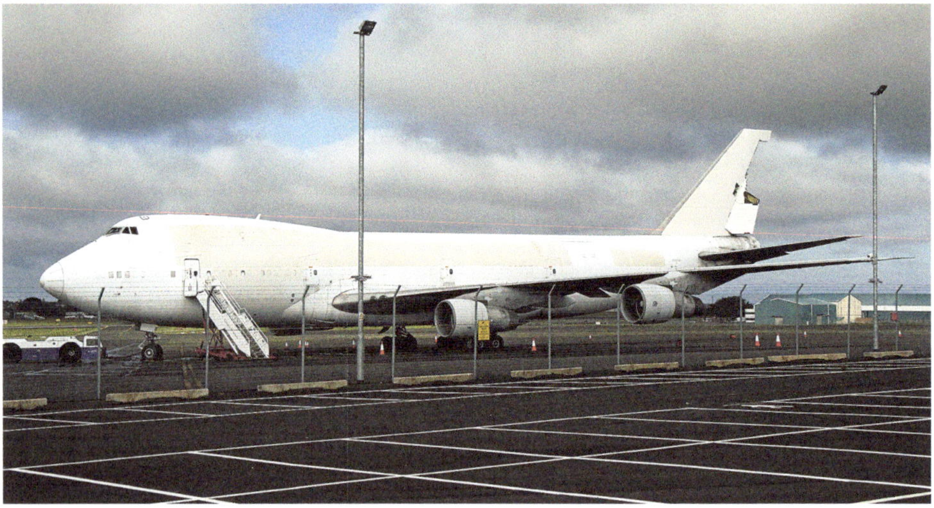

Ex-Polar Air Cargo Boeing 747-122(SF) N852FT was used as an airfield training aircraft. (Paul Fallon)

By 2000 the airport hit the 2.5 million passengers per annum mark, and the cargo and military customer base continued to grow, but Stagecoach, announcing that it was focusing on its core rail and bus businesses worldwide, sold the airport on 20 January 2001 to the New Zealand-based Infrastructure & Utilities NZ Limited (Infratil) for £33.4 million.

Infratil completed a £3 million refurbishment of the terminal building in April 2005, which was projected to be able to handle up to 3 million passengers a year. A Travelex outlet was also installed near the entrance of the departure hall. However, the company was strongly criticised for its re-branding of the airport using the Glaswegian-style slogan 'Pure Dead Brilliant', which stood as its moniker for the next eight and a half years.

Prestwick Airport became the entry point into Scotland on 6 July 2005 for the world's most powerful leaders on the eve of the three-day G8 Summit, which was being held in Gleneagles. Amid an unprecedented level of security, officers (including armed officers) were drafted in from police forces throughout the UK to assist in the operation – by far the biggest security operation ever mounted on Scottish soil – and included manning the airport's 14-mile perimeter in preparation for the landing of Air Force One, carrying American president George W. Bush. All commercial flights were grounded and all trains were halted, and the A77, which runs past the end of the main runway, was controversially closed while the aircraft was on final approach.

When BAE Systems was formed in 1999, their unit at Prestwick became part of BAE Systems Regional Aircraft, which offered nose to tail parts and maintenance support for the Jetstreams, the Hatfield and Woodford-built 80- to 112-seat Avro RJX (formerly the BAe-146) regional jetliner, the sixty-four-seat Advanced Turboprop (ATP) and earlier BAe-748 turboprops. With the end of production in 2002, Regional Aircraft was re-launched as a service and support business based at Prestwick, a task it continues to this day.

Prestwick International Aerospace Park opened in 1999 on a 247-acre site adjacent to the airport after the greenbelt status was removed. Its prime position accommodates Aerospace Service Industries, which enables it to maintain its position as a major aircraft servicing and engineering base.

2000 to 2010

In 2000, Ryanair introduced the Boeing 737-800 (the larger 189-seat variant of the 737 Next Generation family) to Prestwick, with three being based at the airport, which for the first time provided Scottish consumers with direct low fare flights to Europe (Paris and Frankfurt), in addition to low fare flights to Dublin and London. Ryanair continued to be the main scheduled carrier at Prestwick, with Aer Arann and Air Wales working on behalf of Bmibaby.

The 63,873 square foot (5,934 square metre) 747 hangar south of the main terminal building was completed in 2000. Accessed via an internal airport roadway with controlled security access, it can accommodate a Boeing 747 or a minimum of three Airbus A320s with its fully open door span of 764 feet (71 metres) wide by 215 feet (20 metres) high.

Spirit AeroSystems (Europe) Limited (headquartered in Wichita, Kansas, USA) was established at Prestwick in 2005 and acquired the BAE Systems Aerostructures UK business unit. The company is one of the largest airframe suppliers to Airbus and is a key supplier of major wing structures for the Airbus A320, A330, A340, A380 and A350 families of aircraft, as well as wing components for the Boeing 787 and 777.

Prestwick Airport unveiled its latest facelift in September 2007 following a decade of growth in terms passenger traffic. New shops and a bar were included as part of the re-vamp, and the departures lounge had a new tax and duty-free store, but it was a touch of nostalgia that marked the occasion with the unveiling of a plaque in honour of Elvis Presley, set Sunset Boulevard-fashion in the concourse floor.

In the face of very challenging times, with volatile fuel prices and unfavourable economic conditions that affected the aviation industry as a whole, a draft master plan for Prestwick was published by Infratil in 2008, outlining the stages of projected growth in both passenger (from the current year's projection of 2.5 million passengers to around 5.7 million passengers in 2018, and around 12 million by 2033) and freight business (which was expected to grow at an average rate of 4 per cent each year).

The holiday airlines varied from season to season and included companies such as My Travel, Britannia Airways, Balkan Holidays and LTE operating flights to Spain, Portugal, Bulgaria and the US, but considerably more freight was handled than passenger traffic at this time. Cargolux, Polar Air Cargo (which also has maintenance hangars at the airport), Atlas Air, British Airways World Cargo, Air France Cargo, and Singapore Airlines Cargo all operated Boeing 747-400F, with occasional flights by Air Foyle HeavyLift and Volga-Dnepr with Antonov An-124 aircraft.

2010 to 2017

With the opening of the new National Air Traffic Services (NATS) Centre in 2010, air traffic control was consolidated, reducing the requirement of four centres down to two to reduce costs and increase security and operational efficiency. The operations room in Prestwick combines the Manchester Area Control Centre (MACC), which controls aircraft over much of the north of England, the Midlands and North Wales Centre, from 2,500 feet up to 28,500 feet, the Scottish Area Control Centre (ScACC), which controls aircraft over Scotland, Northern Ireland, Northern England and the North Sea from 2,500 feet up to 66,000 feet, and the OACC, which controls the airspace over the eastern half of the North Atlantic from the Azores (45 degrees north) to a boundary with Iceland (61 degrees north).

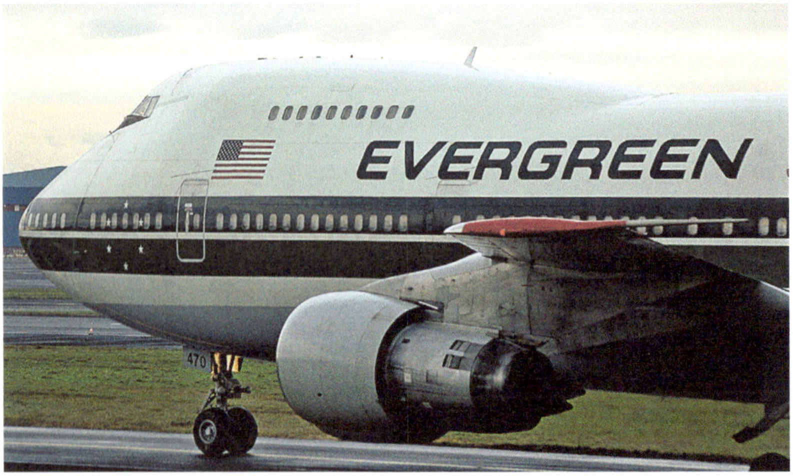

Evergreen International Airlines Inc. Boeing 747-273C N470EV at Prestwick on 18 November 2007. (Scott Wright)

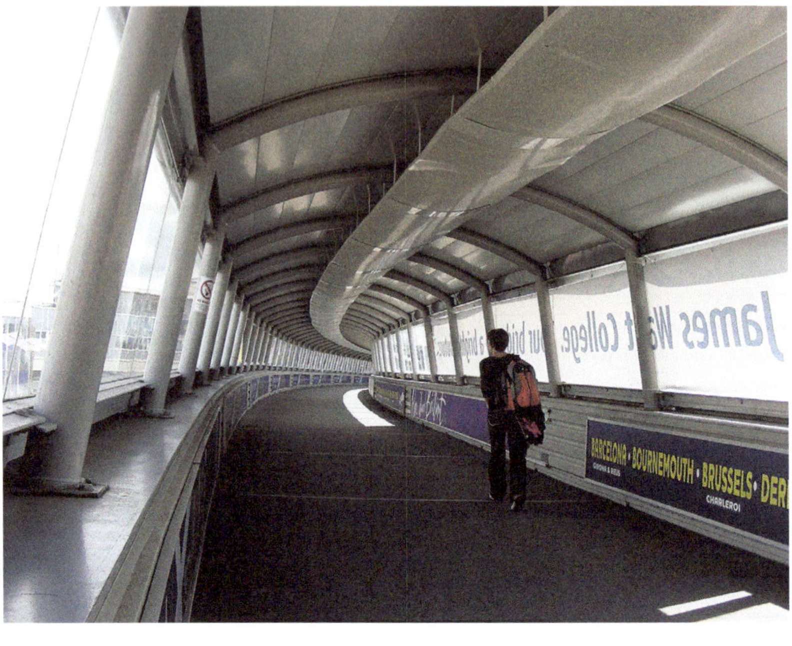

The enclosed footbridge from Prestwick International Airport railway station to the terminal building on 19 July 2009. (James Benedict Brown)

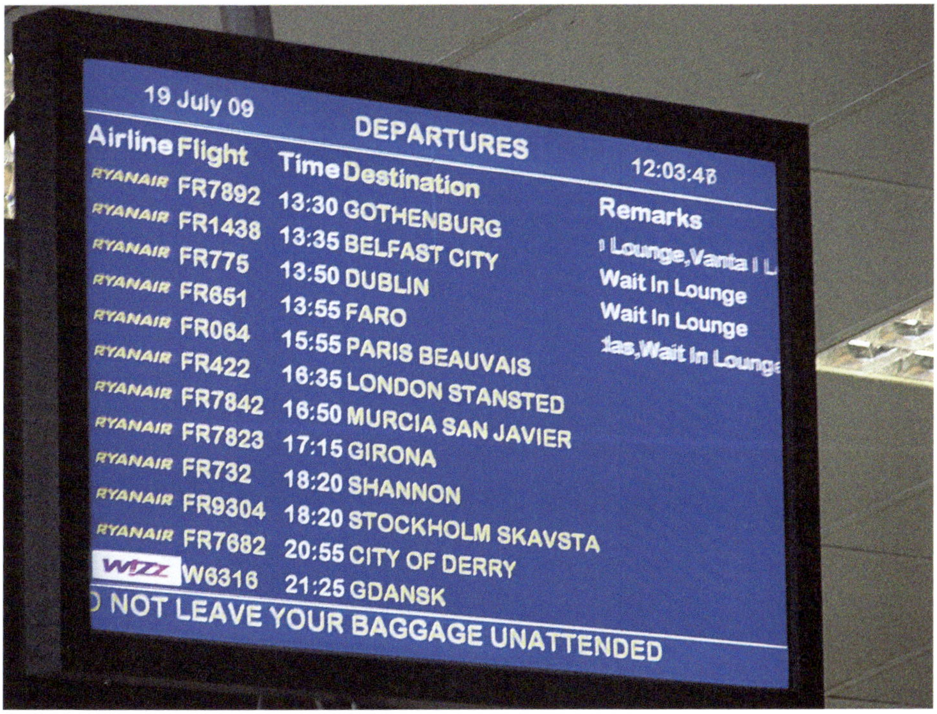

The departure screens at Prestwick International Airport on 19 July 2009. Hungarian airline Wizzair has a single departure light showing on this board, which is otherwise dominated by Ryanair. (James Benedict Brown)

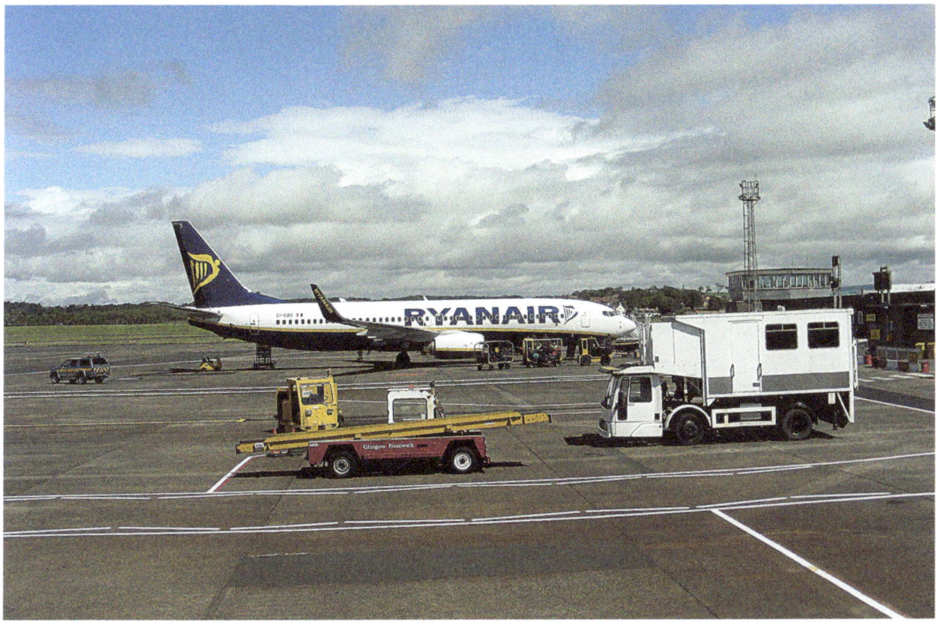

Ryanair Boeing 737-8AS EI-EBO is seen preparing for a flight to Gothenburg City on 19 July 2009. (James Benedict Brown)

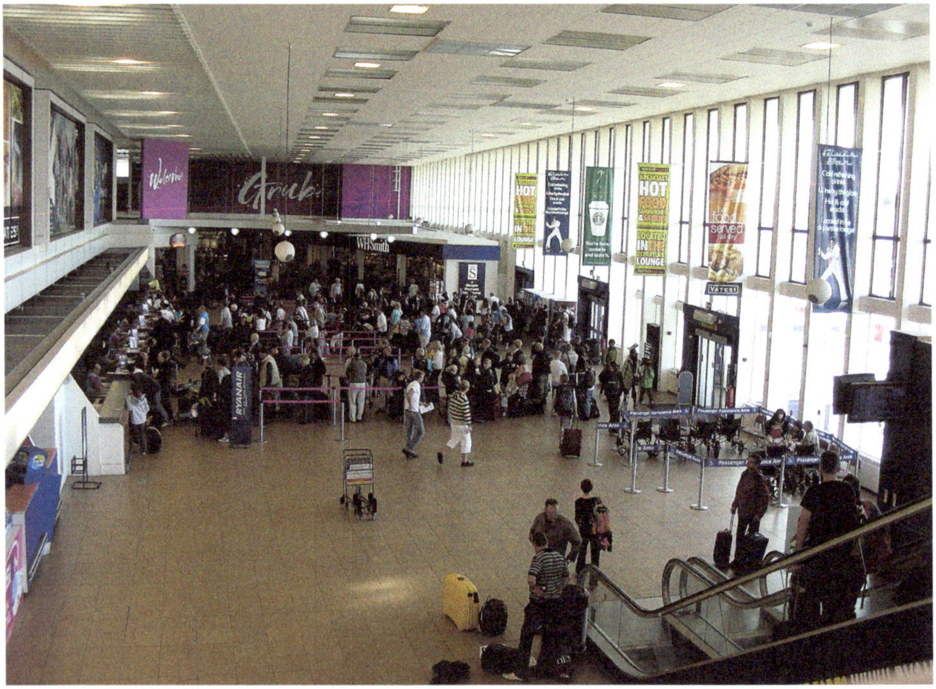

The check-in hall of this once grand airport on 19 July 2009. Now reduced to an almost entirely Ryanair schedule, it became even quieter when Ryanair moved to online check-ins. (James Benedict Brown)

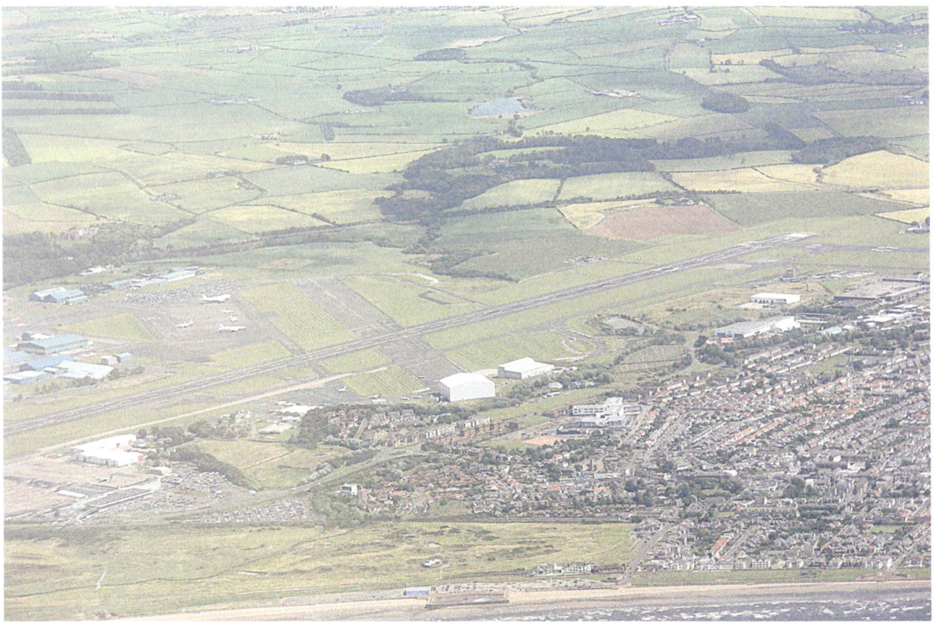

A look back at Prestwick and the adjacent airport after take-off from runway 31, turning south along the coast towards Ayr on 19 July 2009. The passenger terminal is at the bottom left. (James Benedict Brown)

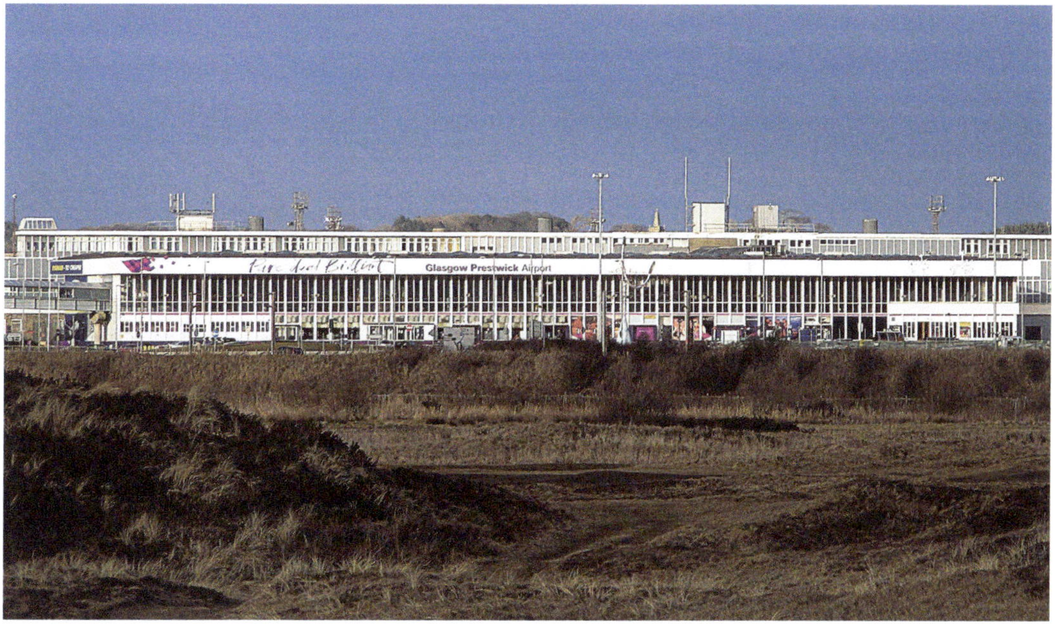

2010

Pure Dead Brilliant. The terminal, designed by Joseph L. Gleave, was opened by the Queen Mother on 22 September 1964. The Prestwick Golf Club course in the foreground was home to the first British Open in 1860. This photograph was taken on 6 March 2010. (Stephen Wagstaff)

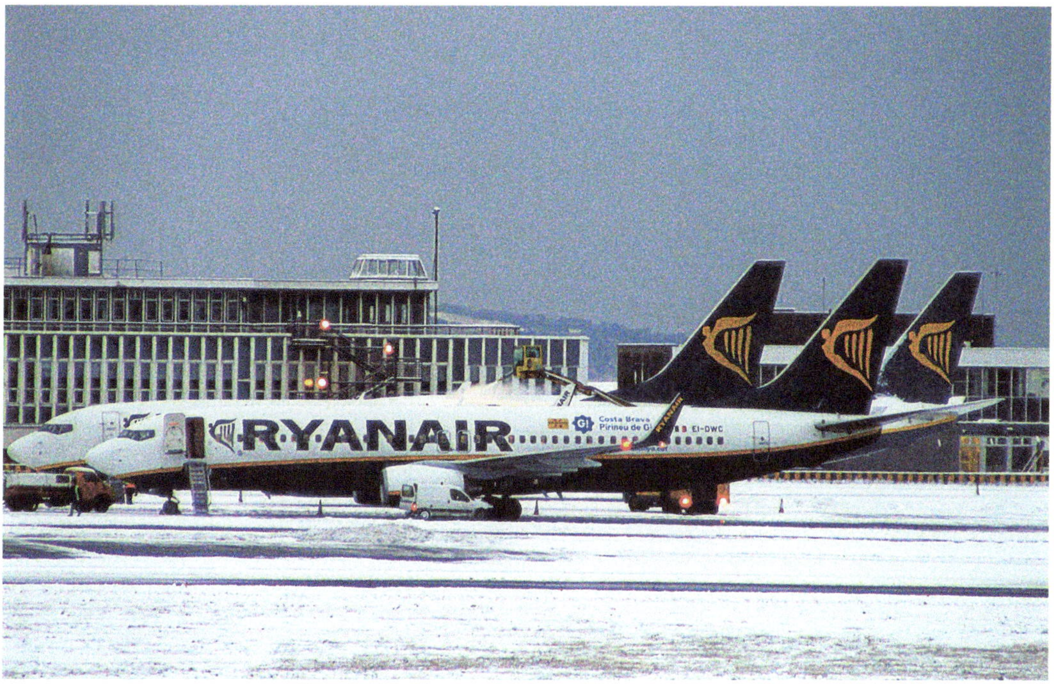

On a rare occasion when snow settled at Prestwick, on 18 December 2010, a line-up of Ryanair Boeing 737s receive de-icer treatment. (Stephen Wagstaff)

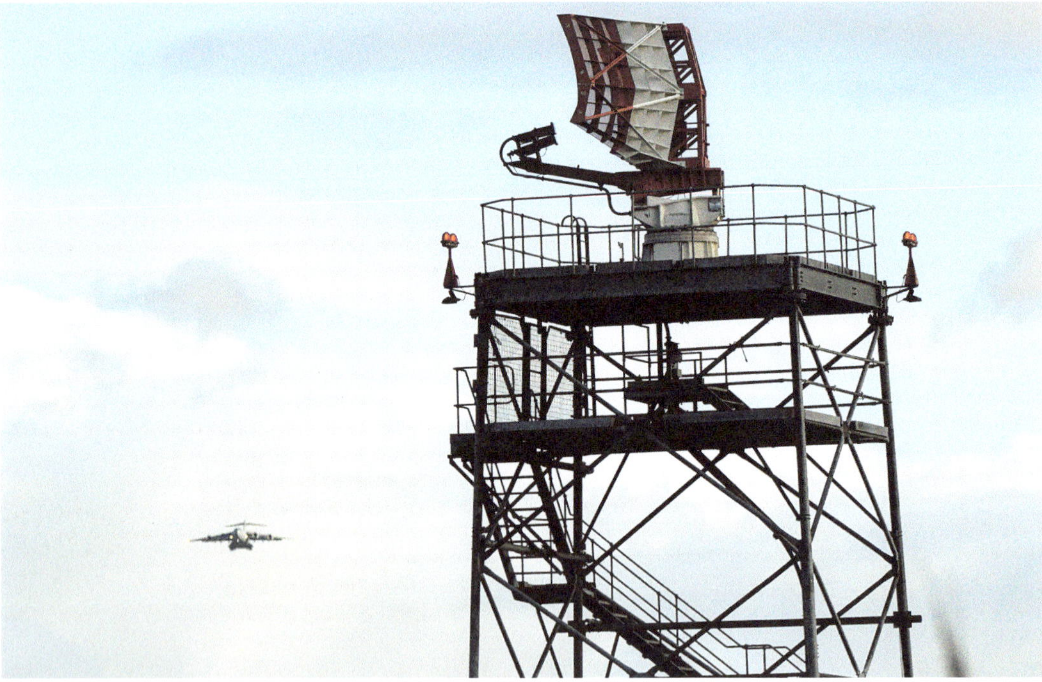

2011
A Boeing C-17 Globemaster III military transport aircraft on final approach on 26 February 2011. (Jim Ramsay)

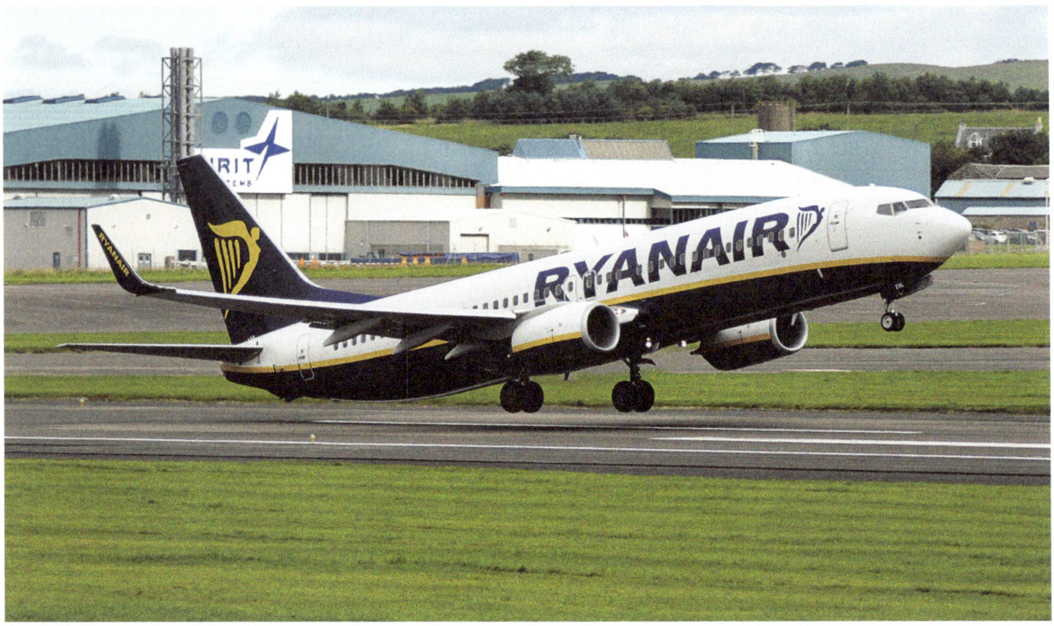

2012
Ryanair Boeing 737-8AS EI-EVL departs Prestwick on 7 August 2012. The 737-800 and 737-900 had extended fuselage lengths, increasing the seating to 189. (Robert McCulloch)

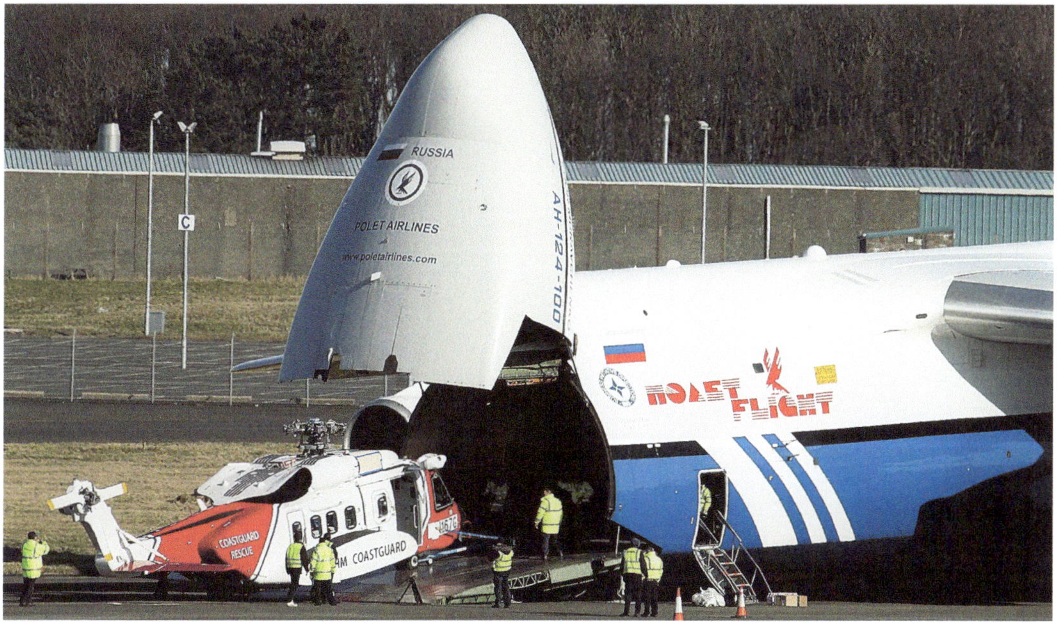

2013
Bristow Sikorsky S92 G-MCGB/N167G being unloaded from Volga-Dnepr Airlines' Antonov An-124 RA-82077 on 21 February 2013. (Bob Smith)

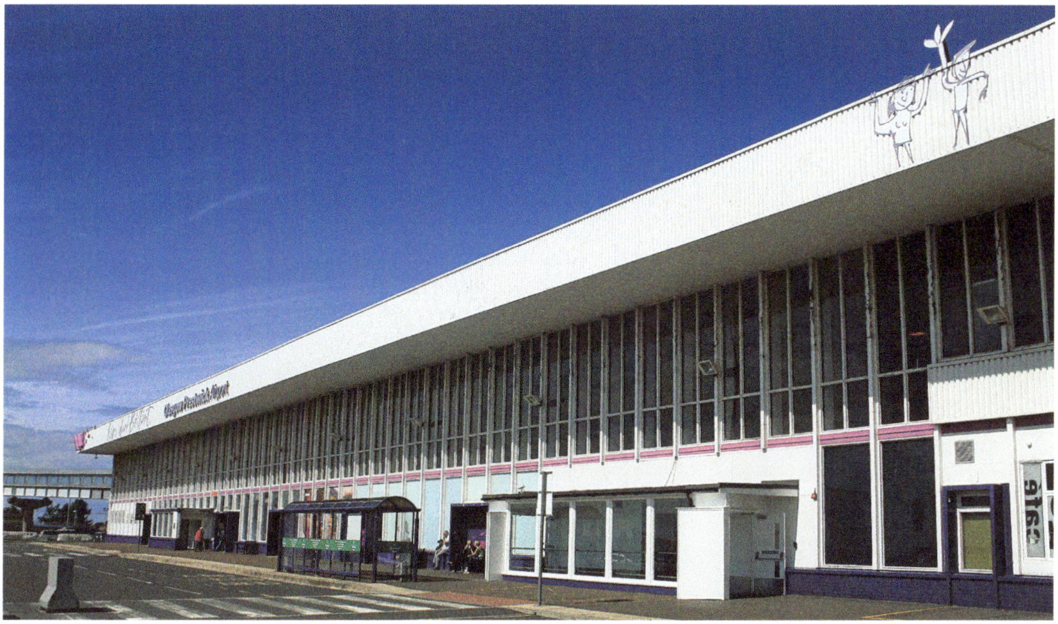

Prestwick Airport was the main Scottish airport for international/transatlantic flights until these flights were transferred to Glasgow. The airport doesn't look its best here, with paint peeling on the outside and indoors. The door frames, ceiling and paintwork look old and dated. Every flight on the arrival and departure screens (and there weren't that many) were Ryanair flights. 13 August 2013. (Peter Edin)

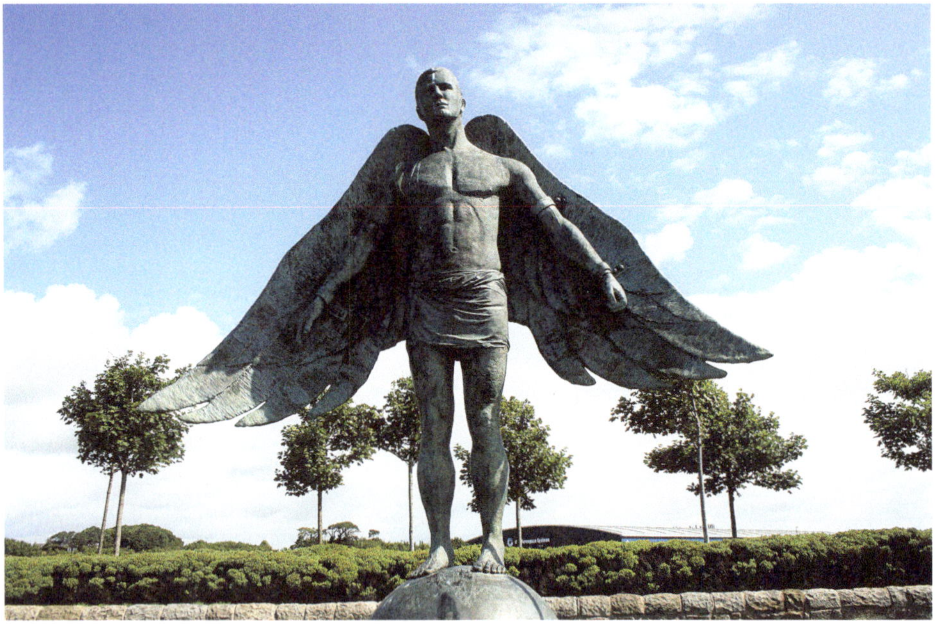

Andy Scott's bronze piece, the *Monkton Icarus*. This landmark sculpture was commissioned for the aerospace technology park near Prestwick Airport and was developed from school children's designs. It is seen on 13 August 2013. (Peter Edin)

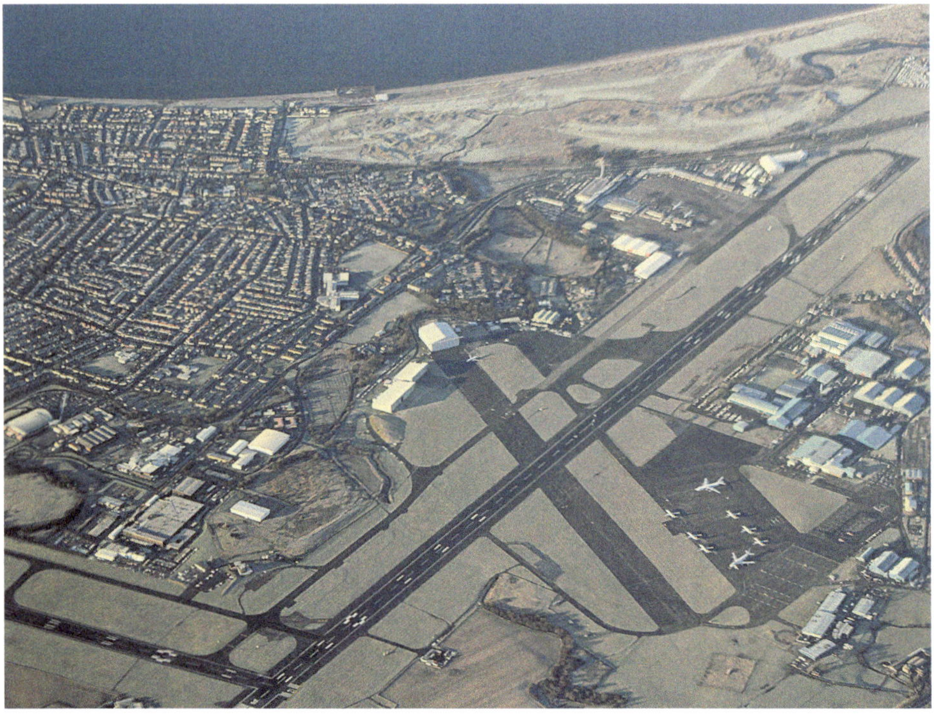

A view of Prestwick Airport from a flight from Glasgow to Tenerife on 11 December 2012. (Graham Speirs)

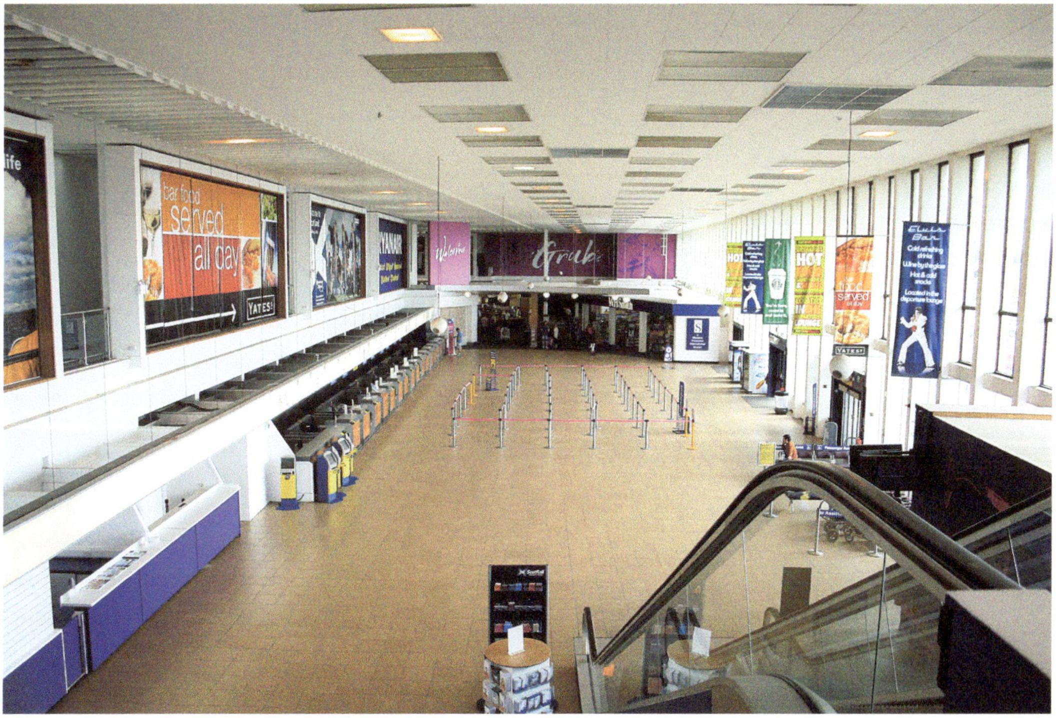

An inside view of the terminal building on 13 August 2013. Built in 1964 as a part of major expansion work, its arrival and departure halls can handle up to 3 million passengers a year. (Peter Edin)

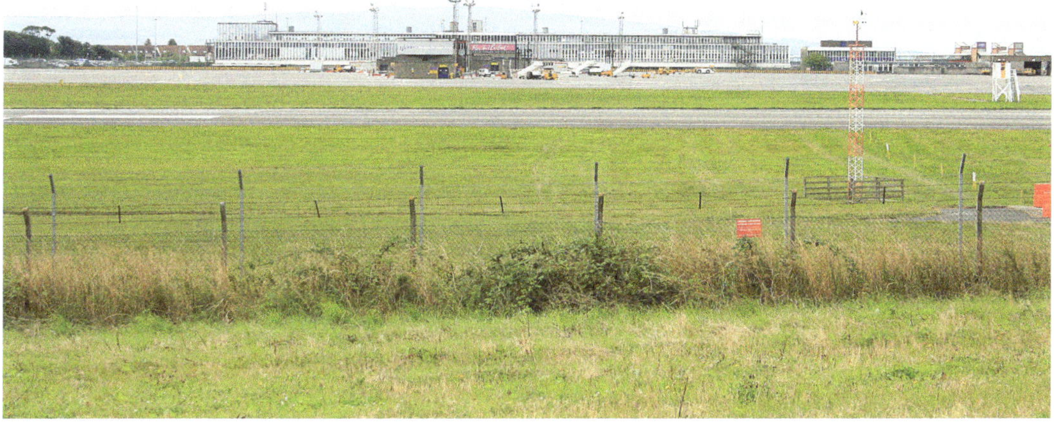

A view of Prestwick Airport on 13 August 2013. (Peter Edin)

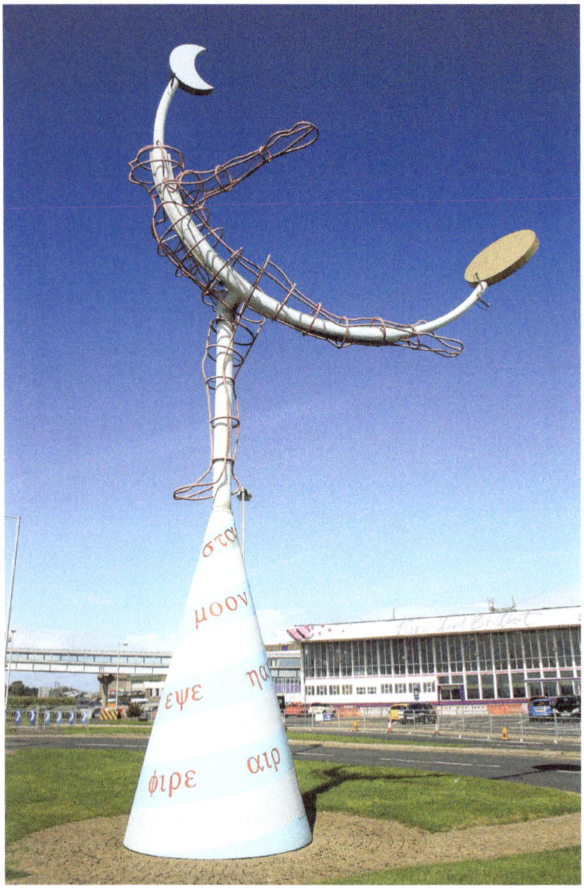

The Celestial Navigator at the airport entrance on 13 August 2013. The 15-metre-high sculpture by the Aberdeen-based artist Professor Carole Gray was created as part of a commission from Prestwick Airport through Art in Partnership. (Peter Edin)

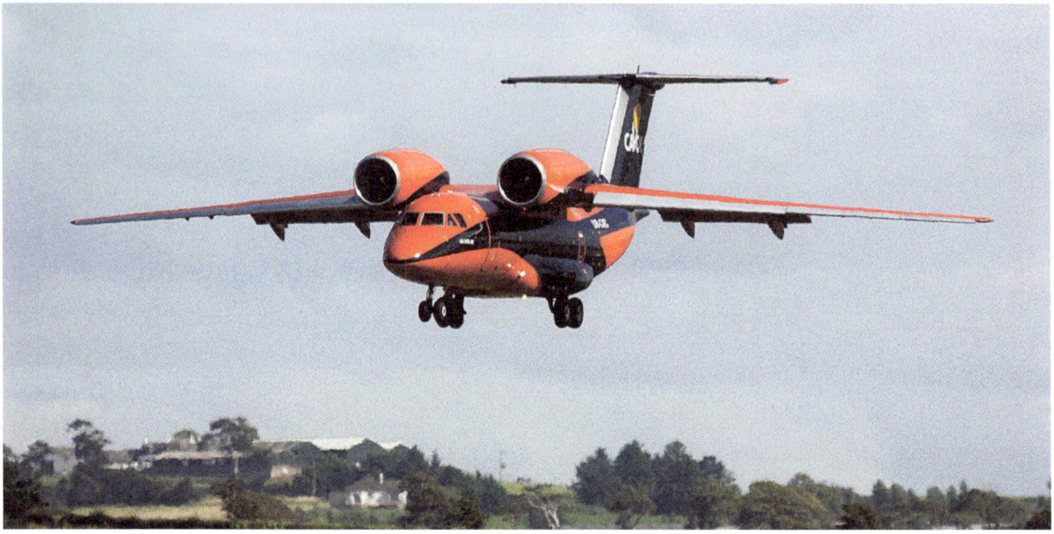

An unusual visitor to Prestwick was this Cavok Airlines Antonov An-74TK-100 cargo aircraft, UR-CKC, on 5 September 2013. UR-CKC was damaged beyond repair in an accident caused by bird strikes during take-off at São Tomé International Airport on 29 July 2017. (Jim Fulton)

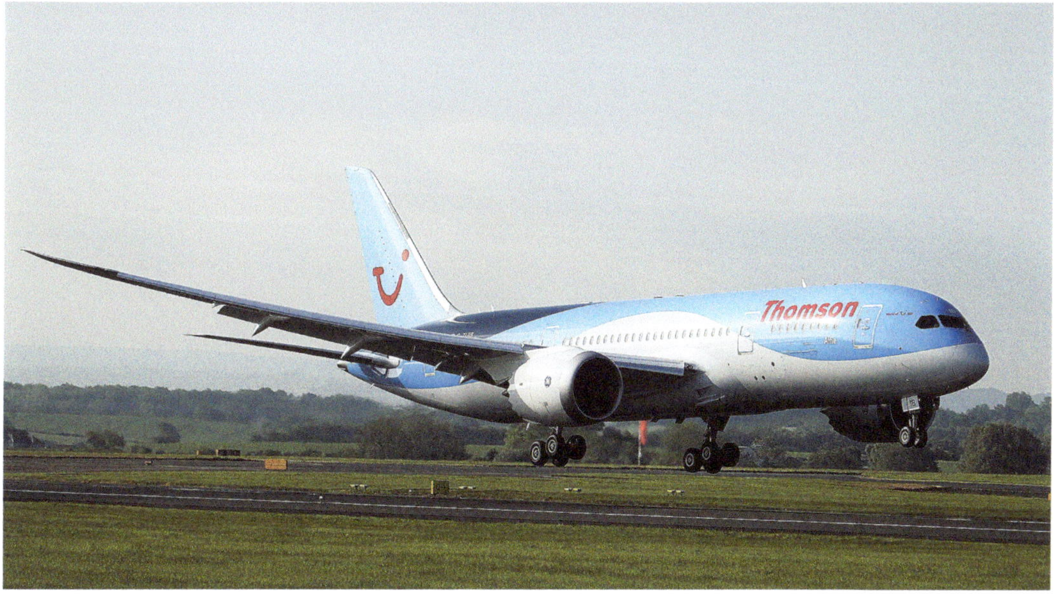

Thomson Airways Boeing 787-8 Dreamliner G-TUIB *Alfie* landing on runway 31 on 6 June 2013. It made its first appearance in Scotland at Prestwick Airport two days previously for test flights ahead of the launch of services in July to Mexico and Florida from Glasgow. (Bob Smith)

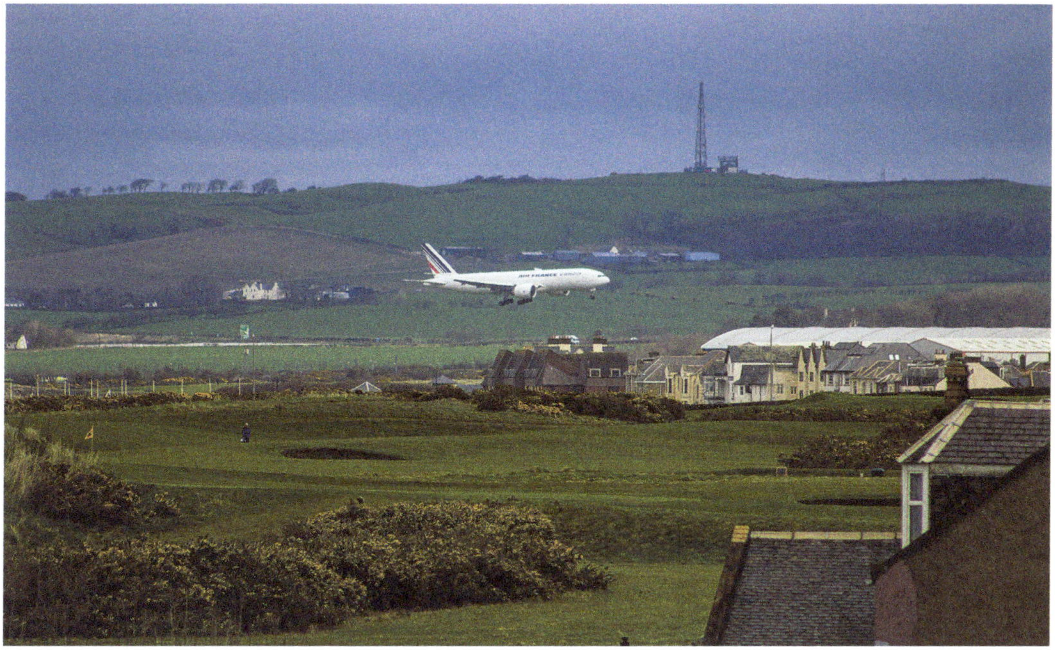

2014

Air France Cargo Boeing 777-F28 F-GUOC is captured on arrival at Prestwick on 6 April 2014. The 777 was the first commercial aircraft designed entirely by computer, which created three-dimensional drawings that allowed engineers to assemble a virtual aircraft, check for interference and verify that the thousands of parts fitted properly. (Barry Young)

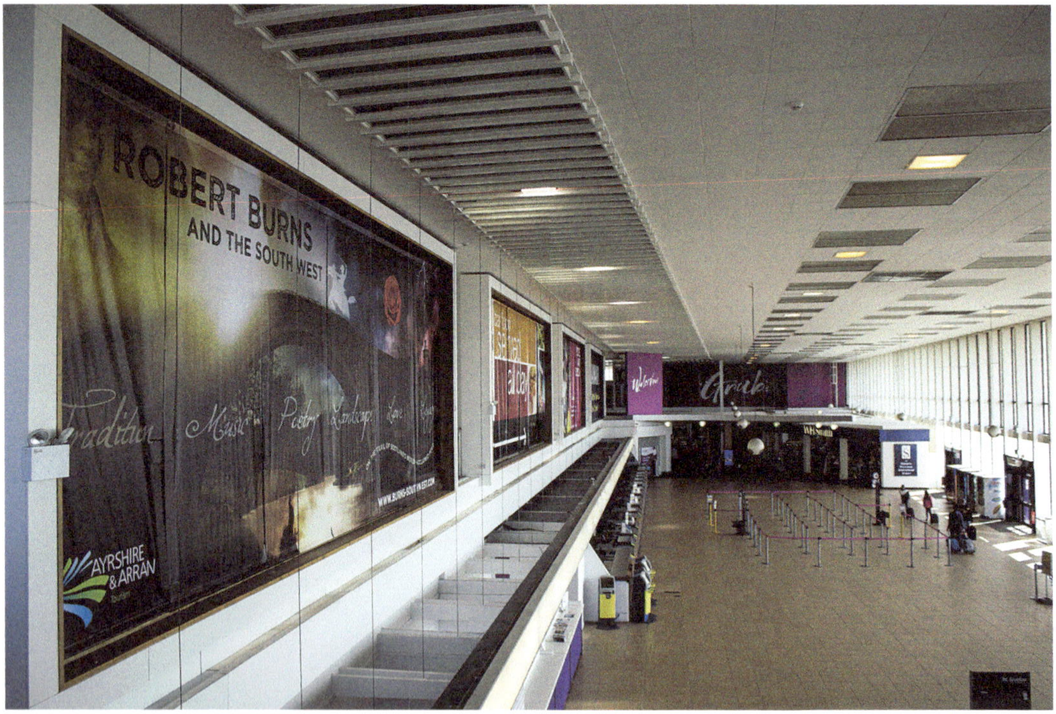

Terminal 2 on 12 April 2014. (Barry Young)

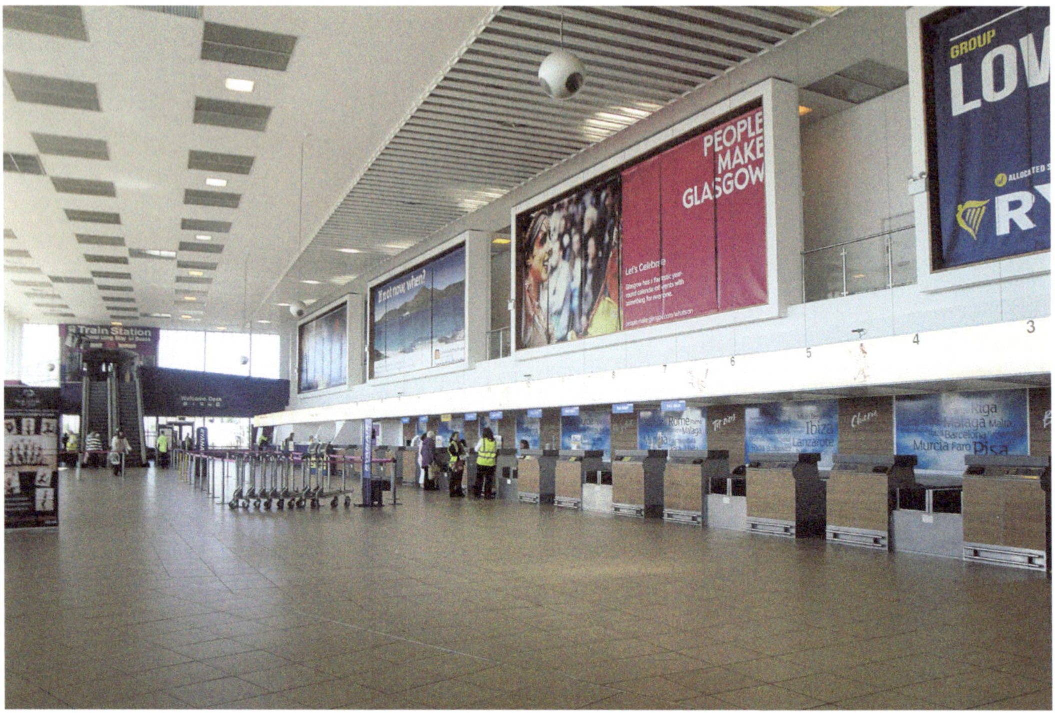

The check-in hall at Prestwick on 7 September 2014. (Bill Johnston)

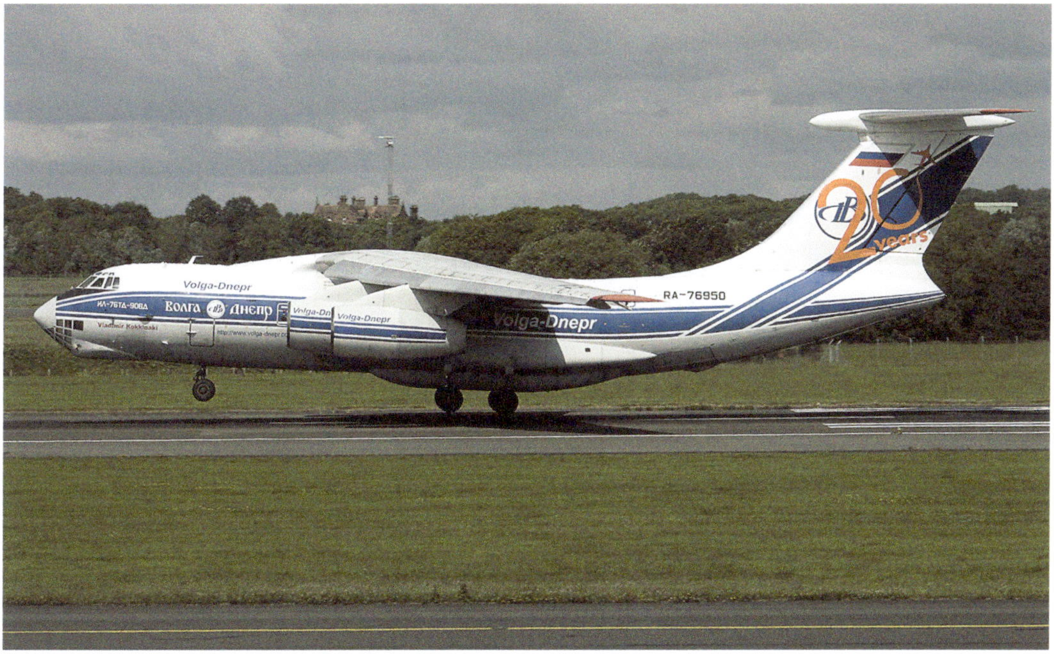

Volga-Dnepr Airlines Ilyushin IL-76TD-90VD RA-76950 arriving at Prestwick Airport on 22 June 2014. The Ulyanovsk-based airline provides global air charter services for the movement of oversized, unique and heavy air cargo. (Scott Wright)

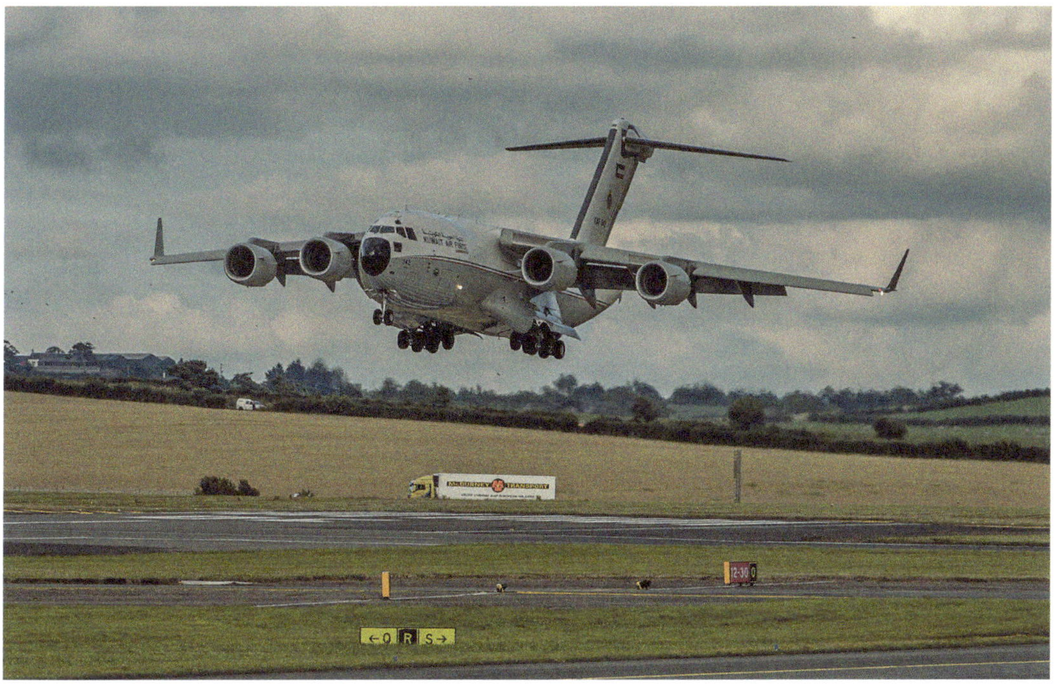

Kuwait Air Force C-17A Boeing Globemaster III KAF 342 is seen arriving on 6 August 2014. (Jim Ramsay)

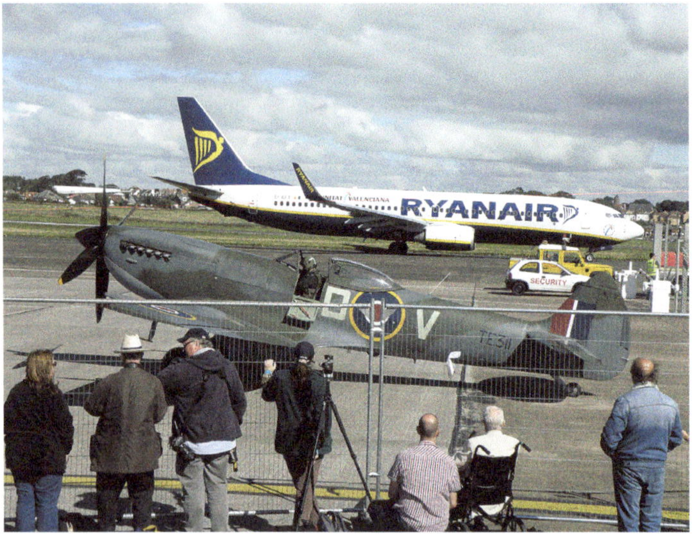

Boeing 737-8AS EI-EFT of Ryanair taxiies out at Prestwick for departure to Dublin while the pilot of the Battle of Britain Memorial Flight Spitfire prepares his aircraft for departure on 7 September 2014. (Alexander Cunningham)

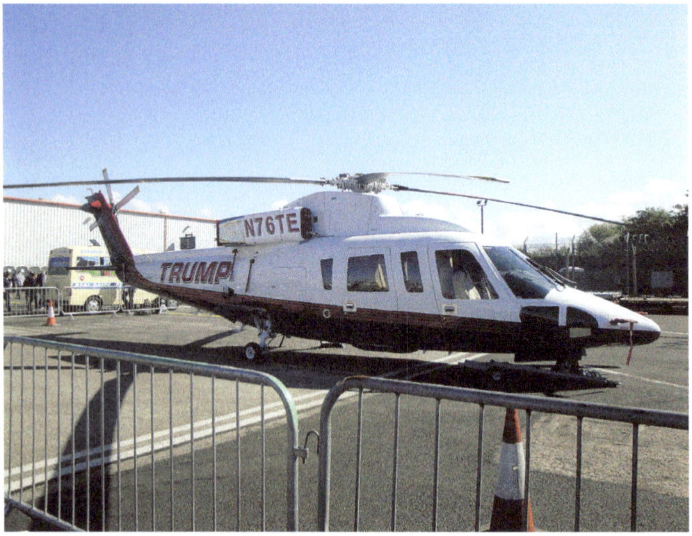

Donald Trump's Sikorsky S-76B helicopter N-76TE on 7 September 2014. Based in the UK to transport customers to Trump's golf club investments around Scotland and Ireland, it was re-registered G-TRMP in June 2015. (Bill Johnston)

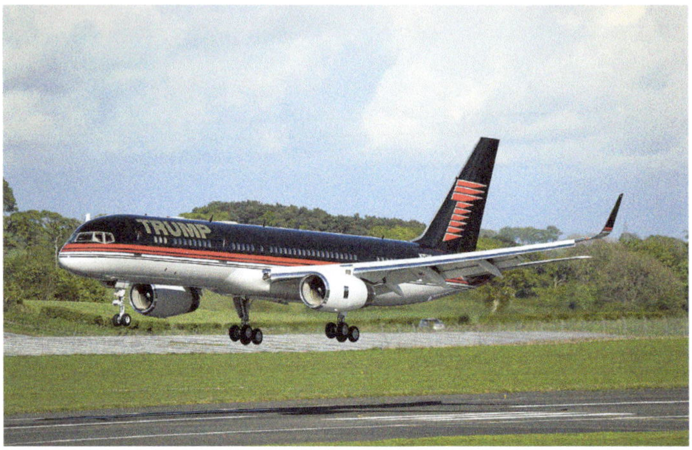

Donald Trump's Boeing 757-200 N757AF business jet about to touch down at Prestwick on 13 May 2014 on a visit to see his new acquisition, the Turnberry Golf Course Resort. (Gerry Rudman)

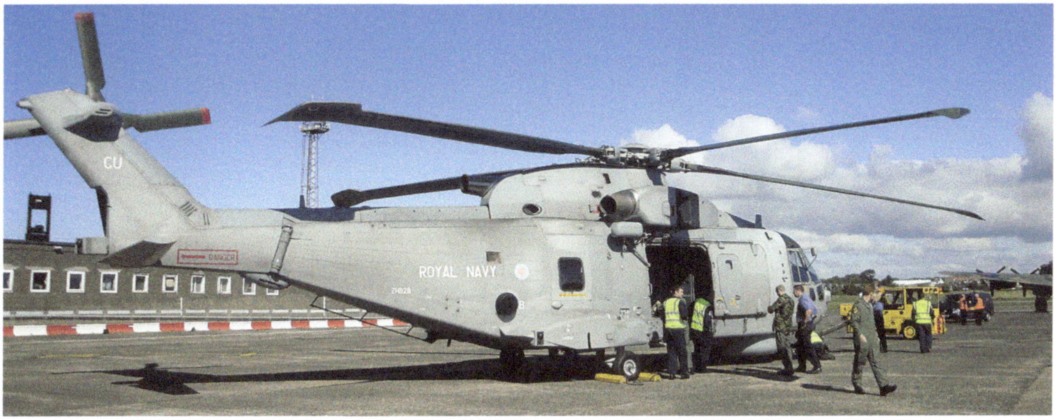

AgustaWestland EH101 Merlin HM.1 medium-lift helicopter ZH828 of the Fleet Air Arm (Royal Navy) took part in the Scottish Airshow on 7 September 2014. (Bill Johnston)

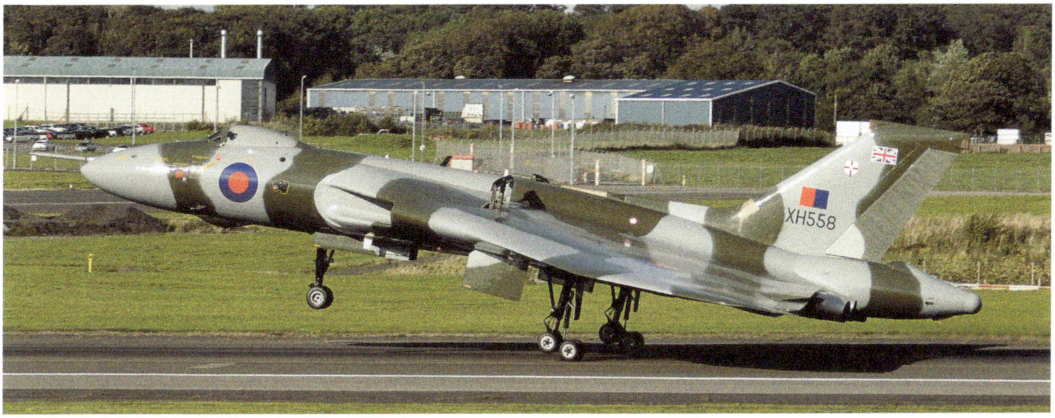

Avro Vulcan B2 XH558/G-VLCN touches down at Prestwick on 6 September 2014. Now kept in taxiiable condition, *The Spirit of Great Britain* was the last Vulcan in military service. (Robert McCulloch)

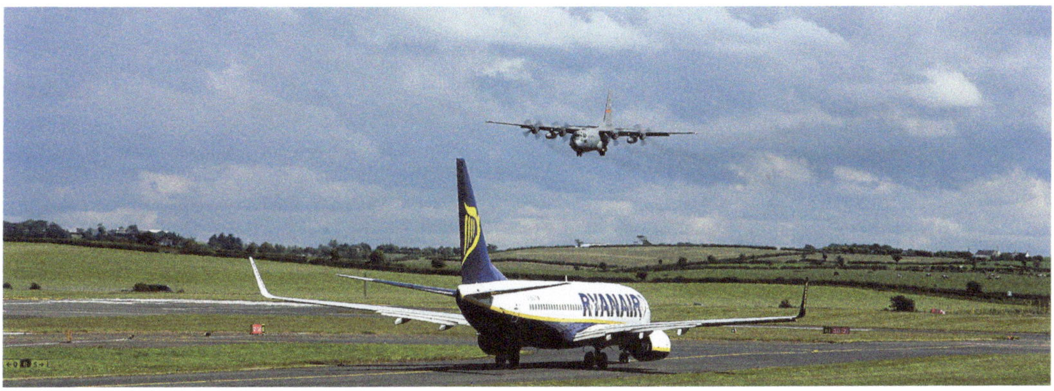

USAF Hercules C130H 92-1451 of the 182nd Airlift Wing, Illinois Air National Guard, is seen coming in to land on 6 July 2014. (Nam Seif Eddine Boukhris)

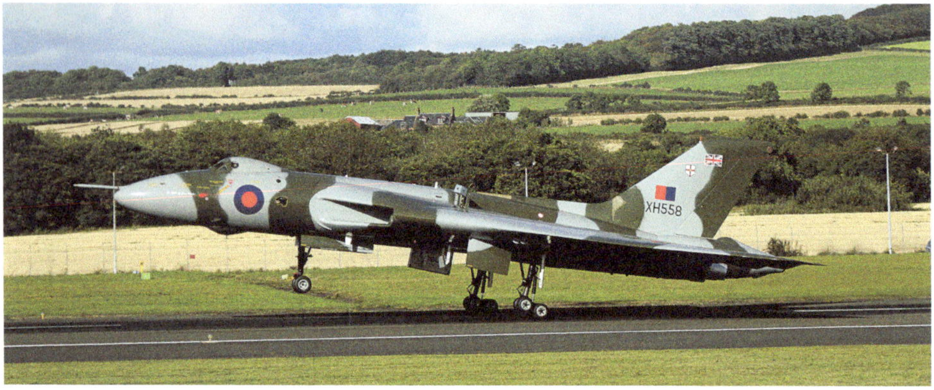

The last remaining airworthy Avro Vulcan, XH588 *The Spirit of Great Britain,* lands on runway 30 on 6 September 2014. XH558's final ever flight took place on 28 October 2015, and it is now permanently grounded at Doncaster Sheffield Airport. (Leslie A. Rodger)

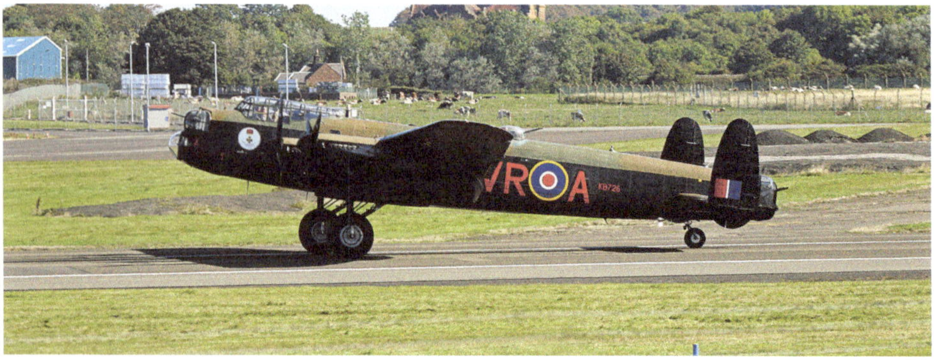

The 'Mynarski Lancaster', KB726/VR-A, landed on runway 30 in company with the Battle of Britain Memorial Flight Lancaster, PA474, on 6 September 2014. (Leslie A. Rodger)

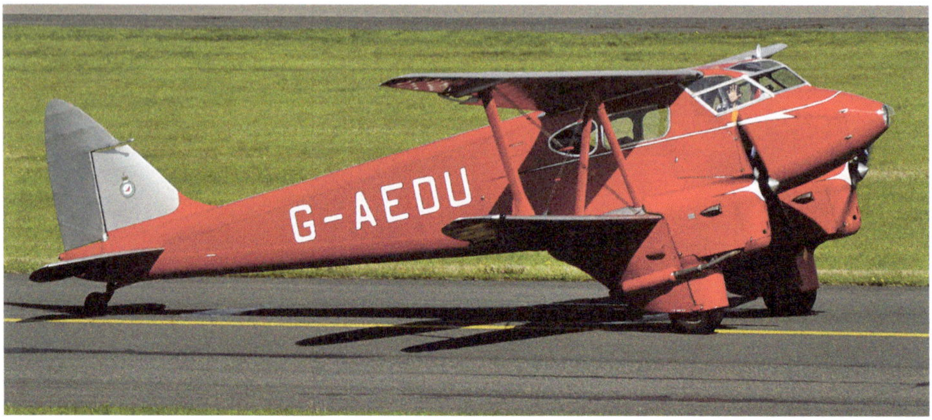

2015

De Havilland DH90A Dragonfly G-AEDU is photographed during the airshow on 5 September 2015. The 1937-built Dragonfly is owned by the Norman Aeroplane Trust and has previously been registered CR-AAB, ZS-CTR and N190DH. (Robert McCulloch)

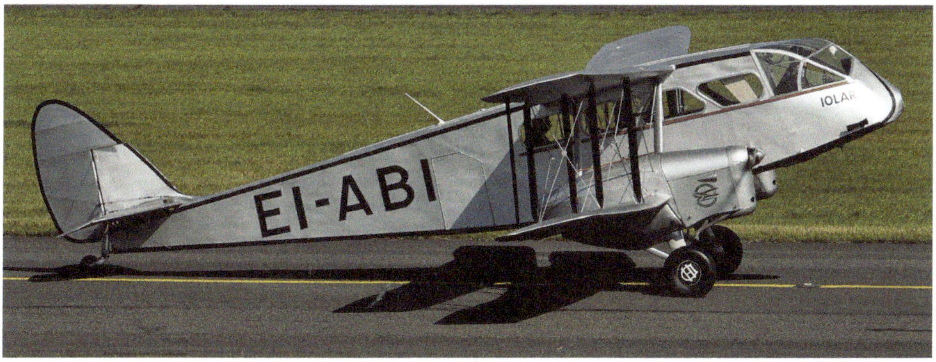

De Havilland DH.84 Dragon EI-ABI *Iolar* ('Eagle') during the airshow on 5 September 2015. The 1936-built Dragon is operated by the Irish Historic Flight and has previously been registered G-AECZ, EI-AFK and AV982. (Robert McCulloch)

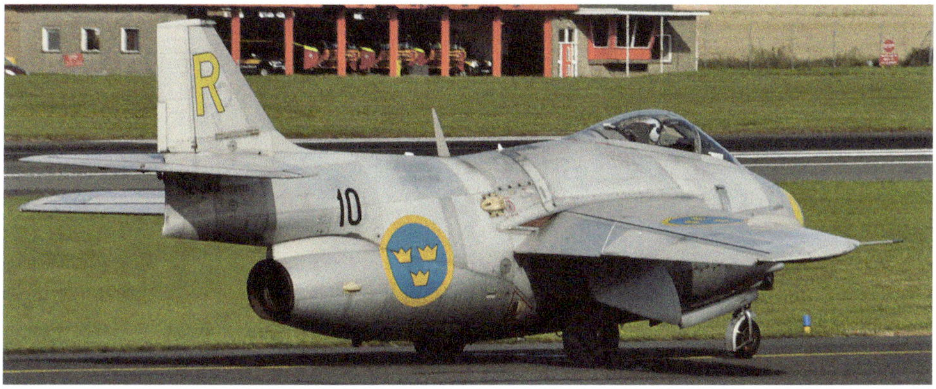

Swedish Air Force Historic Flight Saab J29 Tunnan SE-DXB *The Flying Barrel* on 5 September 2015. This was the first Western European fighter to be produced with a swept wing after the Second World War. (Robert McCulloch)

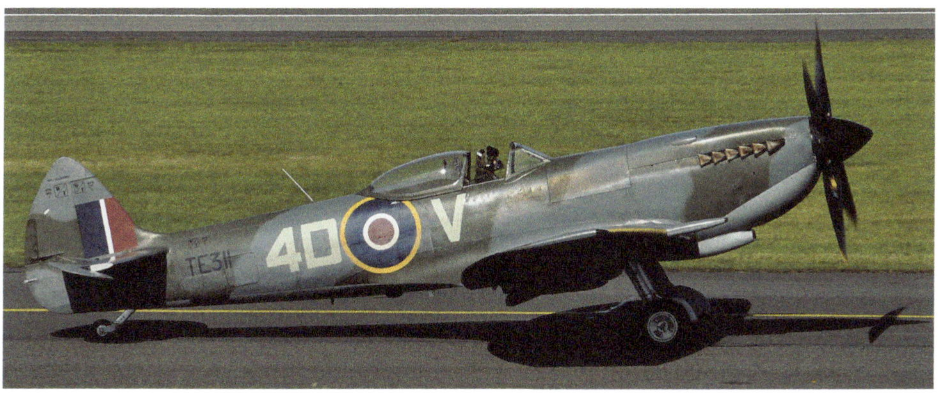

Royal Air Force Battle of Britain Memorial Flight Supermarine Spitfire Mk LF XVIE TE311 (4D-V) during the airshow on 5 September 2015. Built in June 1945 and used mainly for pilot training, it received a false rear fuselage to resemble a Mk 1 Spitfire for the filming of ground sequences for the 1968 film *The Battle of Britain*. (Robert McCulloch)

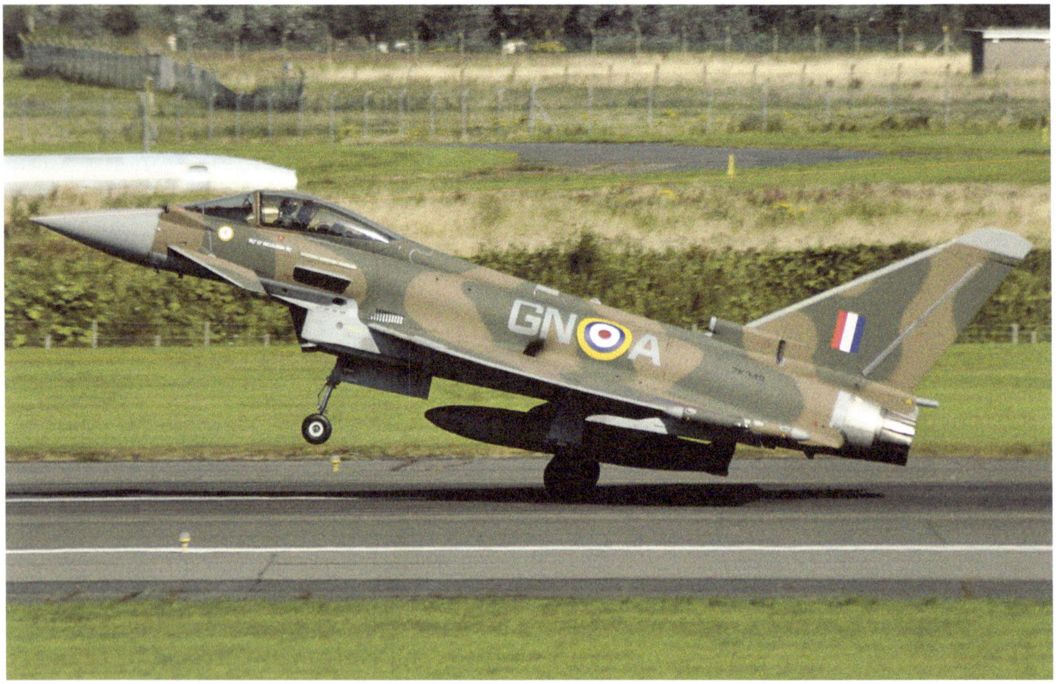

Royal Air Force Eurofighter Typhoon FGR4 ZK349 (GN-A) touches down at Prestwick having completed its display at the Scottish Airshow on 5 September 2015. (Robert McCulloch)

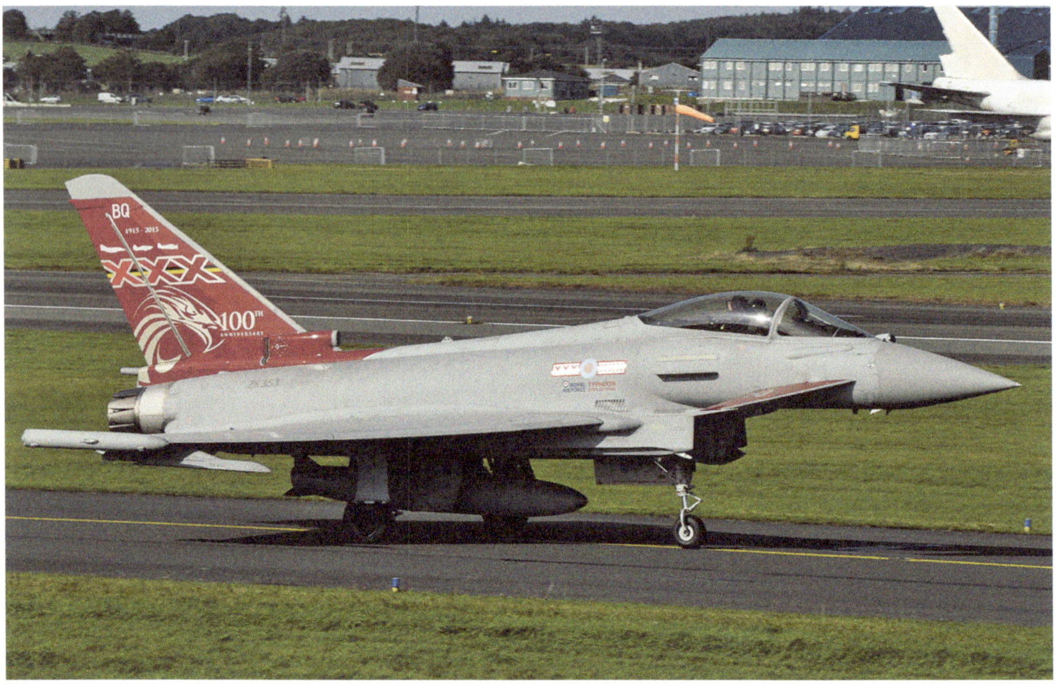

Royal Air Force Eurofighter Typhoon FGR4 ZK353-BQ is seen wearing the centenary colour scheme of No. 29 Squadron on 5 September 2015. (Robert McCulloch)

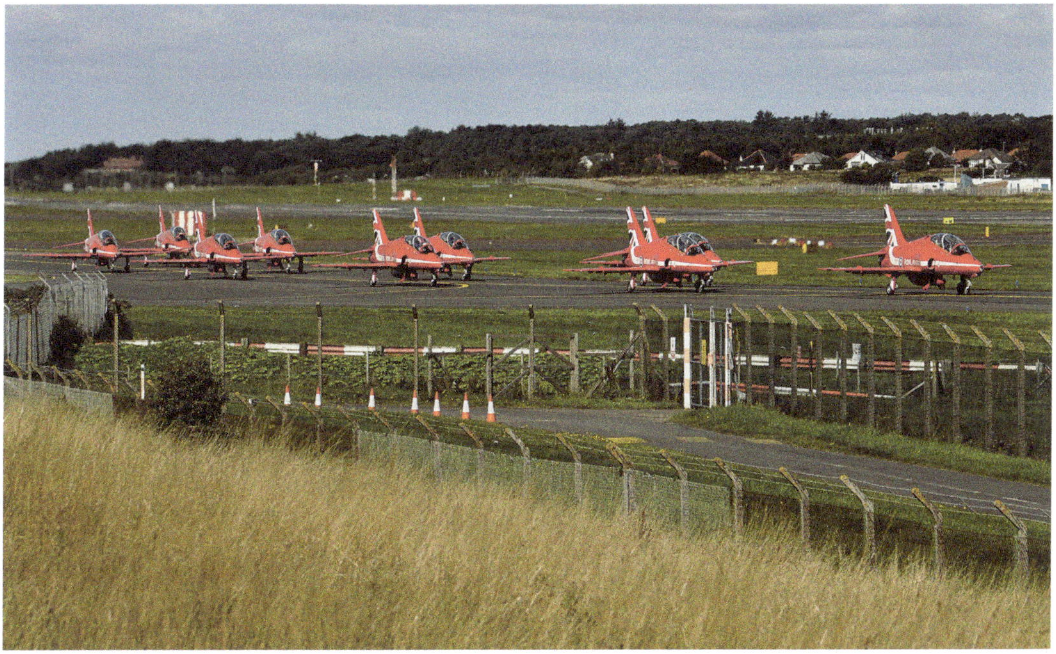

The dual-control BAE Systems Hawk T1s of the Royal Air Force Red Arrows aerobatic team taxi at Prestwick prior to departure to display at the Portrush Airshow on 5 September 2015. (Robert McCulloch)

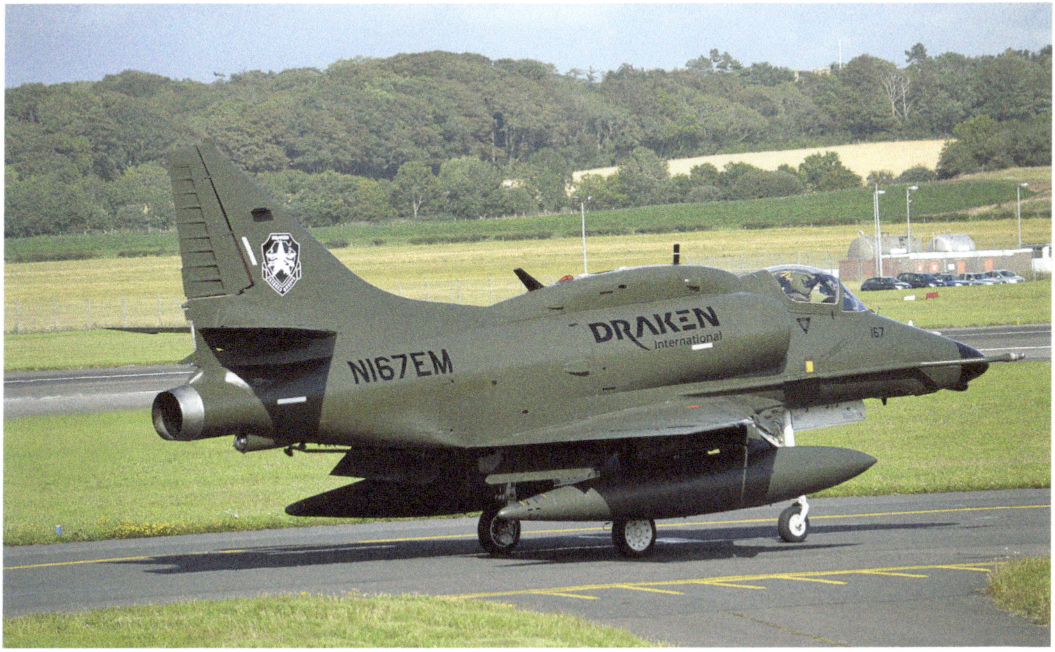

McDonnell Douglas A-4N Skyhawk N167EM of Draken Int. is seen at Prestwick departing after a refuelling stop en route from the USA to France for a contract assignment on 6 August 2015. (Gerry Rudman)

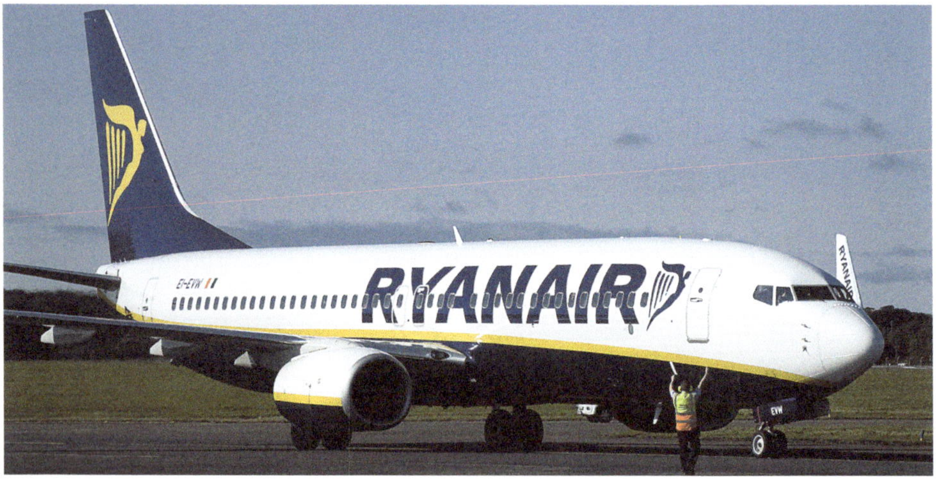

Ryanair Boeing 737-8AS EI-EVW on 6 September 2015. (Scott Wright)

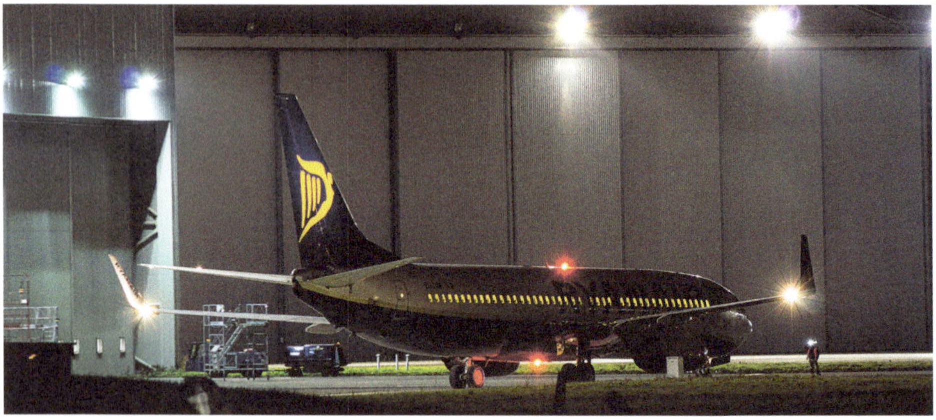

Ryanair Boeing 737-8AS EI-DAE is photographed during maintenance at Prestwick on 19 October 2015. (Barry Young)

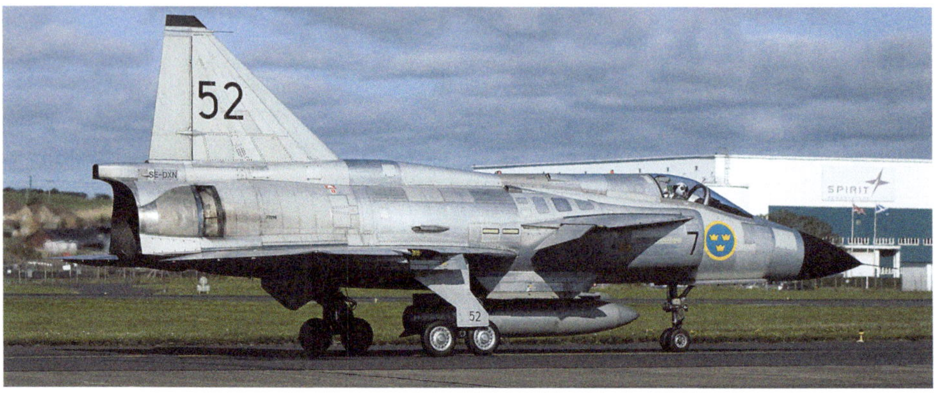

Swedish Air Force Historic Flight AJS-37 Viggen SE-DXN during the airshow on 6 September 2015. (Scott Wright)

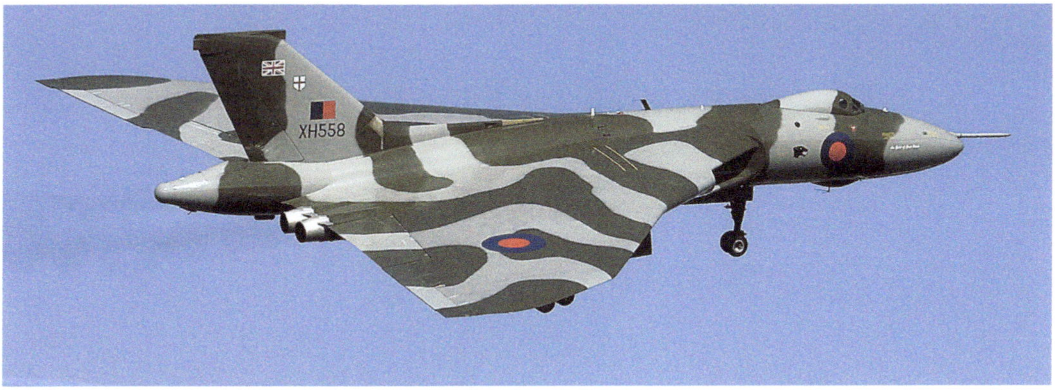

Avro Vulcan B.2 XH558 *The Spirit of Great Britain* is seen at Prestwick on 6 September 2015, during its last ever flying season. (Scott Wright)

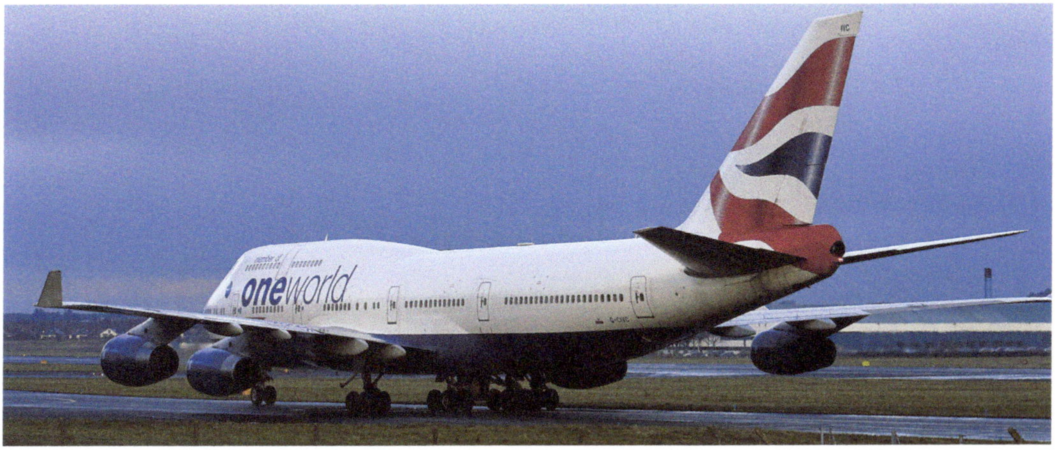

British Airways' Boeing 747-436 – the best-selling model of the Boeing 747 family of jet airliners – G-CIVC is captured in 'One World' livery on 15 December 2015. (Nam Seif Eddine Boukhris)

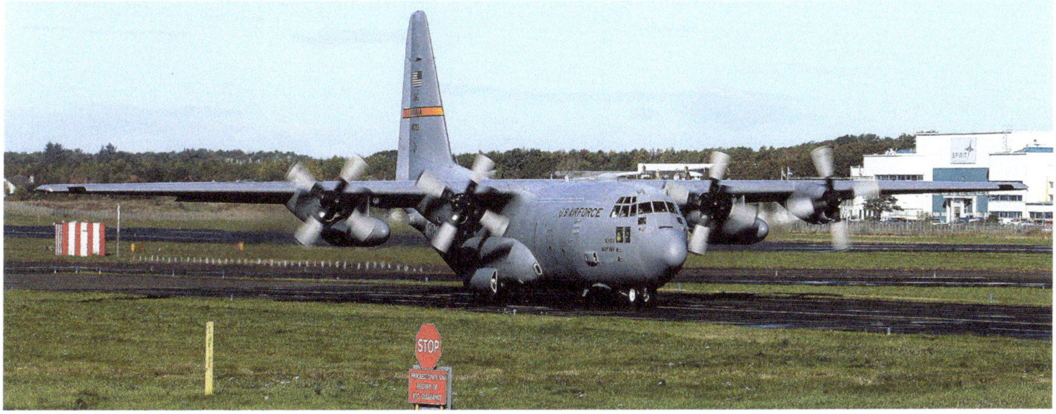

Illinois Air National Guard Lockheed Hercules C-130 H46703 of the 182nd Airlift Wing is photographed leaving apron H for runway 30 on October 2015. (Leslie A. Rodger)

NATS is a public private partnership between the Airline Group, which holds 42 per cent, NATS staff, who hold 5 per cent, UK airport operator LHR Airports Limited (which owns and runs London Heathrow, Southampton, Glasgow, and Aberdeen airports) with 4 per cent, and the UK Government, which holds 49 per cent.

The airport's two runways, designated 13/31 (9,799 feet (2,987 metres) in length and 150 feet (46 metres) in width) and 03/21 (6.525 feet (1,989 metres) long and 147 feet (45 metres) wide) are surfaced with concrete/asphalt. In November 2013 the main runway was re-designated 12/30 from 13/31 due to the drifting of the magnetic North Pole.

The world's largest airplane, the six-engined, 590-ton Ukrainian Antonov An-225 Mriya AN 225, which can transport the equivalent of ten battle tanks, landed at Glasgow Prestwick airport on Saturday 10 March 2012. Its Ukrainian operator set up a base at Stansted Airport for the giant aircraft to tour landing-capable airports as part of a drive to expand their presence to airports in the UK.

In March 2012, Infratil made the decision to sell Glasgow Prestwick Airport owing to its declining commercial and financial performance. The airport was losing £7 million a year, and although a number of potential investors showed interest in the airport, none submitted an acceptable bid. After the last potential buyer withdrew interest in September 2013, the Scottish Government bought the airport two months later (and the 'Pure Dead Brilliant' moniker was removed straight away) for the nominal price of £1 in order to protect around 1,400 jobs in an area where unemployment was above average in Scotland, and to safeguard what it considered to be a strategic infrastructure asset. Prestwick was the second UK airport to enter public ownership in 2013 after Cardiff Airport, being nationalised by the Welsh Assembly.

Donald J. Trump arrived in his signature Boeing 757 at Prestwick on 14 November 2014 to announce the Trump Organisation's official partnership with the Scottish-based aviation group. Earlier this year, Trump finalised his purchase of the legendary Turnberry golf resort, now known as Trump Turnberry, and Prestwick Airport had been selected as the Scottish base for all Trump aviation operations.

In 2015, Ryanair was the only passenger carrier connecting Prestwick to holiday resorts in Spain, Greece, Portugal and Malta, despite operating a reduced number of destinations from the previous year. Passenger flights (including some charter flights) account for only around half of the airport's revenue, with freight and retail accounting for the rest.

The Royal Navy Search and Rescue Flight at HMS *Gannet* finished its operations from Prestwick Airport on 1 January 2016 after forty years of lifesaving missions. Its Westland HAS5 ASW Sea King helicopters made a final farewell fly past of Scotland on 14 January 2016, having been involved in thousands of rescues since the first unit was established. Civilian-operated Bristow Helicopters took over the responsibility for delivering search and rescue coverage across Scotland, northern England and Northern Ireland, with two Sikorsky S-92 helicopters (the most advanced aircraft in Sikorsky's civil product line). Leonardo introduced two new AgustaWestland Search and Rescue AW189 helicopters to operate from the Coastguard base at Prestwick Airport, and spent the three months flying in the area on crew transition missions before it began operational duties from July 2017.

Glasgow Prestwick Airport manages air traffic services for all airspace up to 6,000 feet and 42 nautical miles of the airport – handling 22,924 flights each year with 24-hour approach radar service with secondary surveillance radar – and in July 2016 its new state-of-the-art air traffic control system entered full operational service. Following hundreds of hours of testing and fine tuning, and ten months of training for the full complement of air traffic controllers, the new Interoperability Through European Collaboration (iTEC) system, went live for limited operational service at busy times prior to the full switch-over.

The iTEC system was developed by Indra Sistemas (a Spanish information technology and defence systems company) and was designed to increase airspace capacity and improve safety by automatically detecting potential aircraft conflicts ahead of time from its huge database of trajectories combined with meteorological and other data to support human decision making. It also helps reduce aircraft fuel burn and emissions by giving pilots greater flexibility to fly the best and most direct routes above 28,000 feet instead of following the existing network of rigid waypoints and airways. While the system was used initially to only control aircraft at high altitude over Scotland, northern England and Northern Ireland, it is expected to be employed (through NATS investing £600 million in the new technology) across the entire UK operation at NATS' Prestwick and Swanwick centres over the next five years. Exploring integration with compatible systems on the continent to create a single European sky is also intended.

A strategic plan produced by the airport's executive team for the loss-making Ayrshire airport was unveiled at the end of June 2017 to return the airport into private hands within five years. Loans to the value of £39.2 million in support and upgrades will be repayable once the airport becomes profit-making again, and despite a contract with the US Defence Logistics Agency creating an increase in income of 37 per cent from military flights (according to last year's Audit Scotland report), it seems likely that it may take until 2023 to repay the loans. The key points highlighted to attract investors include having Scotland's longest commercial runway and parallel taxiway, and that it is the only airport in Scotland with a railway station on the site.

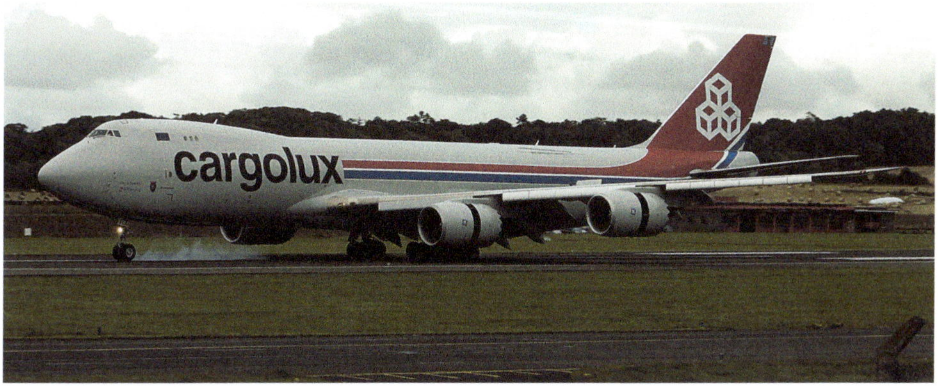

2016

Cargolux Airlines International Boeing 747-8R7(F) LX-VCG on 2 September 2016. Cargolux is Europe's biggest all-cargo airline, with a fleet of modern Boeing 747-8 and 747-400 freighters. (Scott Wright)

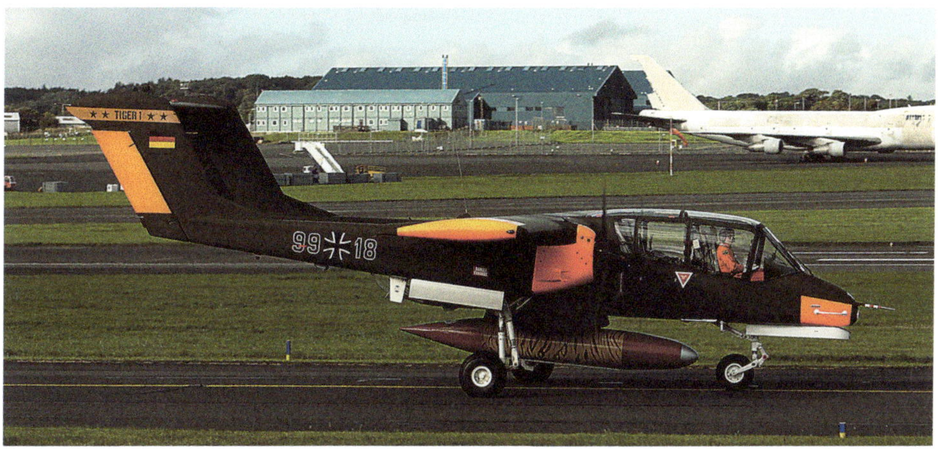

The North American Rockwell OV-10 Bronco G-ONAA turboprop light attack and observation aircraft was specifically designed for the Vietnam War. It has been on static display at the International Aviation Museum (Manfred Pflumm) since 1991. It is pictured here on 2 September 2016. (Scott Wright)

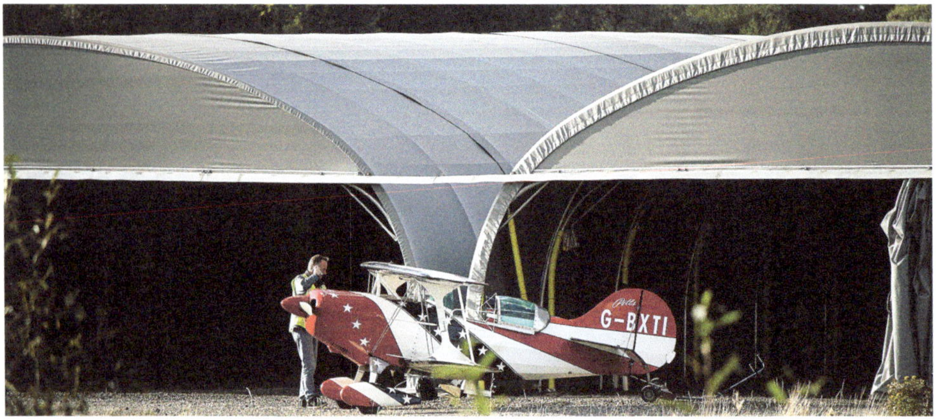

Pitts S1 Special G-BXTI outside Prestwick Flying Club's poly tunnels on 9 October 2016. (Craig Durwood)

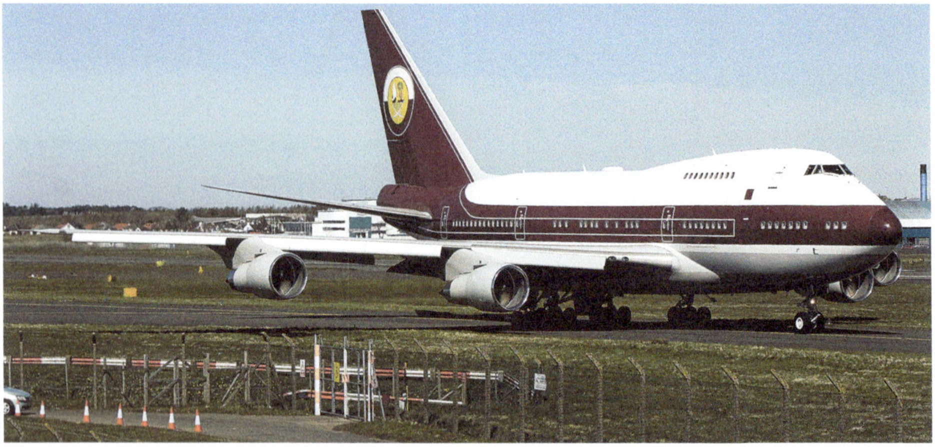

Boeing 747SP-21 VP-BAT in the livery of the Qatar Amiri Fleet on 20 April 2016. (Scott Wright)

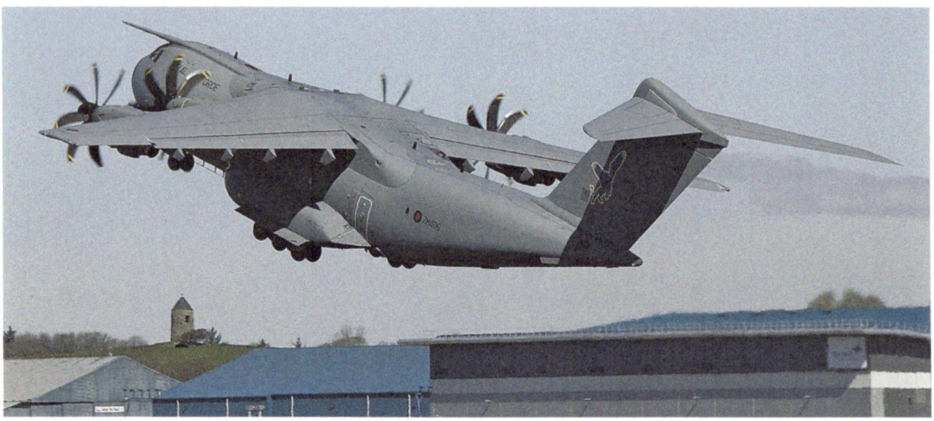

Royal Air Force Airbus A400M-180 Atlas four-engine turboprop military transport ZM406 is seen on 20 April 2016. (Scott Wright)

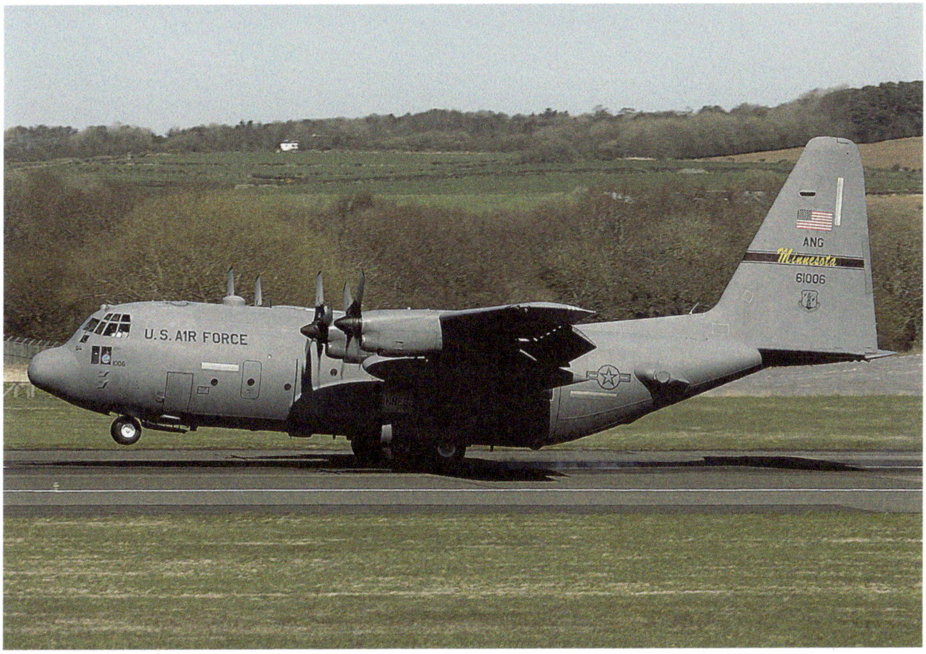

USAF Lockheed Martin Hercules C-130H 96-1006 is photographed on 20 April 2016. The medium-size transport aircraft has assumed a wide range of military tasks such as airlift, airdrop, reconnaissance, special operations and close air support since first becoming operational in December 1956. (Scott Wright)

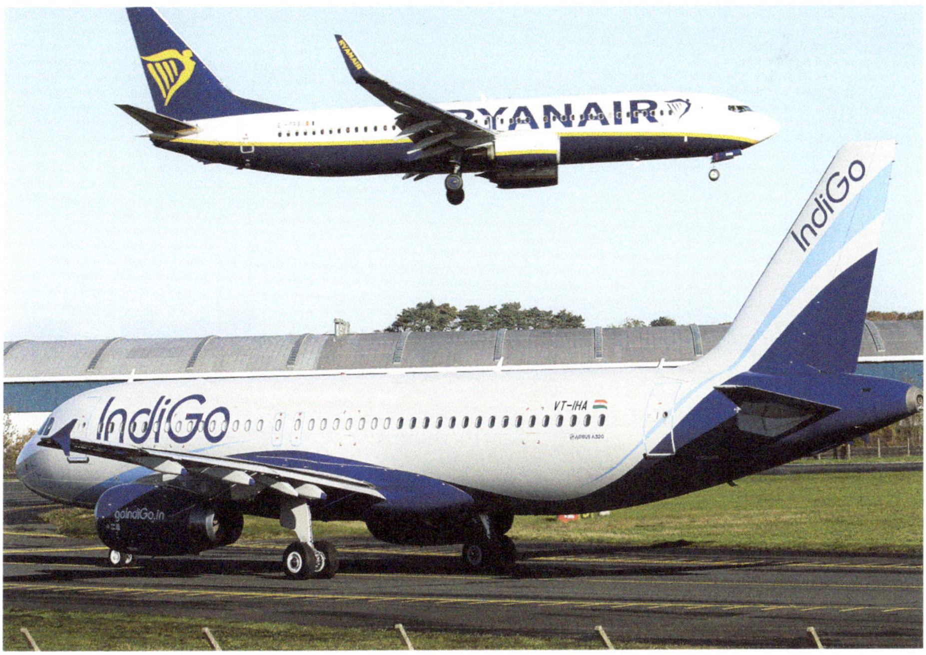

IndiGo Airbus A320 VT-IHA and Ryanair Boeing 737-8AS (WL) EI-FRB on 1 November 2016. (Dougie Edmond)

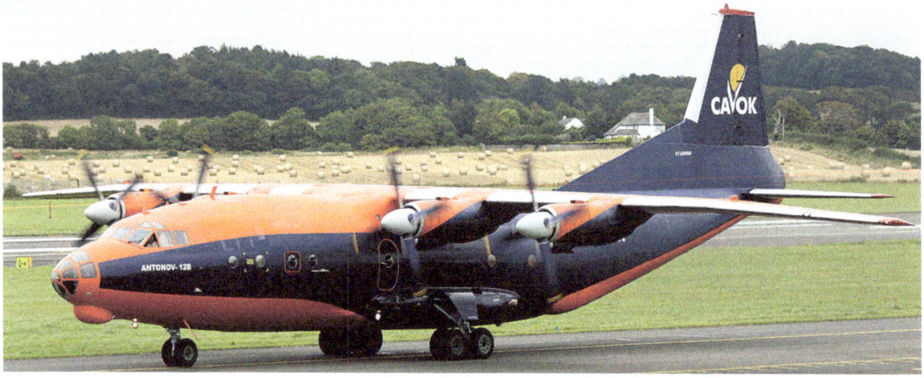

Cavok Air Antonov An-12B on 6 September 2016. The Ukraine-based Cavok Air operates cargo charters. (Dougie Edmond)

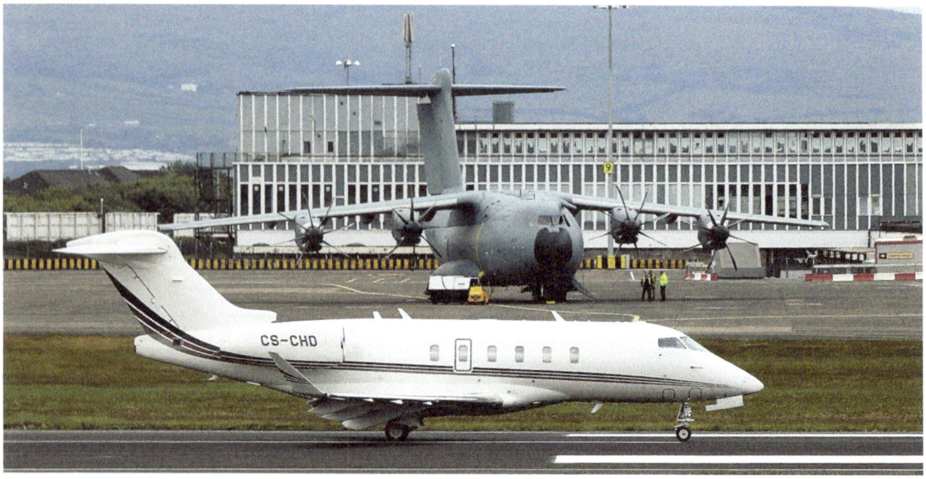

Netjets Transportes Aereos Bombardier BD-100-1A10 Challenger 350 CS-CHD on 30 June 2016. Founded in 1964 as Executive Jet Aviation, the company sells part ownership or shares of private business jets. (Dougie Edmond)

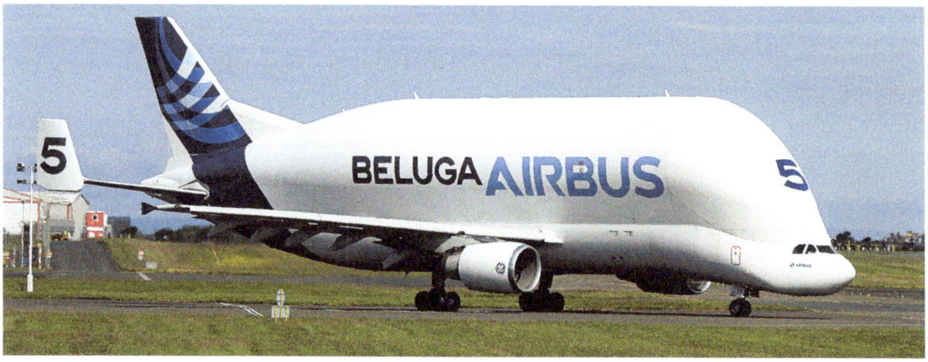

An Airbus A300-600ST (Super Transporter) Beluga leaving apron H for runway 30 on 17 June 2016. (Leslie A. Rodger)

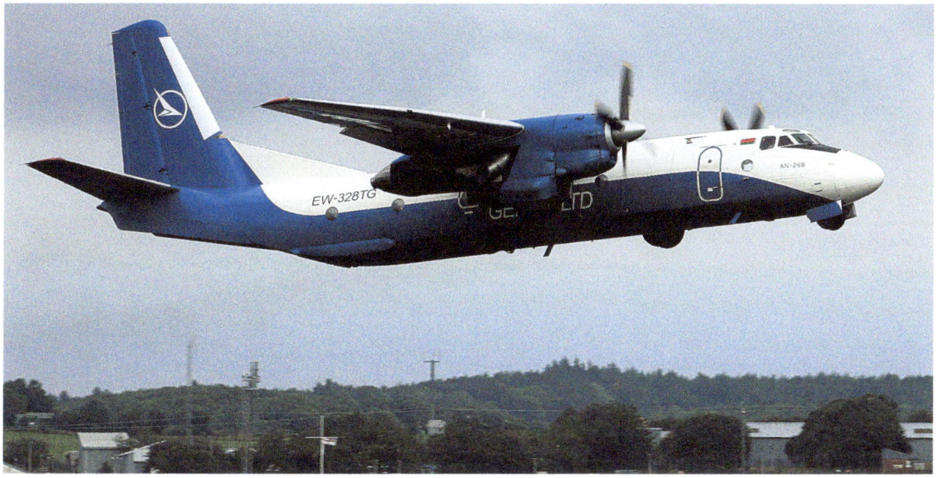

Genex Ltd Antonov An-26B EW-382TG on 19 August 2016. The civil cargo version of the An-26, the prototype AN-26B was retrofitted as a mobile civilian emergency hospital. (Dougie Edmond)

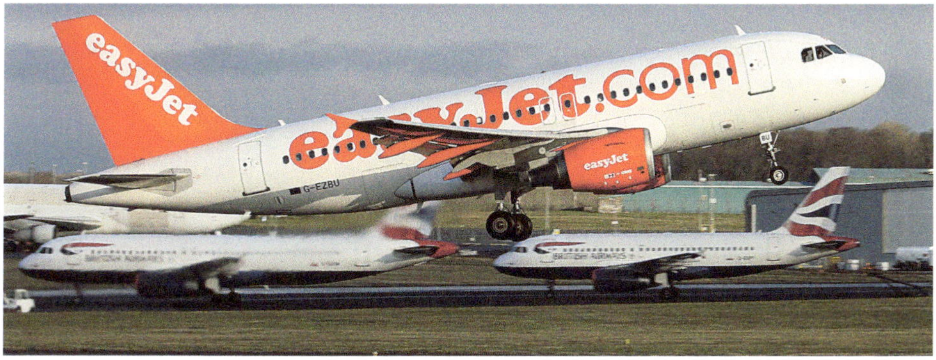

Easyjet Airbus A319-111 G-EZBU on 6 January 2016. Formerly D-AVWW (test registration), the aircraft was new to Easyjet in 2007. (Dougie Edmond)

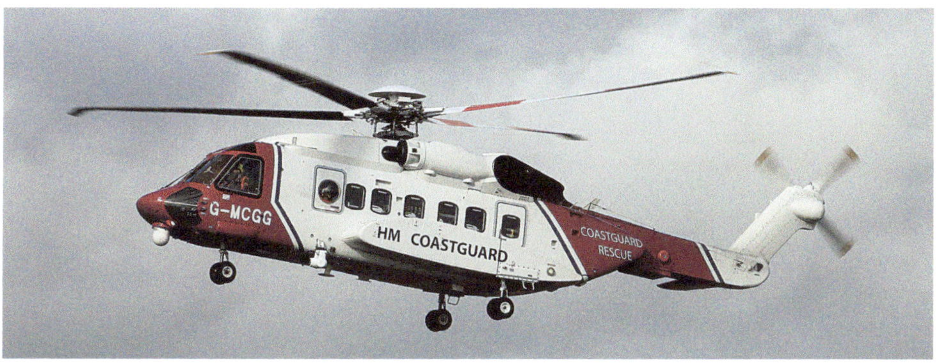

Coastguard Rescue Sikorsky S-92 Helibus G-MCGG on 13 August 2016. It was one of two S-92s operated by Bristow Helicopters while the new Leonardo AW189s were being put through their trials. (Dougie Edmond)

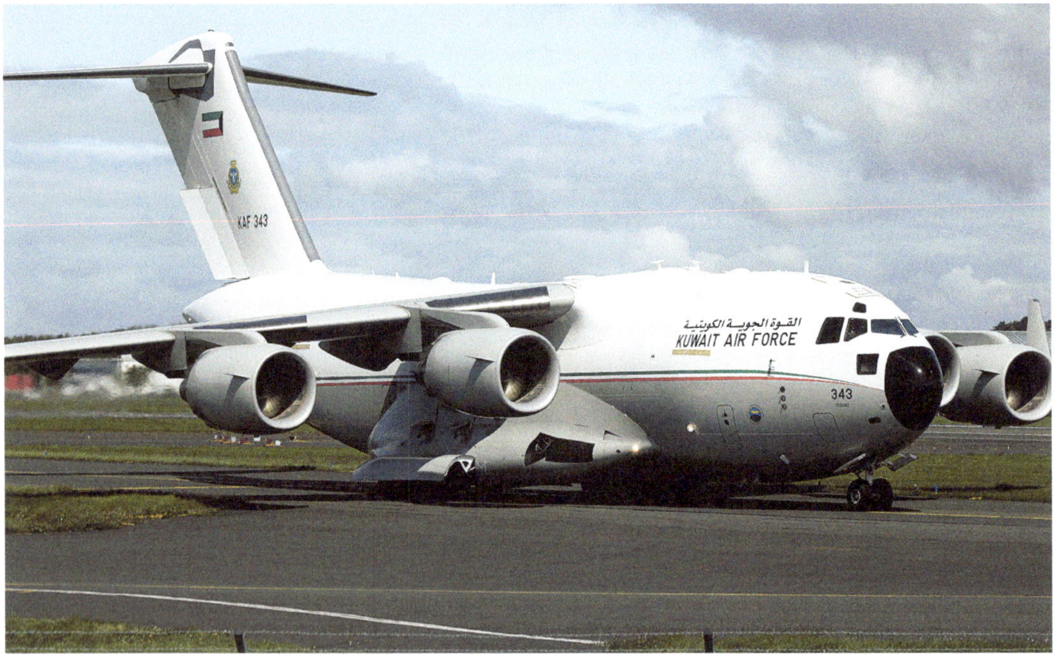

KAF 343, a Kuwait Air Force Boeing C-17A Globemaster III long-range strategic heavy-lift transport aircraft, on 23 May 2016. Used for combat, peacekeeping or humanitarian mission operations, it is declared part of the Joint Rapid Reaction Force. (Dougie Edmond)

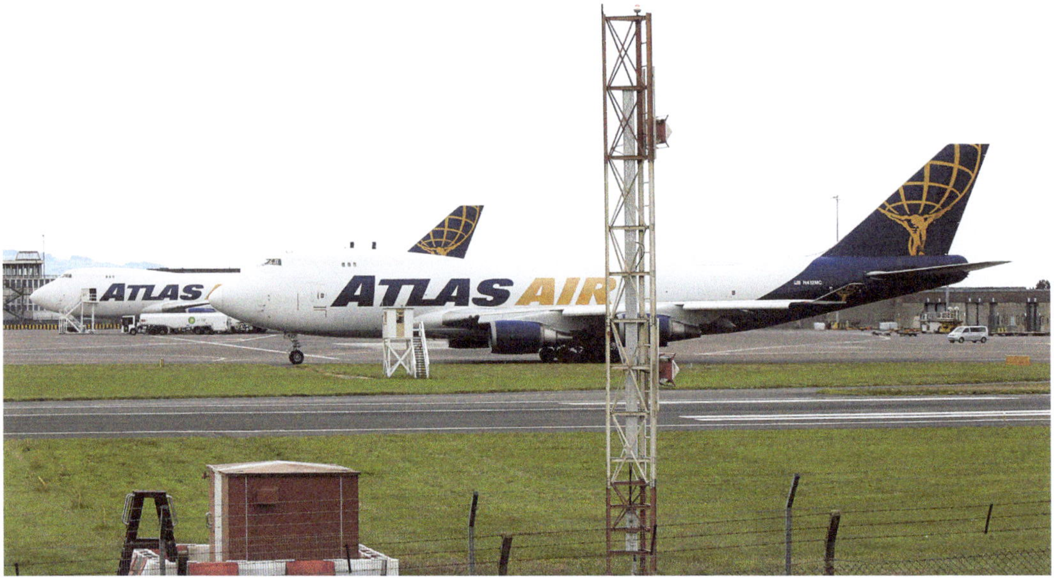

Atlas Air Boeing 747-47UF (SCD) N412MC on 17 June 2016. The 'SCD' designates Side Cargo Door. (Dougie Edmond)

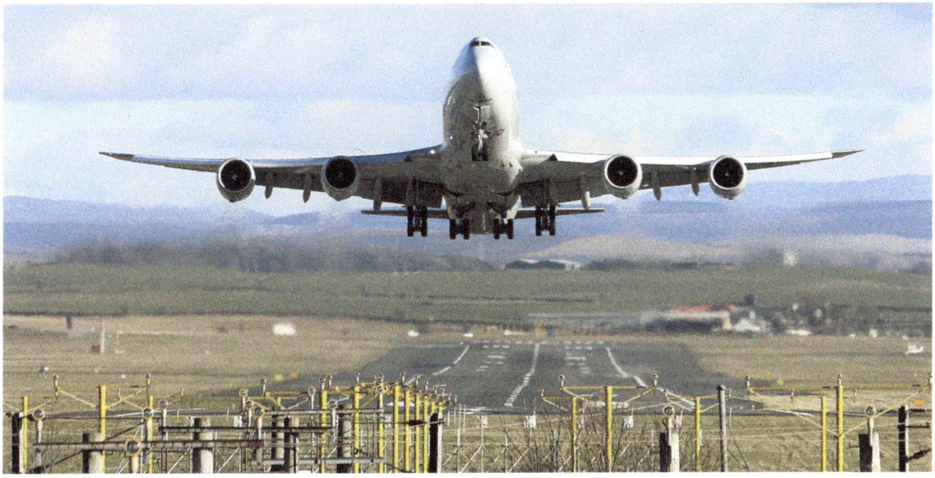

From Europe's biggest all-cargo airline, this is Cargolux B747-8R7F LX-VCD on 9 March 2016. (Dougie Edmond)

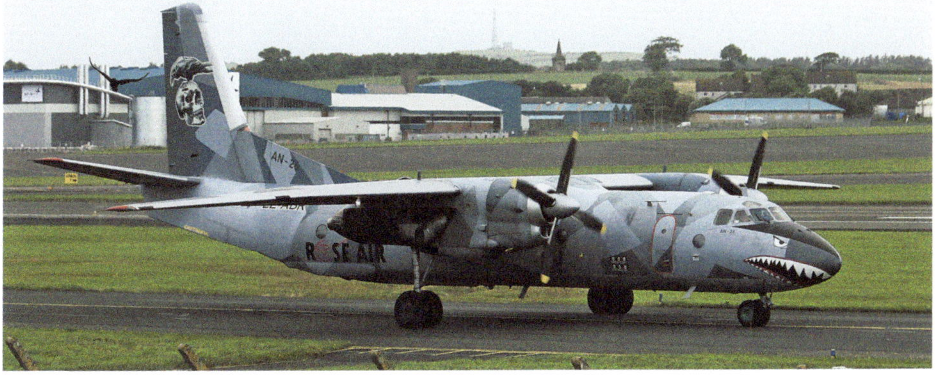

Rose Air Ltd Antonov An-26 LZ-ABR/ABJ on 7 August 2016. The aircraft became pretty well known after being involved in the filming of the action movie *The Expendables 3* during 2013. (Dougie Edmond)

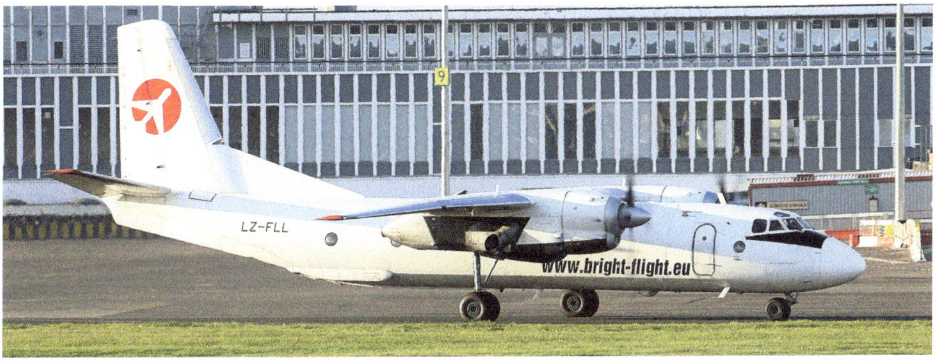

Bright Flight Antonov An-26B LZ-FLL on 24 October 2016. It was originally registered with Aeroflot as CCCP-26114 in 1982. (Dougie Edmond)

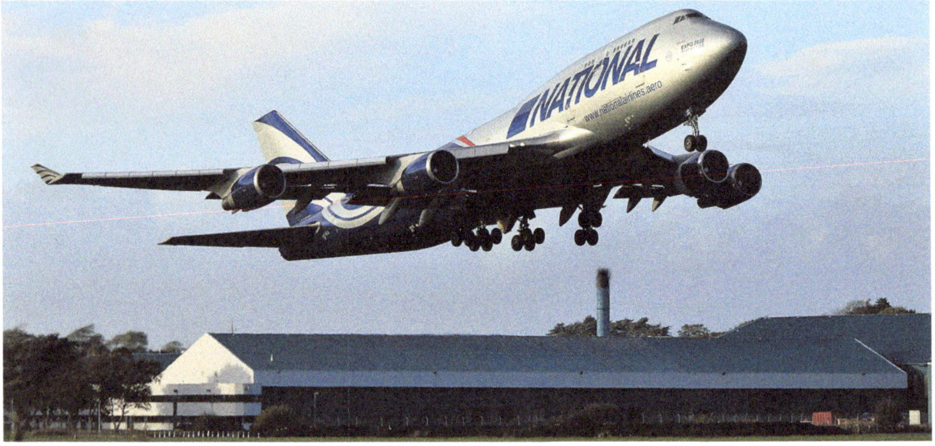

National Air Cargo Boeing 747-428 (BCF) N919CA on 16 October 2016. (Dougie Edmond)

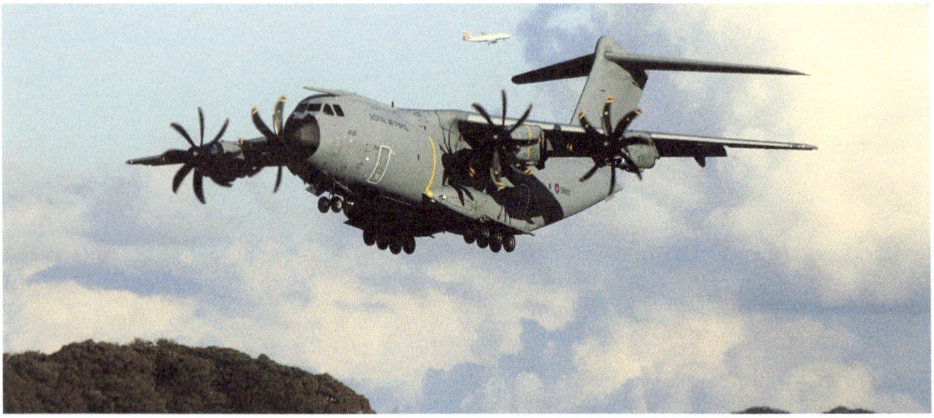

RAF Airbus A400M-180 Atlas tactical airlifter ZM400 *City of Bristol* on 1 October 2016. (Dougie Edmond)

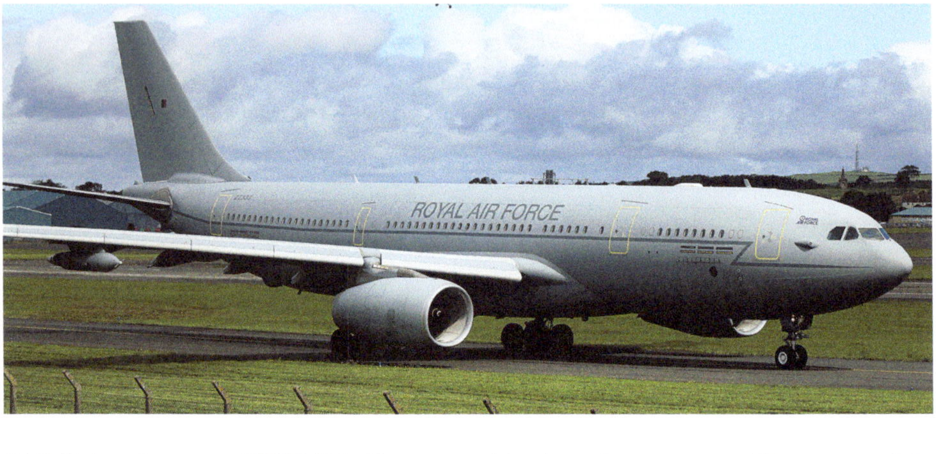

RAF Airbus A330-243 MRTT KC2 Voyager multi-role tanker transport ZZ333 on 27 July 2016. (Dougie Edmond)

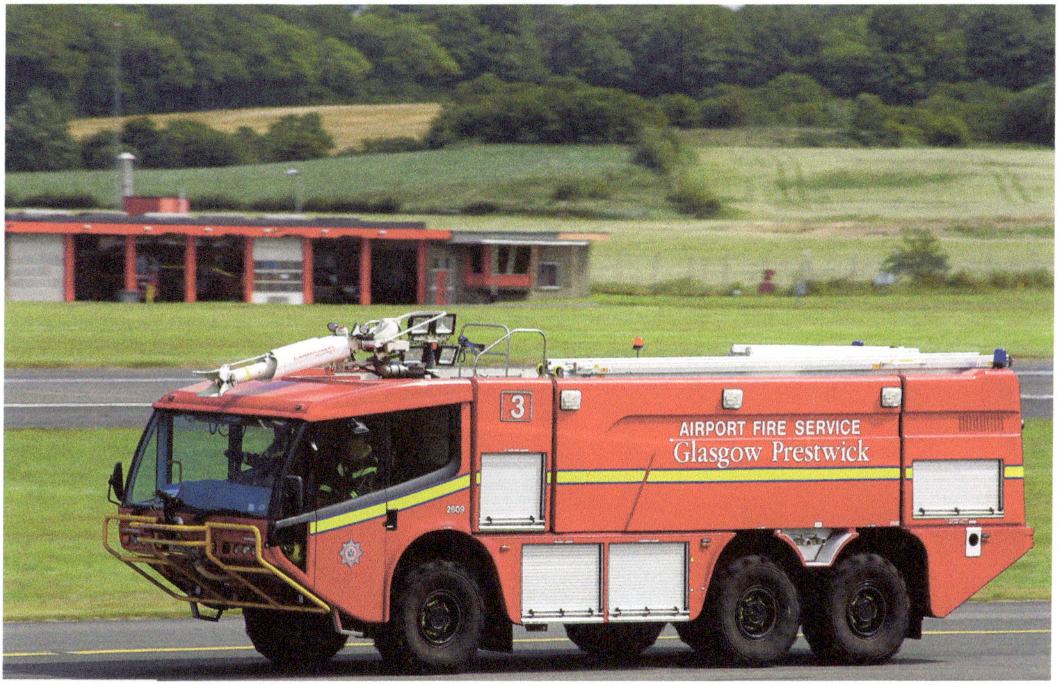

Carmichael Cobra 2 6×6 foam tender SG52 XLK at Prestwick Airport in 2014. (Nam Seif Eddine Boukhris)

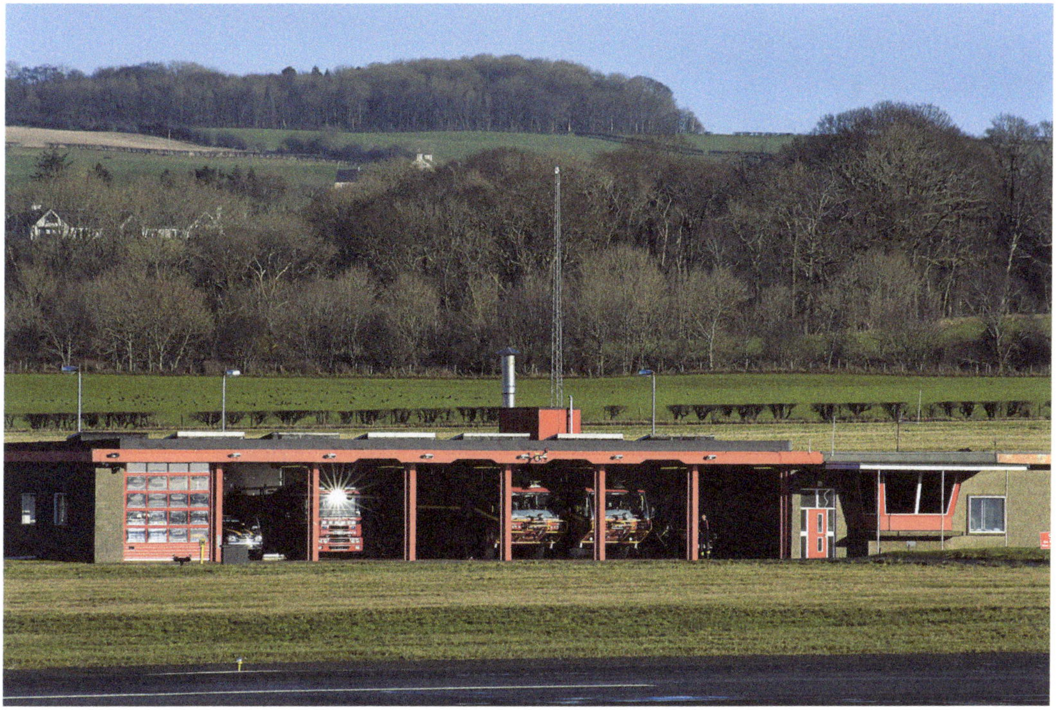

Glasgow Prestwick Airport's fire service station on 14 January 2016. (Nam Seif Eddine Boukhris)

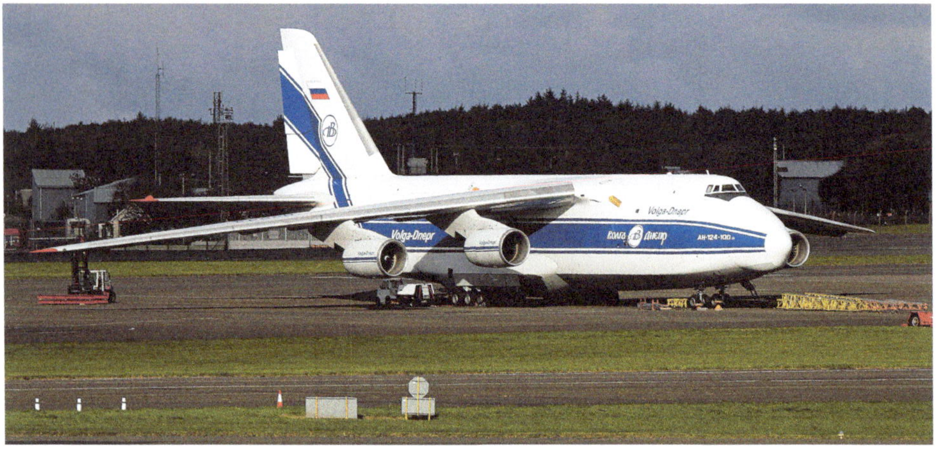

Volga-Dnepr Airlines' Antonov An-124-100 Ruslan strategic airlift jet is the world's largest civil cargo aircraft. It is seen here on apron Charlie on the north side of the airport on 24 October 2016. (Leslie A. Rodger)

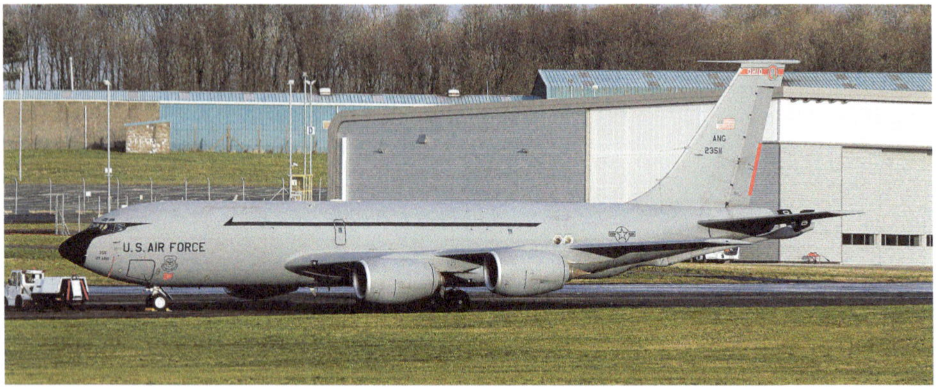

US Air Force Boeing KC-135 Stratotanker 23511 on apron Foxtrot (Northside) following a fog diversion into Prestwick in December 2016. (Leslie A. Rodger)

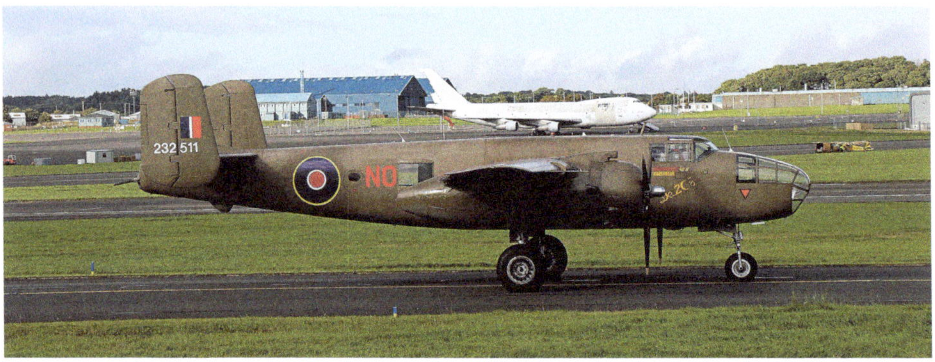

North American Aviation B25 Mitchell PH-XXV/232511/N5-149 *Sarinah* of the Royal Netherlands Air Force Historical Flight Foundation is captured taxiing in September 2016 from apron H for runway 30. (Leslie A. Rodger)

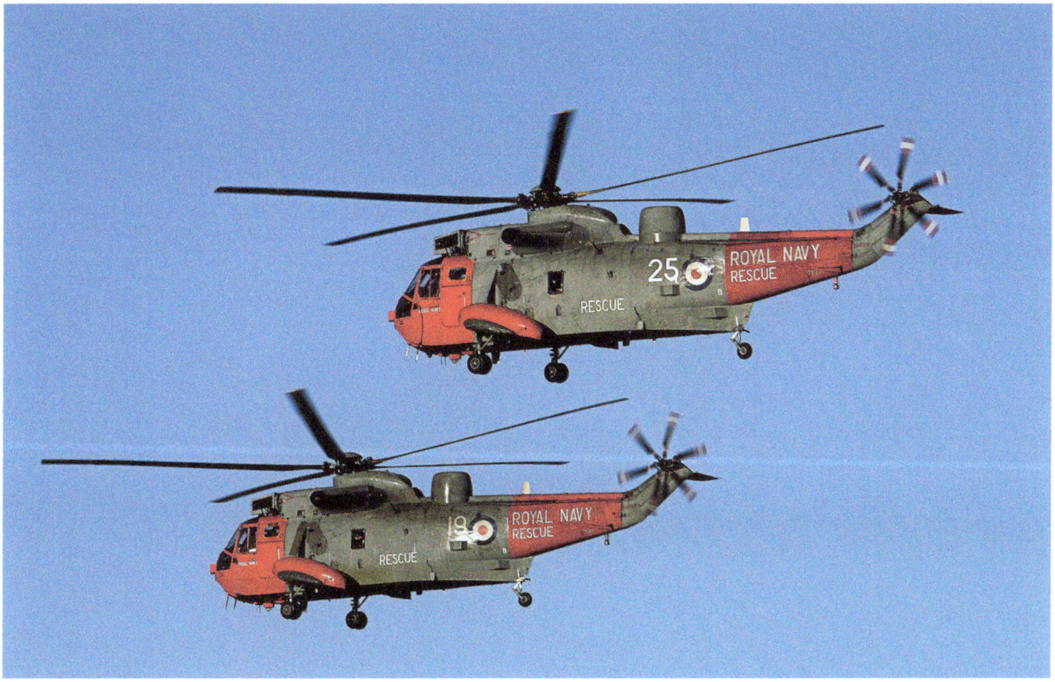

HMS *Gannet*'s Royal Navy Westland HAS5 ASW Sea King helicopters were replaced by a civilian team at Prestwick Airport on 1 January 2016. (Leslie A. Rodger)

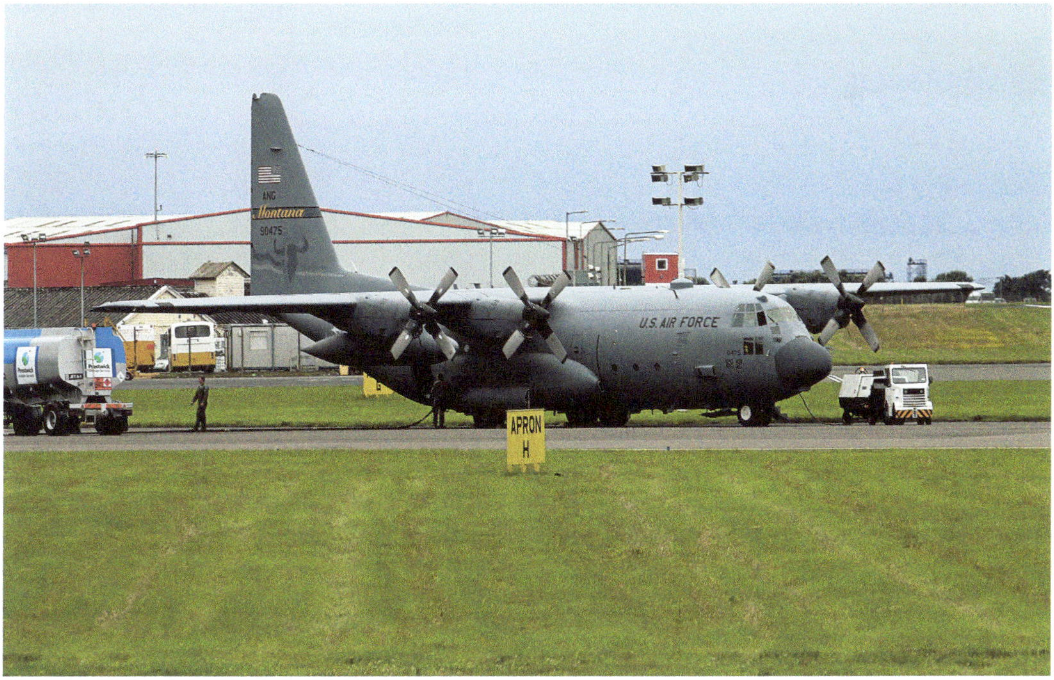

Montana Air National Guard Lockheed Hercules C-130H 79-0475 of the 120th Airlift Wing being refuelled on apron H on 15 July 2016. (Leslie A. Rodger)

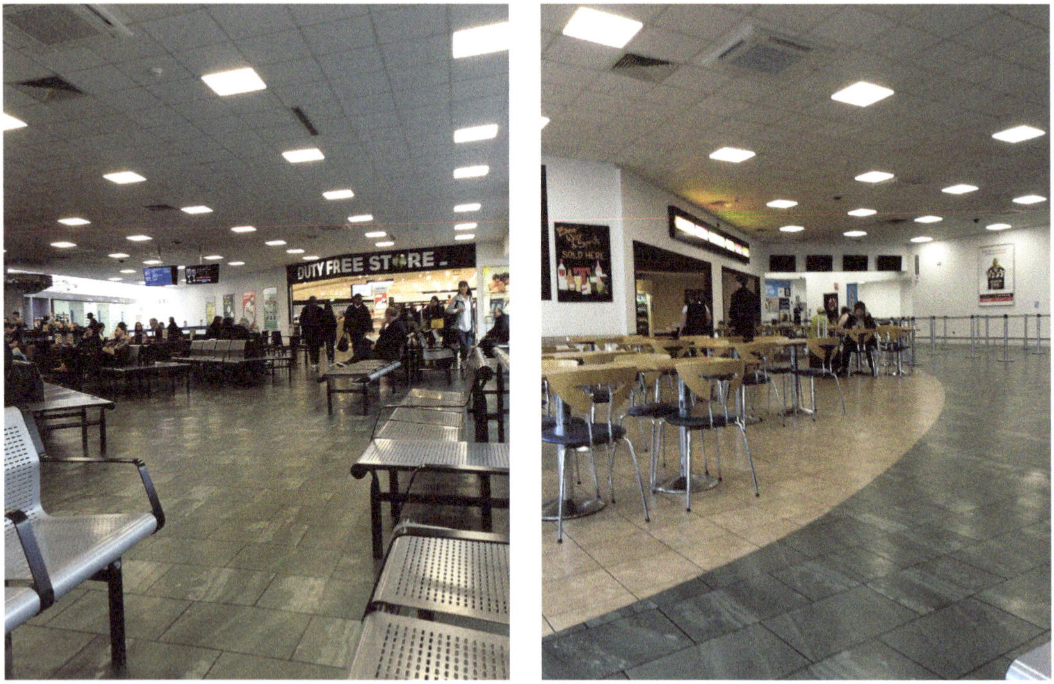

2017
The departure lounge on 19 April 2017. (Bill Johnston)

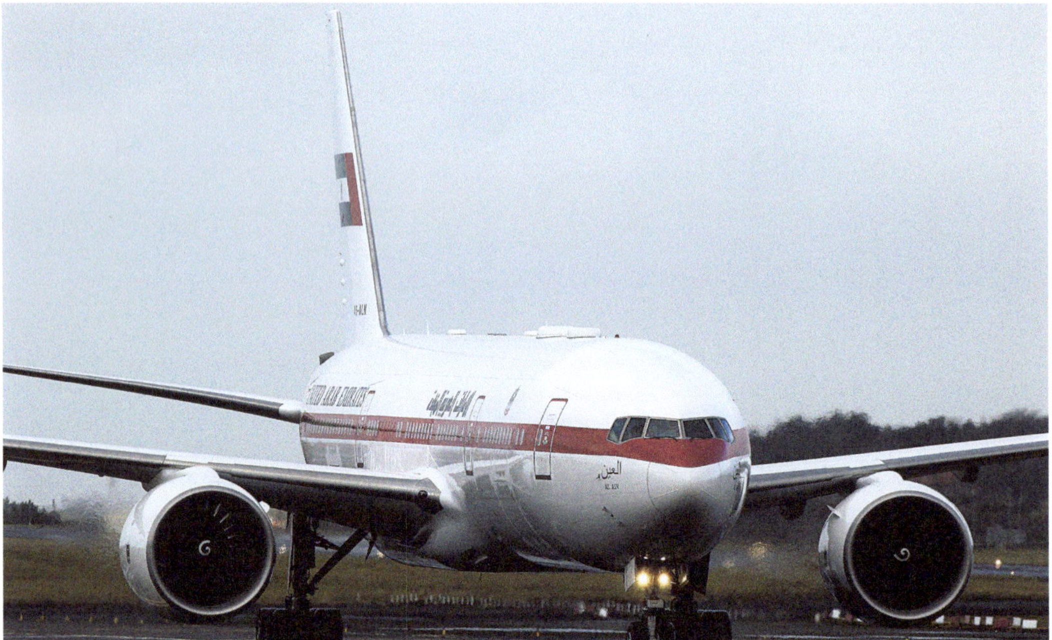

Abu Dhabi Amiri Flight Boeing 777-2AN(ER) A6-ALN *Sultan 04* arriving for a night stopover on 9 January 2017. (Dougie Edmond)

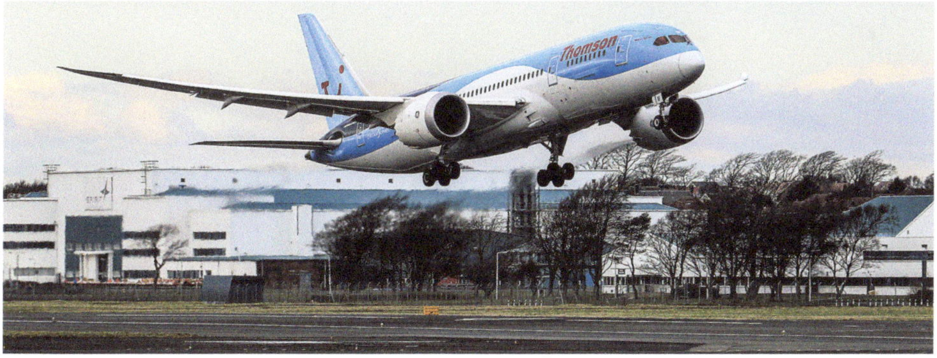

Thomson Airways was the UK launch customer for the Boeing 787-8 Dreamliner, with crew training flights being carried out at Prestwick from 20 June 2013. (Dougie Edmond)

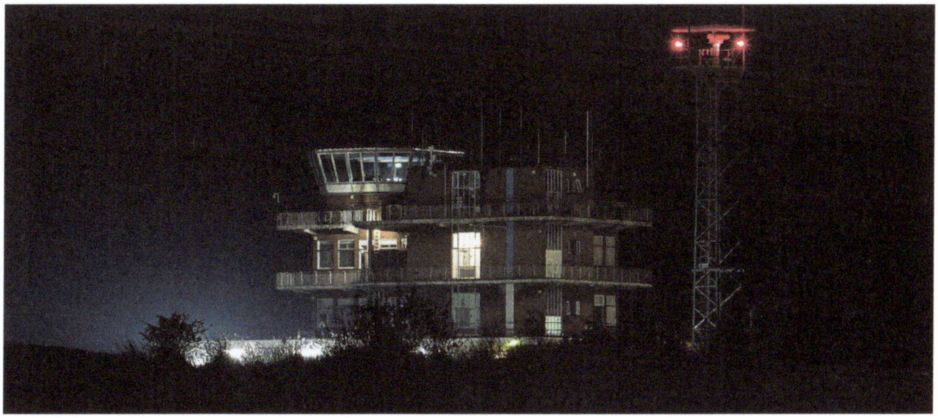

Above and below: Prestwick Airport's control centre on 16 September 2017, where the new iTEC system first went live for limited operational service on 28 July 2016. (Dougie Edmond)

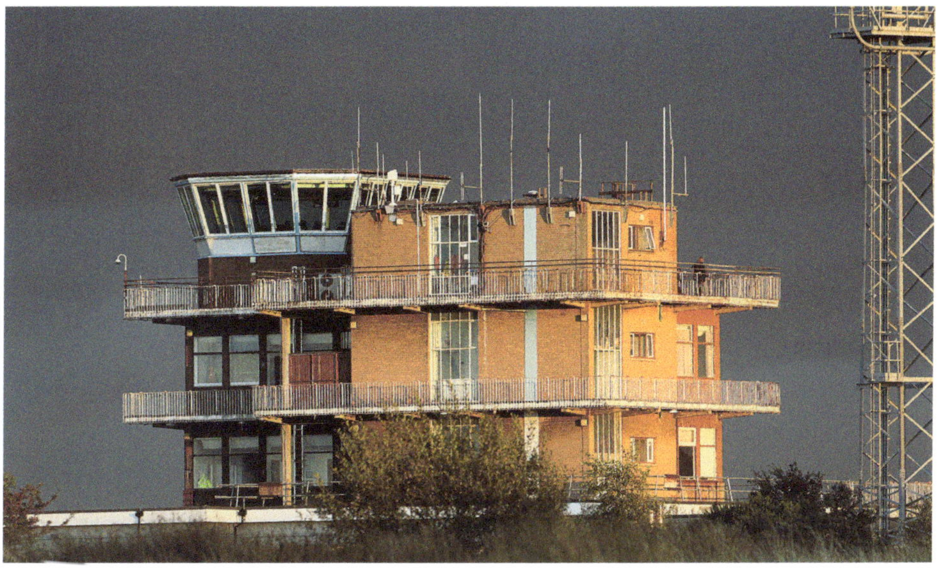

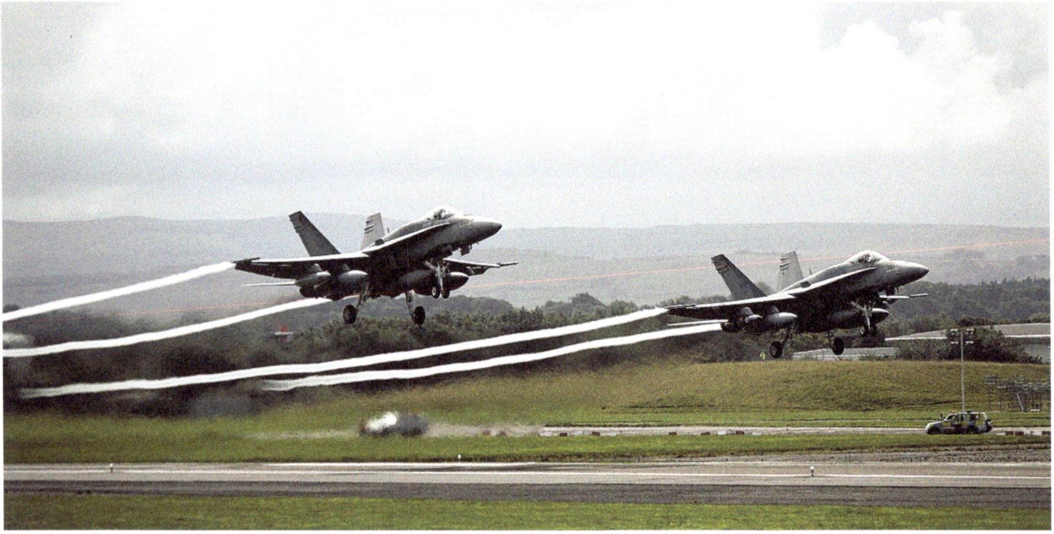

A pair of CF188A Hornets of No. 409 Tactical Fighter Squadron, RCAF, get airborne from runway 30 on 20 August 2017. They would shortly be formatting with their CC150 Polaris tanker and would head to Romania for a NATO air policing mission. (Craig Durwood)

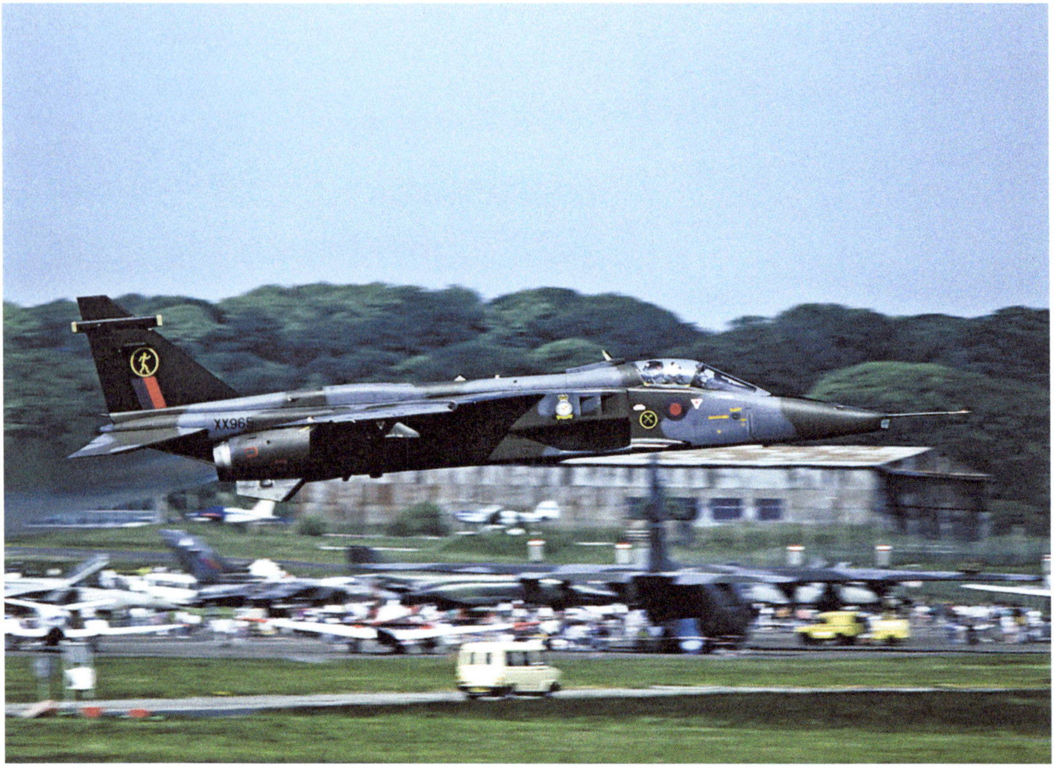

No. 16 Squadron Sepecat Jaguar GR-1 XX965 performing at the Prestwick airshow. One of twenty-three Jaguar variants, the Sepecat ground attack fighter aircraft has been in service with the Royal Air Force and the Armée de l'Air since 1973. (Leslie A. Rodger)

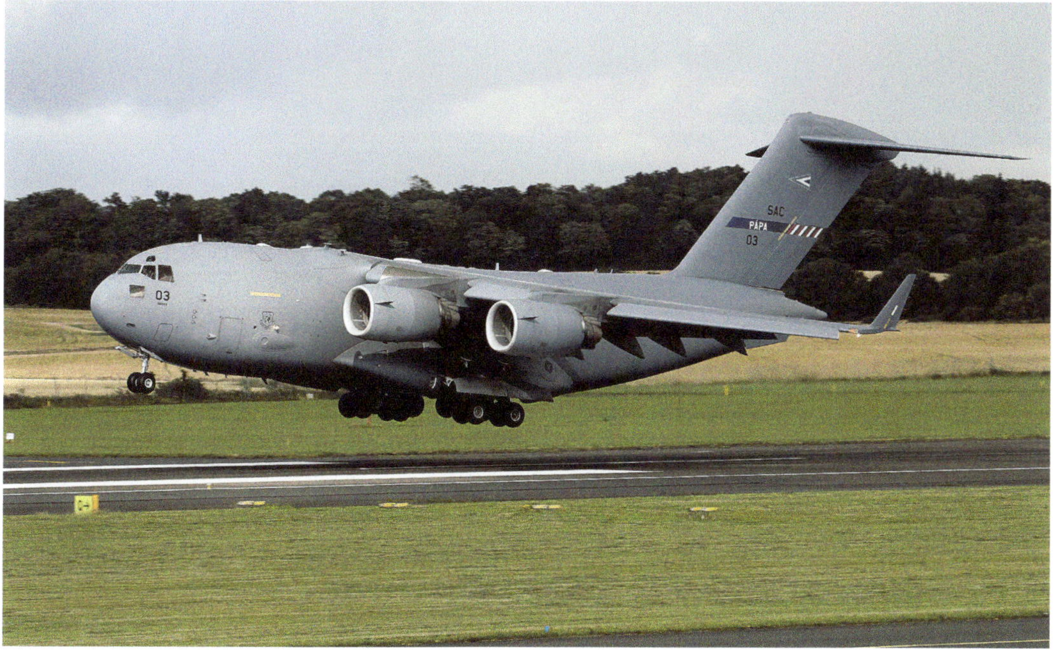

NATO Strategic Airlift Capability (SAC) 03 Boeing C-17A Globemaster III 080003 is seen landing on runway 30 on 27 July 2017. (Leslie A. Rodger)

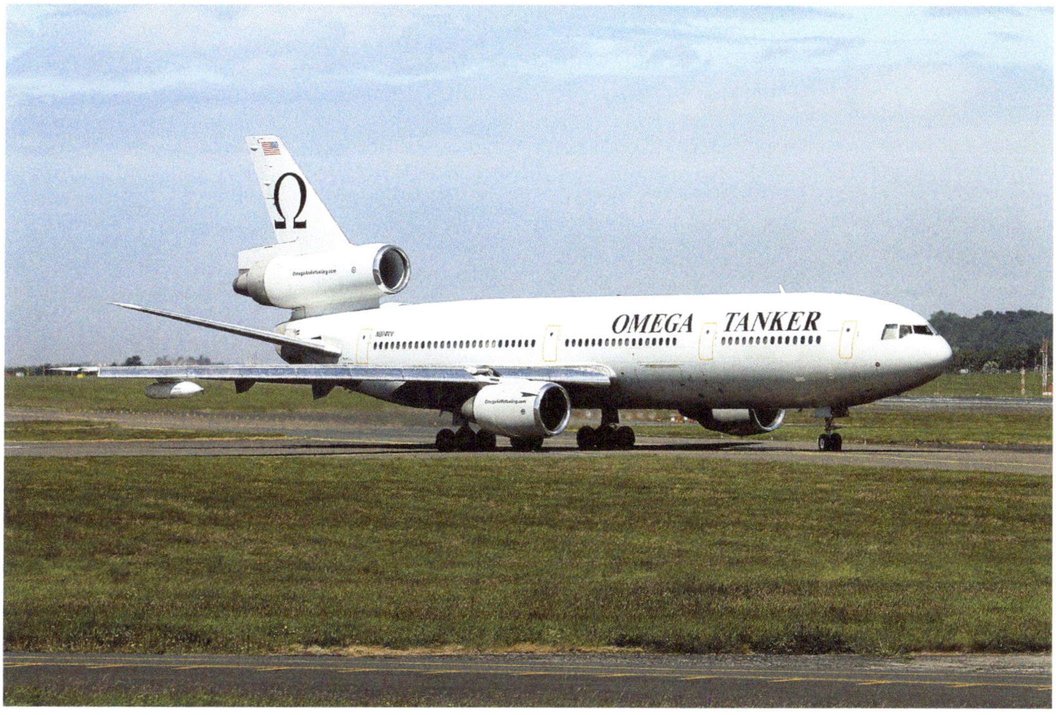

Omega Air McDonnell Douglas DC-10 N974VV is seen taxiing from apron H for runway 30 on its return to the USA from Finland on 17 June 2017. (Leslie A. Rodger)

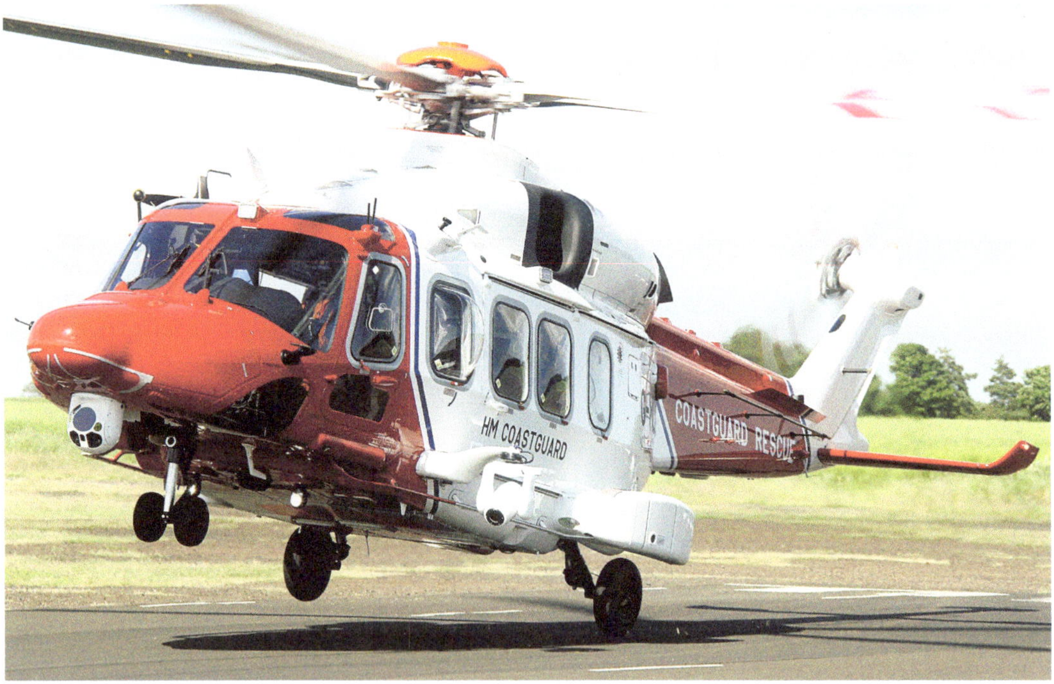

AgustaWestland AW189 G-MCGT, photographed on 17 June 2017. This helicopter is operated by Bristow Helicopters on behalf of HM Coastguard. (Iain Scobie)

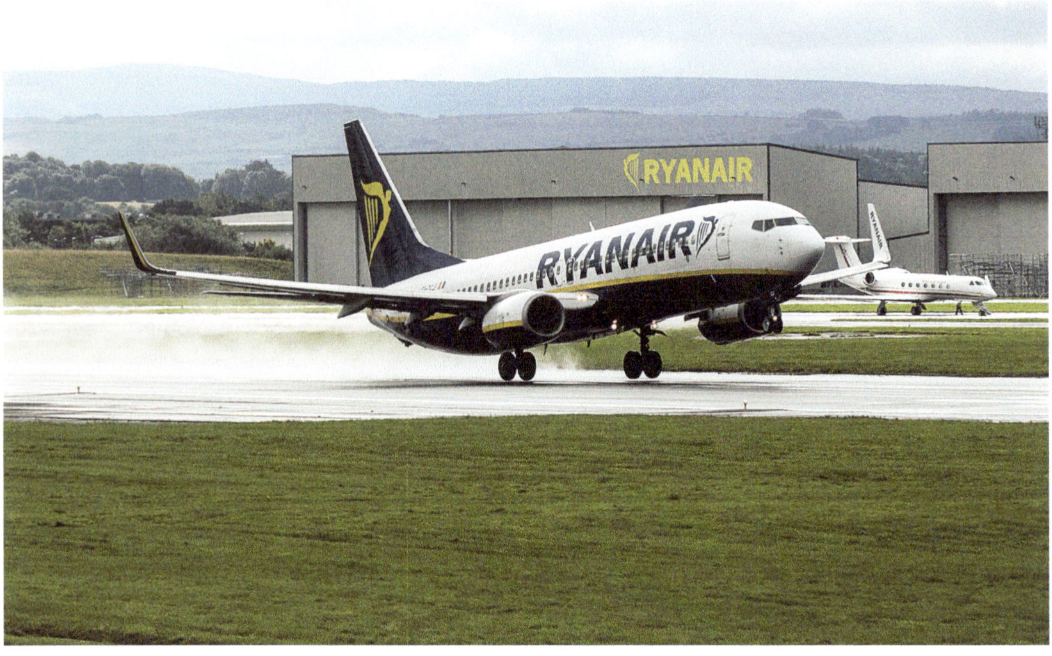

Ryanair Boeing 737-8AS (WL) EI-DCJ with Prestwick Aircraft Maintenance (PAM, the heavy aircraft maintenance provider for Ryanair) in the background on 26 August 2017. (Dougie Edmond)

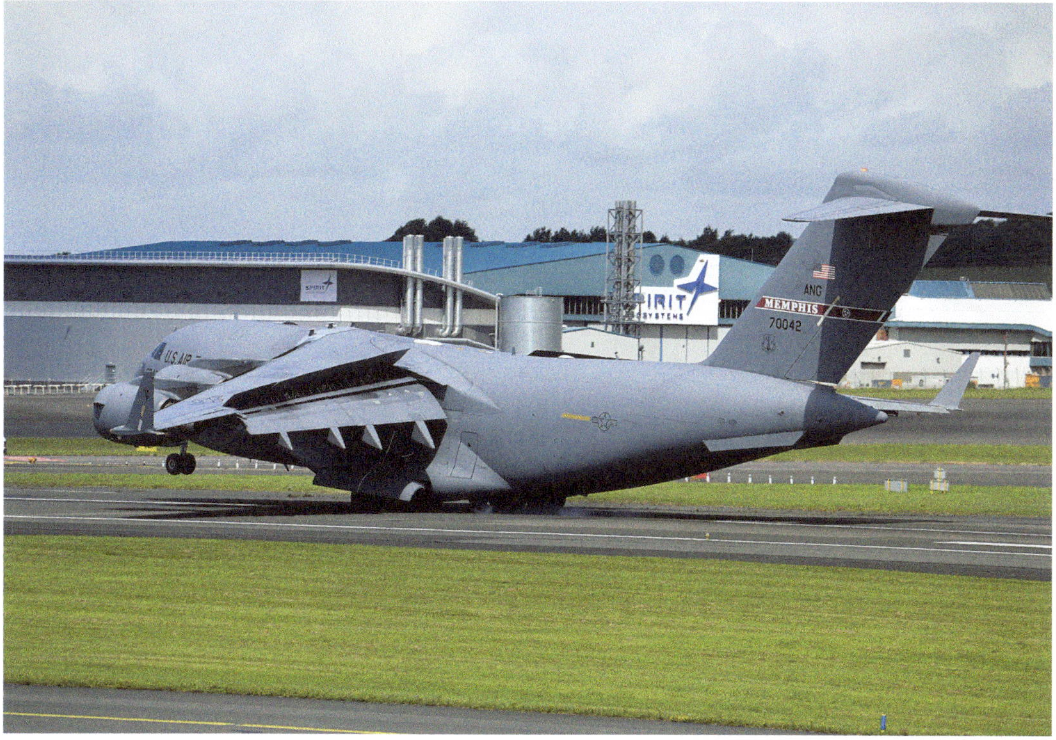

Tennessee Air National Guard Boeing C-17A Globemaster III 97-0042 touching down on a fuel stop at Prestwick on 1 August 2017. (Gerry Rudman)

Fire and Rescue Service

A separate entity from the Scottish Fire and Rescue Service, the Glasgow Prestwick Airport Fire Service operates from a fully equipped, state-of-the-art building located on the north side of the airport, with four watches covering 24 hours a day, seven days a week, 365 days a year. Three modern Carmichael Cobra 2s (6x6), SG52 XLK, SG52 XHK, and SG52 XHJ, are based on site to meet the Rescue and Fire Fighting Services' (RFFS) category 7 requirements (aircraft with an overall length of 160 feet (49 metres) and 16 feet (5 metres) fuselage width), with upgrades to categories 8 (200 feet (61 metres) and 23 feet (7 metres)) and 9 (249 feet (76 metres) and 23 feet (7 metres)) also available at short notice.

In November 2016, Chevron Aircraft Maintenance invested £8.5 million into Prestwick Airport with the aim of creating a 'world-class centre of excellence' for various aspects of the airport such as aircraft engineering and maintenance and training. As a growth industry, Prestwick continues to be very heavily used by freight transport, NASA, military flights from the US, Canada and the UK, and private jets, and remains one of Scotland's major engineering hubs, with five major aerospace companies (Spirit Aerosystems, BAE Systems, Woodward, GE Caledonian and UTC), which, together with other aviation and auxiliary companies, provide local employment. The terminal building can accommodate up to 2.5 million passengers with a large check-in area that has thirteen check-in desks and ample space for self-service check-in facilities.

The ex-Polar Air Cargo Boeing 747-122(SF) (N852FT, ex-N4712U) that acted as a vital training tool for security and rescue services and became a familiar feature on the horizon was dismantled for recycling in September 2017 after being a part of the Prestwick skyline for fifteen years. Originally named *The Original Eight*, it was the sister ship to Flight 103, which was blown up over Lockerbie in December 1988.

One Small Step for a Man...

Scottish businessman Stuart McIntyre, the grandson of the visionary David Fowler McIntyre (who predicted as far back as 1944 that jet propulsion and other advances in aviation would make trips possible between Canada and Britain in only three and a half hours, and who founded Scottish Aviation Ltd and Prestwick Airport itself), established the Prestwick Spaceport Consortium in 2013 in order to drive forward the Ayrshire bid; his next task was to convince the government their facility is best placed to deliver a dramatic departure from Prestwick's current fate at the mercy of Ryanair.

With six locations being considered for Britain's first spaceport (which includes Campbeltown, Argyll and Bute; Glasgow Prestwick; Stornoway, Isle of Lewis; Newquay, Cornwall; and Llanbedr, Gwynedd), technical feasibility studies showed that Glasgow Prestwick Airport could be the frontrunner to provide the launch pad for launching and receiving spacecraft, providing business opportunities for customers such as small satellite companies who are looking at alternative, reliable (and lower cost) orbital launches and opportunities for sub-orbital flights carrying fee-paying passengers and space tourism. The intergalactic travel firm SpaceX and Virgin Galactic (a spaceflight company within the Virgin Group) have expressed interest in the huge potential, with anticipation that the facility could be operational from 2019.

Glasgow Prestwick has over 900 acres of land and is currently working closely with Scottish Enterprise and South Ayrshire Council to support the further development of the Aerospace Campus at Prestwick. If the airport is successful in securing a spaceport operator's license, it could lead to the creation of 2,000 additional jobs and generate a projected £320 million for the UK economy.

Accidents

The first serious air accident at Prestwick was on 28 August 1944, when a USAAF Douglas C-54A-1-DC Skymaster, flying too low on a night approach to the airfield, struck the roof of a house and crashed into other houses short of the runway at Hillside Avenue, Glenburn. Twenty-five people were killed (the crew of six, fourteen passengers and five civilians on the ground).

About forty minutes after midnight on 21 October 1948, a KLM Lockheed L-049 Constellation (PH-TEN) crashed some 2 miles from Prestwick airport after attempting to land in poor weather conditions. There were thirty passengers and ten crew on board the aircraft, none of whom survived the crash. At the end of a normal flight from Amsterdam to Prestwick while en route for New York the commander of the aircraft, Captain K. D. Parmentier, asked for a GCA let-down. The visibility was about 4,000 yards (3,657 metres) and the cloud base was down to 300 feet (91 metres). The circuit and approach were, however, quite normal, and Captain Parmentier then informed Control that he intended to make an overshoot and proceed on a visual circuit. As far as can be determined the aircraft struck some high-tension cables, with the result that the machine was set on fire. The aircraft continued but eventually crashed.

On Christmas Day 1954, the Captain of BOAC 377 Stratocruiser *RMA Cathay* G-ALSA started his final approach to land at too steep an angle and flared out too late and too severely, striking the ground 127 feet (38 metres) short of the threshold of Runway 31 and sustaining damage. It then ran on to the runway and proceeded for some 90 feet, where it was again airborne for another 400 feet (121 metres), before contacting the runway again, forcing the port landing gear into the wing and causing the aircraft to overturn and burst into flames. Four of the crew of eleven and twenty-four of its twenty-five passengers were killed.

A British European Airways Vickers 802 Viscount, G-AORC, struck the ground close to the Prestwick beacon on 28 April 1958. The aircraft had taken off from London for a positioning flight to Prestwick, and was cleared to pass the Prestwick radio beacon at 4,000 feet (1,219 metres). The crew reported descending through 11,000 feet, and shortly afterwards the aircraft hit the ground, skidded for about 1,300 feet (400 metres) and caught fire. The five crew members were unhurt and evacuated the aircraft before it was destroyed. The probable cause was the Captain, W. H. Hankin, misreading the altimeter by 10,000 feet.

A Douglas DC-7C on charter from KLM made a safe landing at Prestwick on 28 May 1963 after a fire, which started 200 miles out over the Atlantic, had destroyed its port outer engine. The aircraft, which had seventy-three passengers and a crew of eight, was at 17,000 feet (5,181 metres) when the fire broke out. There was fierce vibration, caused by propeller windmilling after failure of the feathering mechanism, and the pilot, Captain Wilhelm Bellink, rapidly dived the aircraft to 1,000 feet (304 metres) in an effort to put out the flames. The damaged engine tore itself loose, narrowly missing the aircraft's tailplane.

British Airtours Boeing 707-436 G-APFK suffered an engine failure and crashed on landing at Glasgow Prestwick Airport on 17 March, 1977, during a training flight. All four people on board escaped uninjured, but the aircraft was destroyed in the post-crash fire.

British Aerospace BAe Jetstream 3201 G-SUPR crashed shortly after take-off on a test flight from Glasgow Prestwick Airport on 6 October 1992. An engine failure was simulated during take-off, and the aircraft climbed steeper than normal with the gear still extended. Ten seconds airborne, the co-pilot attempted to find out which engine was simulated as having failed. The pilot reminded the co-pilot about the gear and retracted it. The stall warning sounded and the pilot took over control to add power on the retarded engine, but the Jetstream continued to roll to the right and struck the ground inverted. Both crew were killed.

Three bottles of cocktail and one bottle of sherry were responsible for the safe landing of a Loftleiðir (Icelandic Airlines) Skymaster at Prestwick on 15 August 1950. By using the alcohol to replenish the hydraulic system, which had developed a leak, it was possible to obtain enough pressure to effect an emergency landing.